FIFTH EDITION

CONGRESS, THE BUREAUCRACY, AND PUBLIC POLICY

FIFTH EDITION

Congress,
THE
Bureaucracy,
AND
Public Policy

RANDALL B. RIPLEY
Professor and Chairperson
Department of Political Science
Ohio State University

GRACE A. FRANKLIN

BROOKS/COLE PUBLISHING COMPANY
PACIFIC GROVE, CALIFORNIA

Brooks/Cole Publishing Company
A Division of Wadsworth, Inc.

Printed in the United States of America

10   9   8   7   6   5   4   3   2   1

Library of Congress Cataloging-in-Publication Data

Ripley, Randall B.
    Congress, the bureaucracy, and public policy / Randall B. Ripley, Grace A. Franklin.—5th ed.
        p.   cm.
    Includes bibliographical references (p.) and index.
    ISBN 0-534-14454-3
    1. United States. Congress.   2. Civil service—United States.   3. United States—Politics and government.   I. Franklin, Grace A.   II. Title.
JK1067.R53   1990
328.73—dc20   90-2022
                                                                                            CIP

Sponsoring Editor: *Cynthia C. Stormer*
Editorial Assistant: *Cathleen Sue Collins*
Production Editor: *Marjorie Z. Sanders*
Manuscript Editor: *Alan Hislop*
Interior and Cover Design: *Vernon T. Boes*
Art Coordinator: *Cloyce J. Wall*
Interior Illustration: *Cloyce J. Wall*
Typesetting: *Execustaff*
Printing and Binding: *Malloy Lithographing, Inc.*

To F. J. R. and V. G. R.

PREFACE

We expect a student who reads this book to come away with an understanding of the nature of the relationship between Congress and the federal bureaucracy and the centrality of that relationship in the making of national public policy in the United States. The policy examples we have used should give the student a sense of part of the substantive business of the U.S. government and should also give him or her a better sense of how and where to seek additional examples. We think the student who uses this book should be able to explain complex relationships in straightforward and meaningful English.

Public policy making at the national level in the United States is both important and complicated. It is important because it affects the daily lives of all residents of the United States, and it sometimes affects the lives of people in other nations as well. It is complicated because of the vast number of items on the agenda of the national government and because of the large number of individuals and institutions that get involved in making policy decisions.

Central to the complex and important business of making public policy is the interaction between Congress and the federal bureaucracy. Existing books about public policy usually either ignore this relationship or merely allude to it, implying that it is too mysterious to be comprehended. In fact, it is comprehensible and—happy thought!—there are patterns in the relationship that help reduce the confusion surrounding national policy making. We have sought to portray those patterns in clear terms. And, above all, we have sought to give concrete, interesting, and timely examples of the relationships that illustrate the patterns.

A further comment about our choice of examples is needed. Because of the necessities of the publishing process, we could include no examples occurring later than the end of 1989. We have sought to use examples from the last few decades rather than concentrating them all in any single period. We have chosen examples for analytical purposes; we are not trying to tell chronological stories that end at the moment of writing. We are seeking to analyze patterns of behavior.

An introductory comment on the nature of change in American institutions and politics is also relevant to the notion that patterns of behavior are present and require analysis. To be sure, every short period of time—whether measured by the tenure of a specific president, by the two-year tenure of a specific Congress, or annually—will have its own variations. But the patterns we seek to find transcend all of these artificially created time periods. We are not oblivious to changes. American politics is not a static phenomenon, but neither is it a world in which "revolutions" occur frequently and represent "profound" and "dramatic" change. Even the "Reagan revolution" represented only an acceleration of normal incremental change in some areas. "New eras" are rare events in human history in general; they are extremely rare in the daily give-and-take of American politics and policy making.

We comment on the fact of change and the nature of change where it has occurred. But we think it would be a serious mistake to pretend that change is always more important than stable patterns of interaction. Both are important. Distinguishing what changes a lot, what changes a little, and what changes almost not at all presents many challenges. But those are challenges that teachers and students of American politics must constantly meet.

We make no attempt to describe all that either Congress or the bureaucracy does with regard to public policy. Our focus is on those areas and activities in which constant interaction occurs between them and has at least the potential for major substantive results. Our attention is primarily directed to *policy formulation and legitimation*. The *implementation* of policy by bureaucracy and other actors is a vast and important topic by itself, but implementation is not considered in this volume.

We are grateful to the Mershon Center at Ohio State University for providing a good location in which to write and think and interact with each other and with other scholars interested in public policy. This book stems both from a number of projects on policy making in which we have been involved since 1970 that were sponsored in part by Mershon, and from our teaching—both formal and informal and to a number of different audiences—about public policy.

In preparing this fifth edition we benefited from thoughtful reviews by Joel Aberbach, University of California, Los Angeles; T. R. Carr, Southern Illinois University at Edwardsville; Diana R. Gordon, City College of New York; Steven Koven, Iowa State University; Robert W. Kweit, University of North Dakota; Harvey Lieber, American University; Richard Ryan, San Diego State University, Imperial Valley; and James A. Thurber, American University.

Randall B. Ripley
Grace A. Franklin

CONTENTS

CHAPTER THREE

Congressional–Bureaucratic Interaction: Occasions and Resources

51

CHAPTER FOUR

Distributive Policy

72

CHAPTER FIVE

Protective Regulatory Policy
103

CHAPTER SIX

Redistributive Policy
121

CHAPTER SEVEN

Foreign and Defense Policy
151

CHAPTER EIGHT

Congress, the Bureaucracy, and the Nature of American Public Policy

182

List of Figures

List of Tables

FIFTH EDITION

CONGRESS, THE BUREAUCRACY, AND PUBLIC POLICY

CHAPTER ONE

The Nature of Policy and Policy Making in the United States

Policy is a common word, but despite its familiarity, it is a tricky concept to define. Political scientists have filled many pages defining and arguing about the meaning of policy and the related notions of policy making and the policy process.

In this book we endow these core concepts with the following meanings: *Policy* is what the government says and does about matters it wishes to affect. *Policy making* is how the government decides what will be done about these matters. Policy making involves a *process* of interaction among a variety of governmental and nongovernmental actors. *Policy* is the outcome of that interaction.

Figure 1-1 presents a simplified overview of the chain of activities that are required to make and implement policy.

In the first stage of the policy process—*agenda setting*—a problem exists in society. Through various means, that problem comes to the attention of government actors, who perceive it to be an issue that should be addressed by government. Some parts of the government recognize that an issue or problem should receive attention. The agenda of the government can be thought of as the sum of all the issues and problems that the government is addressing at any specific time. In the 1970s, for example, some of the major issues on the national government's agenda included preservation of the environment, conservation of energy resources, unemployment, and inflation. In the 1980s the most visible issues changed. Emphasis was given to defense spending, tax policy, the extent of deregulation, the balance of federal powers with state powers and those of the private sector, the federal budget deficit, and the national trade deficit. In the early 1990s the focus on the federal budget deficit and trade deficit continued. Efforts to cut the defense budget have become prominent as the perceived threat from the Soviet Union and the Warsaw Pact regimes in eastern Europe continues to diminish as major political changes come to these political systems. The drug problem, the cost and provision of adequate health care, and a host of environmental problems will get at a minimum a lot of rhetorical attention and may get some genuine policy-making attention.

Once the government has acknowledged that an issue deserves governmental attention, then it must say what it is going to do about the issue and specify how it plans to accomplish its goals. In the stage of *policy and program formulation and legitimation*, actors from various parts of the government and also from outside of government propose alternative methods of dealing with an issue, and they choose

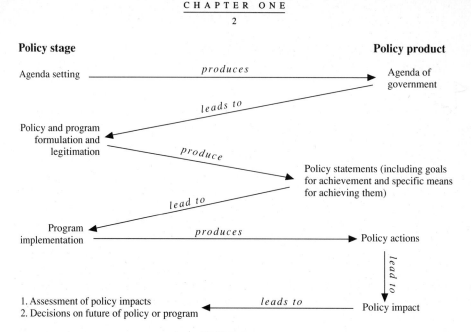

Policy stage   **Policy product**

Agenda setting ————————*produces*————————▶ Agenda of
                                                                                                government

                                        leads to

Policy and program ◀
  formulation and
    legitimation   *produce*

                                                                        Policy statements (including goals
                                                                        for achievement and specific means
                                                                        for achieving them)

                          lead to

Program ◀————————*produces*————————▶ Policy actions
implementation

                                                                                            lead to

1. Assessment of policy impacts   *leads to*
2. Decisions on future of policy or program ◀——————— Policy impact

FIGURE 1–1
An overview of the policy process

a plan of action. In this process, different points of view and preferences are often
expressed, and negotiation and compromise become necessary if a decision is to be
reached. The necessity for negotiation and compromise between competing points
of view also helps explain why policy tends to change relatively slowly and by fairly
small increments most of the time. A typical product at the end of this stage, unless
no product at all is generated, is a statute passed by Congress and signed by the
president that creates a new program or amends an existing one.

Once a plan of action has been selected and a program has been created, then
program implementation must take place. Specific agencies and individuals within
those agencies are formally responsible for that implementation. The agencies must
take a number of specific actions—such as acquiring resources, interpreting the legislation, writing regulations, training staff, and delivering services—in order to put flesh
on the bones of the statute.

The operation of a program will have some *impact* on society. The program
may or may not achieve its intended purposes, even assuming that those purposes
were reasonably clear. It may also have unintended consequences, both beneficial
and detrimental.

Several kinds of *assessment* of impact are always undertaken, even if they are
not explicitly labeled as such and even if they are not formal assessments or evaluations. In fact, most assessments are informal and are dominated by political considerations. On some occasions more formal analyses may be undertaken. The
results of formal analyses may also become incorporated into an adversarial political
process. Government officials who commission formal analyses are often looking
for support for positions they already hold.

A full treatment of the entire policy process is beyond the scope of this book (see Jones 1984, for one excellent introduction to that process). We are going to focus on one part of the process—the formulation and legitimation of public policies and programs. At the heart of the policy-making process at this stage lies the relationship between Congress and the bureaucracy, a relationship that is often given inadequate attention in the literature on American government and policy making. In order to set the relationship in perspective, we will first describe policy making in American national government in terms of major actors, relationships, and characteristics.

The activity portrayed in figure 1-1, the definitions of policy phenomena, and the brief description of the policy process vastly oversimplify the rich variety of the real policy world. Our generalizations impose order on a complex world whose activities and interactions are messy, not neat. On the other hand, we find distinct patterns are present when policy formulation and legitimation at the national level in the United States are analyzed. We present those patterns in the firm belief that a grasp of patterns is far better than a store of unconnected observations or anecdotes. Throughout the book, however, we illustrate the patterns we think are present with policy examples from the last several decades in order to avoid analyzing a fascinating process only in abstract language.

An Overview of the Government Policy Process

Actors and Relationships

The core of the American national governmental policy process is located in Congress and the executive branch. These public institutional entities and actors are often supplemented by nongovernmental institutions and actors, especially the great variety of interest groups active in American politics. These groups are important and influential in many cases, but it is essential to note that their importance is not all-encompassing. It also varies—not just from specific issue to specific issue but also, we argue, from class of issue to class of issue. One of the principal contributions we hope to make is to specify when, where, and how interest groups are important in shaping policy. Despite what the media may suggest, influence does not run just one way, from interest groups to public officials in Congress and the bureaucracy. Instead, there is an interactive relationship between interest groups and public institutions and officials. Interest groups can, under some conditions, help shape policy. The creation of policies also often involves the identification and specification of interests that help generate groups to perpetuate and "refine" those policies. That is, sometimes policies predate the existence of important groups and may help create such groups after the basic policy is already in place.

Both Congress and the executive branch can be understood in terms of key component parts. Congress has party leaders, committee and subcommittee leaders (typically, chairpersons and ranking minority members), and rank-and-file members of the House and Senate. The executive branch consists of the president personally, the presidency collectively in the form of the Executive Office of the President and a variety of presidential appointees, and civil servants throughout all of the agencies.

The civil servants (and we include military officers in this general category) who are important in policy formulation are those high enough in grade to function in a managerial or policy development capacity.

Each of the six component parts of the central Washington policy-making institutions interacts with every other part, but all of the relationships are not equally important. Figure 1–2 indicates the interactions most important to policy making in the national government.

Within the executive branch two relationships are most important—first, that of the president with the Executive Office personnel and presidential appointees throughout the government (the institutional presidency in a broad sense) and, second, that of Executive Office personnel and presidential appointees with civil servants. The bureaucracy is so vast that the president cannot hope to have direct relationships with civil servants except for a handful of career civil servants in the Executive Office and a few career ambassadors in the Foreign Service. Executive Office personnel and presidential appointees, therefore, take on special importance as links between the president and his programmatic preferences and the development and implementation of those preferences in the bureaucracy.

Three relationships are most important within Congress. The first two relationships involve committee and subcommittee leaders, who play an intermediate role between party leaders and rank-and-file members. The third relationship involves direct ties between party leaders and the rank and file, a relationship that is relatively easy to achieve in physical terms because of the limited size of the House and Senate. The committee and subcommittee leaders (especially the latter) are typically the most important individuals in deciding what emerges from Congress in detailed, substantive terms. The party leaders make strategic and tactical decisions about

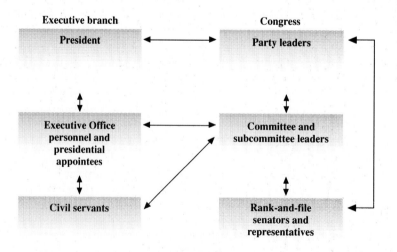

FIGURE 1–2

Most important relationships for policy making in the national government how best to get the work of the committees and subcommittees approved by the full House and Senate. The rank-and-file members are approached by both committee and subcommittee leaders and party leaders to get their support for specific statutory initiatives.

Three relationships between the executive branch and Congress are at the heart of policy formulation and legitimation: first, that between the president and the party leaders, which focuses largely on strategic and tactical matters; second, that between the Executive Office personnel and presidential appointees and committee and subcommittee leaders on substantive matters; and third, that between policy-level civil servants and military officers and committee and subcommittee leaders on substantive matters. This third relationship is central. There is good evidence that neither party consistently dominates the relationship. Both, therefore, require serious attention (Moe 1987). It is this third relationship that will be the focus of this book. Attention to other relationships and actors will, of course, be included when they are important.

In order for substantial and relatively rapid policy movement to occur, the eight relationships portrayed in Figure 1–2 must all be marked by a high degree of mutual confidence and trust, and there must also be a high degree of agreement on the nature of the problems facing society and the proper solutions to those problems. That these conditions are absent more than they are present helps explain why the government moves slowly on only a few problems at a time. Rapid movement on major issues occurs, but when it does, it is unusual enough to warrant special notice.

More often, minor changes are misleadingly touted as major. Policy makers often succumb to the temptation to overstate the importance of limited legislative compromises, attributing to them panacean qualities to create a favorable public image and gain political credit. A classic example of this kind of overstatement occurred in 1989 with regard to the bailout of savings and loan associations. In August, President Bush signed the bailout bill and said that all problems had been handled well and that a new day was dawning for the industry and the American people. Four months later he admitted that the bill hailed as a cure-all was not adequate and did not provide enough money (see Chapter 5 for more information on the policy making that went into the savings and loan bailout bill of 1989).

Principal Characteristics

U.S. policy making is enormously complex for a number of reasons: the sheer size of the government; the number of both governmental and nongovernmental participants that become involved in policy making; the proliferation of specialization within agencies and committees and subcommittees; the involvement of different territorial levels of government; the constitutional separation of institutions that share powers; and the vast range of substantive issues, most of them complicated, to which government addresses itself. Four of the most important elements contributing to this complexity are described in the following paragraphs.

The first is the widespread existence of *subgovernments* in many substantive issue areas. A subgovernment is a small group of political actors, both governmental and nongovernmental, that focuses on a specific, fairly tightly defined policy area. Subgovernments are produced in part by the vast, complex nature of the national policy agenda. They help sustain that complexity. They are most prevalent and influential in the least visible policy areas. Subgovernments do *not* dominate *all* policy making, as is sometimes claimed. The conditions that lead to different amounts of subgovernment influence on different issues are carefully explored in this book.

A second major element is the great variety of governmental institutions—federal, state, and local—that share the responsibility for developing and implementing a number of policies and programs and also have some programs exclusively their own. A so-called national program is likely to require actions not only in Washington but also throughout a number of states and cities in federal field offices and in the offices of state and local governments. Which level of government is responsible for what varies over time, even in the same policy or program area. In general, states were given more responsibility during the Reagan years (Beam 1984; Chubb 1985; Peterson 1984).

A third important contributor to the complexity of national policy making is the existence of separate institutions (the legislative, executive, and judicial branches) that share powers. The separation of institutions stems from a decision by the Founders not to place all powers of government under a single body or person. Instead, the basic governing functions were divided and delegated to three distinct branches. However, in order to limit the autonomy of each branch, the Constitution contains checks and balances that also force the institutions to share their powers. The separation makes some jealousies and conflicts between branches inevitable. The sharing necessitates cooperation among the branches to prevent the government apparatus from ceasing to function effectively. In addition to the separation and sharing of powers prescribed in the Constitution, a commingling of legislative, executive, and judicial powers has evolved as the branches have interacted through the years. Congressional delegation of authority to the executive branch is a particularly notable example of this sharing.

A final major reason why national policy making is complex is the tremendous variety and volume of issues facing government. The substantive spectrum ranges from acreage allotments for cotton growers, to child care, to legal assistance for poor people, to arming and maintaining a vast defense establishment. The degree of specificity of governmental policy varies greatly—some laws spell out infinite details; others are very general. Different policies have different rewards and penalties for various groups, a fact that has a major impact on how policies get made.

The remainder of this chapter will explore these four elements in more detail.

The Subgovernment Phenomenon

Subgovernments are clusters of individuals that effectively make most of the routine decisions in selected, well-defined policy areas. A typical subgovernment is composed of members of the House and Senate, members of congressional staffs, bureaucrats, and representatives of private groups and organizations interested in the policy area. The members of Congress and staff members are from the committees or subcommittees that have principal jurisdiction over the policy area. The bureaucrats in a subgovernment are likely to be the chief of a bureau with jurisdiction paralleling that of the congressional subcommittee and a few of his or her top assistants. The nongovernmental members of a subgovernment are most likely to be a few lobbyists for interest groups with the greatest stakes in the substance of the policy decisions.

Subgovernments are important throughout a broad range of American public policy. They afford an important channel by which nongovernmental actors help determine policy and program content. They are not equally dominant in all policy fields, and their level of influence changes from time to time within a single field. Later in this chapter we relate predictable variations in the level of subgovernment importance to different broad policy types.

Note that we have made three important statements about subgovernments. First, there are lots of them. Second, they are important. Third, they are *not* dominant in all policy areas.

The existence of subgovernments has been documented in a number of studies of American government (see, for example, Cater 1964; Davidson 1977; and Freeman 1965). However, the term is often used too inclusively and authors often imply that subgovernments are uniformly and universally influential.

Most of the policy making in which subgovernments engage consists of routine matters. "Routine" policy is that which is not embroiled in a high degree of controversy. The substance of routine policy changes slowly over time. The participants most interested in any specific routine policy are thoroughly familiar with it and quietly efficient in shaping it to their liking.

Because most policy is routine, subgovernments can often function for long periods without much interference or control from individuals or institutions outside the subgovernment. If the members of subgovernment can quietly reach compromises on policy disagreements that occasionally arise between members, they can reduce the chances of attracting the attention of outsiders. When more participants enter a dispute, the chances of basic policy realignment increase because there are a greater number of interests to satisfy. Such realignments might not be in the best interests of the members of the subgovernment, and therefore strong incentive exists for them to prevent an increase in the number of participants.

The normally closed, low-profile operations of a subgovernment can be opened to "outsiders" in three principal ways. First, as just indicated, if the subgovernment participants themselves arrive at some fundamental disagreement, that disagreement may become publicized and stimulate attention and intrusion from nonmembers of the subgovernment.

Second, the president, other high administration officials, and members of Congress can draw on a variety of resources if they choose to be aggressive in inquiring into the functioning of a subgovernment. Formal resources include budget limitations, limitations on size of staff, vigorous legislative oversight of program activity, and restraints on agency communications (Freeman 1965, 62). Informally, the "meddlers" can use personal influence to intervene, especially the president, who can exert influence on persons he has appointed. Whether the president, administration officials, and members of Congress will be aggressive in relation to a subgovernment's interests depends on the extent to which they perceive interests important to them to be threatened by the subgovernment's behavior. For example, the president or a department secretary may be stirred to take an aggressive stance if the bureau chief member of a subgovernment strays too far too often from officially announced administration policy.

Third, a new issue that attracts the attention of outsiders can be introduced into the subgovernment's jurisdiction. The new issue can upset normal decision making if it is more important than or different in character from the issues the subgovernment is used to dealing with, especially if the issue involves regulation of private activities or redistribution of wealth to one group at the expense of another. In recent years, for example, both the increased concern for the environment and the energy crisis have intruded into the world of the various subgovernments dealing with oil, coal, and natural gas. Now these subgovernments must handle major regulatory issues as well as the familiar issues of subsidy.

American politics minimizes the distinction between governmental and nongovernmental institutions and actors. The line between the two realms is easily crossed, a phenomenon widely approved of by those both inside and outside the government. A corollary is the general belief that individuals most affected by governmental actions should have virtually continual access to governmental officials during the policy-making process (Lowi 1979).

Not only are the lines between governmental and nongovernmental institutions blurred by the norm of open, continual access during policy making, but a constant flow of personnel between governmental and nongovernmental institutions further blurs the distinctions. People from Congress (both the members and staff) and the executive branch agencies move into jobs in the private sector to work in the same substantive policy areas in which they worked during their government tenure. This flow of personnel enhances the importance and stability of subgovernments. The magnitude of this type of personnel movement is so large that subgovernments have also been called "incest groups" (Lewis 1977).

Participation in subgovernments offers the most pervasive and effective channel for interest group impact on policy and program decisions, but the interest groups are not uniformly important (Hayes 1981). Their impact varies by policy area and also in relation to group resources.

When all organized interest groups are considered together, a strong "business or upper-class bias" becomes evident (Schattschneider 1960). The better-off members of society, especially the private business sector, are represented much more strongly than other sectors, which helps explain why much substantive policy that emerges is favorable to these interests.

Federalism in Policy Making

Geographic Dispersion of the National Government

Washington, D.C., is synonymous with the national government, and it is true that much of the decision-making apparatus of the government is concentrated there. But

Washington contains only a small proportion of all employees of the federal executive branch. In 1987, just over 3 million civilians were employed by the federal government, but only about one in ten of those individuals worked in the Washington metropolitan area. Most of the rest worked elsewhere in the United States. About 5 percent of the total worked outside the United States, either in U.S. territories or in foreign countries. Individuals in the regional and local offices of the federal government had primary responsibility for day-to-day delivery of many federal benefits and services. A glance at any local telephone book of any size will reveal how extensively the federal government is represented on the local level.

Federal, State, and Local Government Interaction

Policy making and implementation in the United States is complicated not only because national institutions and employees are dispersed, but also because state and local governments, which are numerous, are important in implementing national programs. Many ties bind federal, state, and local governmental units and employees together: federal money, limited exchanges of personnel, and daily programmatic interactions.

State and local government employment is much larger than federal employment. In 1986, 82 percent of almost 17 million civilian government employees were state and local. The federal share of total civilian governmental employment shrank steadily from the end of World War II (it was 33 percent in 1950, for example) until about 1980, when it stabilized at about 18 percent.

The financial impact of the federal government on state and local governments grew dramatically during the 1950s, 1960s, and 1970s. Table 1–1 summarizes the growth of federal grants-in-aid from 1950 through an estimate for 1994. The amount of aid in this form measured in constant dollars has risen continuously. Until the 1980s this form of spending also represented a continuously increasing percentage of all federal outlays and all state and local spending. The Reagan assault on some of the programs handled through grants, however, helped shrink both of those percentages throughout the 1980s. Moderate shrinkage seems likely to continue during the Bush presidency.

The purposes for which federal grants-in-aid to states and localities are spent have changed considerably. Table 1–2 summarizes the distribution of grant spending by function from 1960 through an estimate for 1990. The table shows that health has been the large gainer throughout the period in terms of purposes served and that transportation has become much less important in relative terms. Education, training, employment, and social services peaked in the 1960s and 1970s and went into decline during the Reagan era. Income security remained important throughout the period, although its relative size fluctuated. The category called *general government* was important only for a limited period of time when the federal government had a general revenue-sharing program (a program that ended completely in 1986). That money was used largely for education by state governments and for public safety and transportation by local governments.

The grant system was altered in the early 1970s by the development of several major "special revenue-sharing" programs, particularly in community development

TABLE 1–1

The Growth of Federal Grants-in-Aid to State and Local Governments, 1950–1994

| Fiscal year | Amount (millions) | Federal grants as a percent of | |
		Total federal outlays	State-local expenditures
1950	$ 2.3	5.3	10.4
1960	7.0	7.6	14.6
1965	10.9	9.2	15.2
1970	24.1	12.3	19.2
1975	49.8	15.0	22.7
1980	91.5	15.5	25.8
1985	105.9	11.2	20.9
1990 (estimate)	123.6	10.7	NA*
1994 (estimate)	138.1	10.5	NA*

*NA = not available.

SOURCE: *Special Analyses, Budget of the United States Government, Fiscal Year 1990* (Washington, D.C.: U.S. Government Printing Office 1989), H–22.

TABLE 1–2

Percentage Distribution of Federal Grants to States and Localities by Function, 1960–1990

	1960	1970	1980	1990 (est.)
Natural resources and environment	2	2	6	3
Agriculture	3	3	1	1
Transportation	43	19	14	14
Community and regional development	2	7	7	3
Education, training, employment, and social services	7	27	24	18
Health	3	16	17	31
Income security	38	24	20	27
General government	2	2	9	2
Total (includes other)	100	100	100	100

SOURCE: *Special Analyses, Budget of the United States Government, Fiscal Year 1990* (Washington, D.C.: U.S. Government Printing Office 1989), H–20.

and employment and training. The system was altered again in the Reagan era by the collapsing of some specific categorical grants into block grants. These altera- tions did not change the percentage distribution of dollars by function, but they did change some of the patterns of control and some programmatic relationships between the levels of government.

Regardless of how much flexibility and influence is granted to state and local governments in any particular version of federalism that happens to be in vogue at the moment, two central facts are pertinent to the analysis in this book. First, Congress and the federal bureaucracy are at the heart of the interactions that lead to the statutes prescribing the nature of the relationship between the territorial levels of govern- ment and the scope and objects of the fiscal aid. Second, no version of federalism is likely to be permanent. Congress and the bureaucracy both review what happens during the implementation of various grants, regardless of form. They may diminish their own role, but they rarely eliminate it. They retain the option to change basic intergovernmental relationships. The "natural" dominant pressures on both Congress and the bureaucracy are to keep states and localities dependent on them in many ways so that they can claim credit for programs and spending that benefit their individual constituencies or clients.

Separate Institutions, Shared Powers

Cooperation and Conflict

The Constitution created three branches of government that have distinct identities in terms of their powers and the way in which officeholders are chosen. It also distributed powers in such a way that interaction and cooperation between the branches are necessary if anything is to be accomplished. Institutional jealousies about preserving powers and competition to serve different constituencies mean that the three branches will inevitably have some conflicts. But an overriding desire to achieve some policy goals also means that most participants in all three branches understand and operate on the values of cooperation and compromise much of the time. The existence of subgovernments serves to reinforce the values of cooperation and compromise for the participants (Morrow 1969, 156–158). Institutional jealousies and competition among constituencies remain even within individual subgovernments, but the effects of those jealousies and competition are muted in day-to-day operations. A premium is placed on generating policy that is usually either an extension of the status quo or some small variant of it. More policy generation also creates more bureaucracy, which, in the course of implementing programs, creates more occasions for members of Congress to serve their constituents in dealings with the bureaucracy. Such service benefits the members at election time (Fiorina 1977).

Most of the literature dealing with Congress and the bureaucracy usually focuses on the conflictive aspects of the relationship, and although conflict is a more exciting topic than cooperation, the bulk of policy making is nevertheless based on cooperation. One of the tasks of this volume will be to develop suggestions in the literature about the conditions that promote cooperation or conflict (Bernstein 1958; Bibby 1966; Fiorina 1977; Morrow 1969; Scher 1963; Sharkansky 1965a, 1965b).

A few generalizations specify some of the major conditions promoting either cooperation or conflict.

First, personal compatibility between key agency personnel and key congressional personnel, especially at the subcommittee level, is important. A high degree of compatibility promotes cooperation. Less compatibility (or greater amounts of hostility) promotes conflict.

Second, the degree of ideological and programmatic agreement between key individuals in Congress (usually those on the relevant subcommittee) and in the agency is important. A high degree of agreement promotes cooperation. A low degree of agreement promotes conflict. Similarly, a high degree of unity *between* the individual members of Congress thought by bureaucrats to be important is likely to make the bureaucrats less inclined to pursue interests that may conflict with united congressional opinion. Disunity among members of Congress may tempt bureaucrats to form alliances with those agreeing with them, thus provoking conflict with the other congressional faction.

Third, the amount of genuine participation by Congress (primarily members of a subcommittee) in the development of programs is important. If executive branch officials simply present Congress with finished products—either in the form of proposed legislation or in the form of major administrative decisions—conflict may result. If the executive officials adopt the habit of consultation as they undertake either legislative or administrative courses of action, they enhance the chances of cooperation.

Fourth, if an issue is relatively unimportant to constituents or interest groups, then the chances of congressional–bureaucratic cooperation are enhanced. However, if constituents or interest groups are heavily involved, the potential for conflict increases.

Fifth, agencies that are highly aggressive in seeking to expand their authority and their funding run a greater risk of conflict with Congress, especially committees and subcommittees, than agencies that are less aggressive.

Sixth, if the presidency and Congress are controlled by the same political party, the chances for cooperation are enhanced. If different parties control the two branches, the chances for conflict increase.

Delegation of Authority

Delegation of authority occurs when Congress writes general statutes that necessitate further elaboration before they can be implemented. Career civil servants in executive branch agencies must supplement general statutory language with more specific language in a variety of regulations. The regulation writing process is, in effect, a second legislative process (Rabinovitz, Pressman, and Rein 1976). The process of writing regulations can take a long time, and, over the course of time, the regulations can alter substantially the presumed purposes of the statutes on which they are based.

There is nothing disreputable or unusual about delegation of authority. Some degree of delegation is necessary because of the volume of legislation and because of the complicated nature of individual statutes and the topics they address. In theory, Congress sets clear standards and guidelines in the legislation for the bureaucracy to follow in elaborating the statute through regulations. In practice, however, the clarity and specificity of the standards and guidelines vary a great deal. For example, Congress may direct the National Labor Relations Board (NLRB) to ascertain that the parties in labor negotiations adhere to "fair standards." The meaning of "fair standards" is, however, not provided by Congress but is, instead, left to the determination of the NLRB. Similarly, the interpretation of "maximum feasible participation" of the poor mandated in the Economic Opportunity Act of 1964 was left to the Office of Economic Opportunity and not provided in any way by Congress. On the other hand, Congress may specify precise standards that allow little agency leeway, as was the case with the Securities Act of 1933. The large size of the *Federal Register*, in which regulations generated by the bureaucracy must be published, testifies to the importance of agency-generated regulations. There is a also a large amount of informal, unrecorded administrative rule making on the part of agencies.

Congress sometimes intentionally uses delegation to delay making a final decision. A clear-cut policy decision may penalize or anger some groups. These groups can then manifest their unhappiness by withdrawing their support from selected members of Congress. If the members perceive that they would lose a great deal of support, they may choose not to state a clear policy and leave the policy outcome ambiguous by delegating decision making to parts of the bureaucracy, or to regulatory commissions, or to the courts, with only vague congressional guidance. This way, the perceived winners and losers defined by the policy decision are less clear, and the responsibility for the decision is deflected from Congress to others.

The propriety of congressional delegation of authority was challenged during the New Deal, and the Supreme Court ruled on a few occasions that specific delegations were unconstitutional because of vagueness. But the judicial check has not been exercised since the 1930s. In effect, Congress can follow whatever course it wishes with respect to delegation. In summarizing this fact and the continuing trend toward very broad delegations, Woll (1977, 170) wrote that "it is possible to conclude that there are no constitutional or legal restrictions that have impeded in any substantial way the trend toward greater delegation. This situation has not, of course, resulted from administration usurpation, but from congressional desire." Delegation, in sum, is a result of necessity; but it is also a matter of will, not coercion.

Although the principle of delegation of authority is well established, the question of what form delegation ought to take is not so well settled. Some scholars (for example, Harris 1964) argue that Congress should be only minimally involved in administration. They imply that its delegations of authority should be broad and vague to allow bureaucrats to make interpretations best suited to meeting problems faced in program administration. Other scholars (for example, Lowi 1979) argue that delegation of authority without accompanying clear guidelines limits congressional policy impact to relatively marginal details and represents, in effect, a congressional abdication of responsibility. Congress, in this view, should publish clear expectations and guidelines along with its delegations.

The forms of delegation vary. The reasons for relatively clear guidelines in statutory language in some cases and very broad and vague language in others are numerous and vary from case to case. One important consideration may be the mood of Congress at any given time with reference to the agency to which the delegation is being made. More precisely, the most important consideration may be the attitude of the responsible congressional subcommittees toward the relevant agencies.

A striking example of how patterns of delegation are affected by changing congressional attitudes is provided by comparing the degree of discretionary power allocated to the Federal Trade Commission (FTC) in the Securities Act of 1933 with the degree of power allocated to the Securities and Exchange Commission (SEC) in the Securities and Exchange Act of 1934 (Landis 1938, 52–55). The FTC's discretionary power was severely limited in part because of congressional lack of confidence in the agency's membership. Its duties were defined so precisely that administration was almost a matter of mechanical routine. In contrast, attitudes toward the FTC had changed in a more favorable direction by 1934, and the new confidence was reflected in the broader administrative authority granted to the new SEC.

The type of issue involved also affects the nature of congressional delegation. In dealing with complex issues, especially those in the jurisdictions of the independent regulatory commissions, Congress is often unable or unwilling to arrive at specific language. The result is that the regulatory commissions have a great deal of discretion in interpreting statutes.

A desire to shift responsibility for decision making may also be a factor in congressional delegations of authority to the bureaucracy. Unpopular decisions can be laid at the bureaucracy's door, rather than reflecting negatively on Congress. Landis (1938, 55–60) makes the point that Congress can shift the focus of conflict to administrative agencies and away from itself by avoiding clear policy statements in statutes.

The bottom line with reference to delegation of authority is that a good deal of the detail of public policy gets made by the bureaucracy without any explicit attention from Congress. Congressional access to routine policy matters is limited in practice, if not in theory. Even in initiating new formal statutes, the bureaucracy is important and sometimes dominant (Woll 1977, 170–200).

Legislative Oversight

Congressional delegation of authority does not necessarily mean congressional abdication, however. Congress has access to administrative policy making through a variety of activities collectively known as legislative oversight. This oversight can serve as a counterbalance to congressional grants of policy making authority to the bureaucracy. On the one hand, Congress gives away part of its powers to the executive branch through delegation. On the other hand, it reserves the right to monitor the way the executive branch is exercising that authority. We use "oversight" as a neutral word. Oversight in general is necessary in a representative government. But we do not prejudge any specific exercise of it as either good or bad.

Legislative oversight is not just a single activity that occurs on a regular basis. Oversight, broadly conceived, consists of all of Congress's involvement in the affairs of the bureaucracy (Keefe and Ogul 1985, chapter 12; Ogul 1973). The oversight activities of Congress focus on five objects: the substance of policy, agency personnel, agency structure, agency decision-making processes, and agency budgets. A brief survey of the techniques of oversight follows, and the topic will also receive further treatment in Chapters 3 and 8.

Congressional concern with the substance of policy is manifested in any of three stages: passage of legislation, implementation of programs, and societal impact of the programs. The content of legislation at the time of its passage identifies congressional intents as modified during the legislative process. The legislation may allow the bureaucracy considerable discretion in interpreting and applying the law. To monitor administrative interpretation, Congress can hold regular hearings in connection with both authorization and appropriation decisions and focus on aspects of this issue; it can hold special investigatory hearings; or it can make a variety of personal contacts. If Congress determines that it has overdelegated or underdelegated, it can rewrite a statute. To monitor the impact of legislation on society, Congress can require program evaluations, usually either by the agency itself or by an outside agency such as the General Accounting Office.

The personnel who develop and implement government programs are just as important to policy impact as the content of legislation. Congress is involved with a variety of agency personnel matters—size of total staff or specific components, confirmation of top administrators appointed by the president, compensation for federal employees, and the conduct of personnel in areas such as political activity, loyalty, and conflict of interest.

Congress is involved in agency structure and organization in a fundamental life-and-death sense because it is responsible for creating new agencies or for granting the president reorganization powers while retaining a congressional option for disapproving presidential initiatives. Congress also controls the lifeblood of all agencies—budget—and can kill an agency by refusing to fund it, as it did with the Area Redevelopment Administration in 1963. In addition, Congress becomes involved in the details of agency organization when the president submits reorganization plans. Congressional action killed President John Kennedy's proposal for a Department of Urban Affairs in 1962, for example.

Congress inserts itself into the internal decision-making processes of agencies in at least two ways. First, Congress requires many reports and submissions of data. Congress can review these materials to oversee agency behavior. Second, Congress can use various forms of the legislative veto, which requires an agency to submit its proposals either to Congress as a whole or to a particular committee for approval or disapproval. Although the Supreme Court ruled that the legislative veto was unconstitutional in a 1983 decision, that decision has been largely ignored by both Congress and the executive branch in practice (Chapter 3 provides a bit of detail on this point).

Congressional budgetary oversight can involve authorizations, appropriations, and expenditures. Authorizations establish the legitimacy of a program and set a ceiling on appropriations for subsequent years. Authorizations must be passed before a program can receive appropriations. The authorization process for a new or existing program requires hearings before the relevant House and Senate legislative committees. At these hearings, members review past and expected future program performances by agencies. The frequency of authorization hearings varies from yearly to longer periods, depending on the program. The appropriations hearings held by subcommittees of the House and Senate Appropriations Committees are an annual event for most agencies. These hearings also review agency performance.

It has been difficult for Congress to coordinate the program reviews that occur in the separate authorization and appropriation hearings. The quality of oversight has been criticized for focusing too much on detail and too little on program effectiveness and impact. Detailed questions about spending ("How did you spend the $10,000 for chicken wire at your field office in Ogden?") are raised in appropriation hearings and also in special audits and investigations by the General Accounting Office, an arm of Congress. Considerable funding of agencies also takes place through forms other than appropriations, which further diffuses the congressional potential for focused oversight.

Types of Policy

The national government has assumed responsibility for a mushrooming variety and volume of issues over the years. Discussing governmental policies without using categories of some sort generally produces confusion and meaningless, over-detailed description, and therefore scholars have developed a number of different schemes to help in the analysis of policies. Policies have been categorized in many ways: by specific subject matter (education, agriculture, environment, and so on); by the relative size of the budgets involved; by the beneficiary or target group affected; by the impact on society or some other measure of outcome; or by the process through which the policy is made.

We have developed a sevenfold classification scheme that encompasses most policies of the U.S. government. The scheme is based on the work of other scholars who have analyzed American public policy (Froman 1968; Hayes 1981; Huntington 1961; Lowi 1964, 1967, 1972; Salisbury 1968). In our scheme there are four types of domestic policy: (1) distributive, (2) competitive regulatory, (3) protective regulatory, and (4) redistributive. We identify three types of foreign and defense policy: (1) structural, (2) strategic, and (3) crisis.

These seven categories do not necessarily include all policies easily and perfectly. Nor does the existence of categories prevent genuine hybrids or the movement of policies from one category to another over time. (In fact, we analyze the movement of policies from one type to another later in the book.) There is nothing magic about the categories. They are presented as aids to analysis. They do, however, include most policies to which the national government pays attention at the stage of formulation and legitimation.

Two general sets of policies might seem, at first glance, to fit the categories awkwardly. However, they are accounted for in large part by the categories we use. The first of these potentially undigestible sets of policies is what might be called "constituent issues," or issues involving rules of the political game, a subset of which are constitutional issues. Examples include campaign financing, the regulation of lobbying, and ethics laws. However, most of these specific issues have elements of redistributive policy in them because most of the fights are over how level the playing field should be in terms of economic classes and/or races.

A second cluster of policies that may not fit completely are social regulatory issues. A recent book (Tatalovich and Daynes 1988) on that topic identified six substantive policy areas as examples: school prayer, pornography, crime, gun control, affirmative action, and abortion. The most important issue in that set is affirmative action. It fits our scheme very well as a redistributive issue and generates that kind of politics. Abortion is, for the most part, a redistributive issue. Well-off women can afford safe abortions, short of a complete national ban that is effectively enforced. Poor women are the first to be denied access to safe abortions. To the extent that gun control and pornography are linked to attempts to reduce crime, a form of protective regulation is involved, as are federal crime measures in general. Only school prayer is not accounted for. However, school prayer is dealt with almost exclusively in rhetorical terms, so federal policy is not really formulated.

In short, the categorical scheme we have developed, and which we explain below, addresses quite well even the examples that seem, at first glance, to present analytical problems. Our categories are not perfect. No categories are. But we find the analytical utility of them to be satisfying. We could proliferate categories to account for all policies that do not fit the sevenfold scheme neatly (see Lowi 1988, for one such attempt). We prefer, however, to preserve the values inherent in keeping a scheme with relatively few categories. We think the virtues of parsimony outweigh whatever the costs are of using a scheme that may omit few specific cases.

It should be noted that the emergence of the huge federal deficit and the resulting political fallout did not alter the way in which different types of policy are treated. Much of the concern for the deficit voiced in Congress and the executive branch was rhetorical. Dramatic changes did not take place in relation to concrete decisions or the processes by which decisions were made (Penner and Abramson 1988).

The basic notion behind our scheme is that each type of policy generates and is surrounded by its own distinctive set of political relationships. These relationships in turn help to determine substantive, concrete outcomes when policy decisions emerge. Table 1-3 summarizes the characteristics of the political relationships surrounding policy making for each type of policy. The main features of the political relationships with which we are concerned in Table 1-3 are the identity of the primary actors, the basic nature of the interaction among those actors, the stability of their interaction, the visibility of the policy decisions to individuals not immediately involved or concerned, and the relative influence of different individual actors.

We have excluded competitive regulatory policy from Table 1-3 because it is a type of policy that is rarely formulated and legitimated. In fact, in the last several decades, many areas previously subject to competitive regulatory statutes have been deregulated (for example, various aspects of routes and rates for airlines, truck lines, barge lines, pipelines, and some aspects of communications). Whatever competitive regulatory policy remains is implemented on the basis of very few statutes. The implementers—bureaucratic agencies, regulatory commissions, and courts—focus on decisions about individual cases. Actors involved are relevant bureaucratic, judicial, and quasi-judicial agencies, the individuals or corporate units competing for benefits being awarded, and a few members of Congress who have a specific interest in the outcome. We have included below a brief discussion of competitive regulatory policy to contrast it with other types of policy. It differs from protective regulatory policy at the state level, where it is more frequently a subject of statutes (Nice 1987). But since this book focuses on national formulation and legitimation, we have not included competitive regulatory policy in the analysis in the remainder of the book.

Domestic Policy

Distributive policy   Distributive policies and programs are aimed at promoting private activities that are argued to be desirable to society as a whole and, at least in theory,

TABLE 1–3

Political Relationships in Policy Formulation and Legitimation

Policy type	Primary actors	Relationship among actors	Stability of relationship	Visibility of decision
Distributive	Congressional subcommittees and committees; executive bureaus; small interest groups	Logrolling (everyone gains)	Stable	Low
Protective regulatory	Congressional subcommittees and committees; full House and Senate; executive agencies; trade associations	Bargaining; compromise	Unstable	Moderate
Redistributive	President and his appointees; committees and/ or Congress; largest interest groups (peak associations); "liberals, conservatives"	Ideological and class conflict	Stable	High
Structural	Congressional subcommittees and committees; executive bureaus; small interest groups	Logrolling (everyone gains)	Stable	Low
Strategic	Executive agencies; president	Bargaining; compromise	Unstable	Low until publicized; then low to high
Crisis	President and advisers	Cooperation	Unstable	Low until publicized; then generally high

(continued)

TABLE 1–3 *(continued)*

President, presidency, and centralized bureaucracy	Bureaus	Influence of Congress as a whole	Congressional subcommittees	Private sector
Low	High	Low (supports subcommittees)	High	High (subsidized groups)
Moderately high	Moderate	Moderately high	Moderate	Moderately high (regulated interests)
High	Moderately low	High	Moderately low	High ("peak associations" representing clusters of interest groups)
Low	High	Low (supports subcommittees)	High	High (subsidized groups and corporations)
High	Low	High (often responsive to executive)	Low	Moderate (interest groups, corporations)
High	Low	Low	Low	Low

would not or could not be undertaken without government support. Such policies and programs provide subsidies for those private activities and thus convey tangible governmental benefits to the individuals, groups, and corporations subsidized. A subsidy is a payment of some kind designed to induce desired behavior. Many governmental policies turn out to be subsidies, even if they do not seem to be subsidies at first glance. Decisions about subsidies are typically made with only short-run consequences considered. The decisions are not considered in light of each other; rather, they are disaggregated and each is treated separately. There appear to be only winners in the realm of distributive policy; there are no apparent losers.

The cast of characters (usually individuals or groups that comprise a subgovernment) involved in distributive decisions in a particular field (such as agricultural price supports, water resources, or subsidies for health research) is fairly stable over time, and their interactions are marked by low visibility and a high degree of cooperation and logrolling. The congressional subcommittee generally makes the final decisions after receiving input from other actors. The recipients of distributive subsidies of different kinds are not particularly aware of each other, and there is no sense of competing for limited resources. Anyone is potentially a recipient. Resources are treated as unlimited. Distributive decisions embody the federal pork-barrel in its fullest sense.

Typically, many people, groups, and corporate units are granted bites of the federal pie. Distributive decisions, both within a specific substantive field and across different fields, are made individually, without consideration for their interrelation or overall impact. They are decentralized and uncoordinated. The budget process instituted by the federal government in 1974 and enhanced both by the usage of its reconciliation provisions (especially in 1981) and by the Gramm–Rudman–Hollings law in 1985, with revisions necessitated by a Supreme Court decision in 1986, theoretically brings some budgetary discipline to distributive policy making. That discipline is more apparent than real, however.

Chapter 4 will focus on the nature of congressional–bureaucratic relationships when distributive policies are being made.

Examples of distributive policies include direct cash payments for purchase of agricultural commodities; grants for scientific research in universities and private laboratories; grants to localities for airport construction, hospital construction, sewage facilities, and mass transit facilities; promoting home ownership through tax provisions allowing deductions for interest on home mortgages and local property taxes; and issuing low-cost permits for grazing on public lands.

Competitive regulatory policy Competitive regulatory policies and programs are aimed at limiting the provision of specific goods and services to one or a few designated deliverers, who are chosen from a larger number of competing potential deliverers. Some decisions allocate scarce resources that simply cannot be divided, such as television channels or radio frequencies in available public broadcast bands. Some decisions maintain limited rather than unlimited competition in the provision of goods and services by allowing only certain potential deliverers to provide them and excluding other potential deliverers. Some decisions are aimed at regulating the quality of services delivered through choosing the deliverer periodically and imposing standards of performance. If those standards are not met, a new deliverer can be chosen. This type of policy is a hybrid. It subsidizes the winning competitors and also tries to regulate some aspects of service delivery in the public interest. Examples of competitive regulatory policies include granting and reviewing licenses to operate television and radio stations; authorizing specific airlines to operate specified routes; and authorizing specific trucking companies to haul specified commodities over designated routes.

In recent years, most of the broad decisions leading to a statute have been in the direction of deregulation. Most policy decisions of importance in areas still subject to competitive regulatory policy occur during implementation. Many may occur at the state level. Although it is important to be aware of the existence of this policy area, it is an area of such sporadic and marginal national activity that it will receive no further analysis in this volume.

Protective regulatory policy   Protective regulatory policies and programs are designed to protect the public by setting the conditions under which various private activities can be undertaken. Conditions that are thought to be harmful (air pollution, false advertising) are prohibited. Conditions that are thought to be helpful (the publication of true interest rates on loans) are required.

Protective regulatory policies, unlike distributive policies, establish a general rule of law and require that a certain segment of the population must conform to the law. This means that the policies are broad in impact and, therefore, more visible politically. The actors involved in protective regulatory decisions (coalitions of members of the full House and Senate, executive agencies, and representatives of trade associations) are much less stable than in the distributive arena, partially because of constantly shifting substantive issues. The ultimate decisions get made on the floor of the House and Senate. Chapter 5 examines the congressional–bureaucratic relationship in shaping protective regulatory policy.

Examples of federal protective regulatory policies include the requirement that banks, stores, and other institutions that grant credit disclose true interest rates; prohibition of unfair business practices, unfair labor practices, and business combinations that reduce competition; limits on the conditions under which strip mining can be undertaken and requirements for the postmining restoration of land; the prohibition of harmful food additives; and high taxation to reduce the consumption of such occasionally scarce commodities as gasoline.

It should be noted that the Reagan administration sought eagerly to deregulate in the protective arena. The would-be deregulators did not succeed in terms of statutes, although they could slow down enforcement of protective regulation through administrative action. But the general protective regulatory policy process proved to be, in the words used in a detailed study of two major agencies, "remarkably resilient" (Harris and Miklis 1989, 279).

Redistributive policy   Redistributive policies and programs are intended to manipulate the allocation of wealth, property, political or civil rights, or some other valued item among social classes or racial groups. The redistributive feature enters because a number of actors perceive there are "winners" and "losers" in policies that transfer some value to one group *at the expense of* another group. For example, the rich sometimes perceive themselves to be losers in a program that seeks to confer some benefits on the poor. Anglos sometimes perceive themselves to be losers in relation to a policy or a program that confers special benefits primarily on ethnic and racial minority groups.

Redistribution can run in both directions: from the less advantaged to the more advantaged, as well as from the more advantaged to the less advantaged. However, in the verbal currency of American politics, only programs perceived to redistribute benefits to the less advantaged at the expense of the more advantaged are treated as redistributive policy. In keeping with that fact of American politics, our analysis will focus on such instances. Redistributive policies tend to generate visible and often prolonged political controversy.

Contestants in struggles over redistributive policy perceive the stakes to be high. This means that the policy-making process is often marked by high degrees of visibility and conflict. The coalitions that form in relation to any redistributive issue may change in composition depending on the issue (integrated schools, open housing, welfare programs), but they can generally be identified as a proponent ("liberal") coalition and an opponent ("conservative") coalition. The debate between the coalitions is cast in ideological terms. Whether redistributive policy will actually emerge from the confrontation between the competing coalitions depends on the presence of strong presidential leadership and the willingness of participants to retreat from ideological stances and adopt compromises. The principal political consideration among the participants during the process is who gets what at the expense of whom. Chapter 6 focuses on the congressional–bureaucratic relationship when redistributive issues are at stake.

Examples of redistributive policy include setting progressive personal income-tax rates so that more affluent people pay a higher percentage of their income in taxes than do less affluent people; requiring housing, public accommodations and facilities, and public education to be free of racial discrimination; requiring affirmative action in hiring by federal contractors to increase the employment of women and minorities; and providing employment and training programs, food stamps, or special legal services for the disadvantaged.

Foreign and Defense Policy

Policy typologies dealing with nondomestic issues are less frequent than those in domestic areas. Lowi (1967, 324–325) suggests that there are three distinctive patterns of politics in foreign policy. The first is crisis foreign policy. In this situation, the perception of a threat to national security cuts across normal channels of decision making. An elite of formal officeholders within the executive branch makes the decisions with a minimum of conflict. In the absence of a crisis, there is time for "normal" patterns and concerns to emerge. Institutions become involved, and inter-actions occur over a number of questions. Foreign policy in these "normal" circum-stances is, for Lowi, basically either distributive or regulatory, and the politics surrounding these policies look very much like the politics surrounding domestic distributive or regulatory policy.

In the area of defense policy, which has both domestic and foreign aspects, Huntington (1961) has identified two types—strategic and structural defense policy. Strategic defense policy is oriented toward foreign policy and international politics, and it involves the units and use of military force, their strength, and their deployment. Structural defense policy focuses on domestic politics and involves decisions about the procurement, allocation, and organization of the personnel, money, and materiel that constitute the military forces. Structural decisions are made primarily within the context of strategic decisions to implement those decisions.

We have drawn on both Lowi and Huntington in settling on three categories for the combination of foreign policies and defense policies: structural, strategic, and crisis. All three types will be examined in more detail in Chapter 7.

Structural policy Structural policies and programs aim primarily at procuring, deploying, and organizing military personnel and materiel, presumably within the confines and guidelines of previously determined strategic decisions. Because the federal government has no competitors in providing defense, the element of total subsidy for the enterprise is a given. But the details of that subsidy can vary greatly.

Structural policies are closely related to distributive policies. The process is characterized by the presence of subgovernments, by decentralized decision making, by nonconflictive relationships among the actors, and by decisions that treat internal resources as unlimited and separable. Policy decisions emerge from the formal legislative process (bill introduction, committee hearings, passage by the House and Senate). Although Congress is generally responding to executive requests rather than initiating policy in this area, it nonetheless has final decision power.

Examples of structural policies include specific defense procurement decisions for individual weapons systems; the placement, expansion, contraction, and closing of military bases and other facilities in the United States; the retention, expansion, or contraction of reserve military forces; and the creation and retention of programs that send surplus farm commodities overseas.

Strategic policy Strategic policies and programs are designed to assert and implement the basic military and foreign policy stance of the United States toward other nations. Policy planning and proposals resulting from that planning stem primarily from executive branch activities. A number of executive branch agencies compete, bargain, and sometimes engage in conflict during policy development. Decisions are made by these agencies, with the final approval of the president. Public debate and congressional involvement usually occur after the formal decisions are announced. Committees or individual members of Congress may lobby executive agencies for specific decisions. Congress may respond to an executive request for legislation to implement a decision already made, or Congress may protect and alter an action already completed. Congress does not make strategic choices by itself. Although congressional influence can be important, that influence is often used to respond supportively to executive branch initiatives.

Examples of strategic policies include decisions about the basic mix of military forces (for example, the ratio of ground-based missiles to submarine-based missiles to manned bombers); foreign trade (the absence of tariffs and quotas for specific nations or their nature if present); sales of U.S. arms to foreign nations; foreign aid; immigration regulations; and the number, type, and involvement of U.S. forces overseas.

Crisis policy   Crisis policies are responses to immediate problems that are perceived to be serious, that have burst on the policy makers with little or no warning, and that demand immediate action. The occurrence of crisis situations is unpredictable and tied to external (nondomestic) events. The principal actors are elite executive branch officeholders who work cooperatively together with a minimum of publicized conflict. Visibility of the decision-making process is also low, except to the extent that press releases and press conferences inform the public. The involvement of Congress is informal and limited and is usually made in the mode of consultation with key individuals. The full body may get involved formally, usually after the crisis, to make the action legitimate or to forbid similar exercises of executive power in the future.

Examples of crisis policies include decisions about the U.S. response to the Japanese attack on Pearl Harbor in 1941; the impending French collapse in Indochina in 1954; the Soviet Union's placement of missiles in Cuba in 1962; the North Korean seizure of a U.S. Navy ship in 1968; the Cambodian seizure of a U.S. merchant ship in 1975; the Iranian seizure of U.S. hostages in late 1979; the seizure of a Mediterranean cruise ship in 1985; and the seizure of an American commercial airplane in the Mideast in 1985.

The Rest of the Book

In the remainder of this volume we will develop the notions that have been introduced in this chapter. Our special concerns will be to make clear the varying nature of the involvement of subgovernments in policy making, the need for cooperation and the potential for conflict between Congress and the bureaucracy, and the presence and effect of different major types of policy.

Chapter 2 will discuss the actors in the congressional–bureaucratic relationship: members of the House and Senate; congressional staff; politically appointed members of executive branch agencies; and civil servants (and their military and foreign service equivalents) in policy-making positions in agencies.

Chapter 3 will focus on the occasions for interactions among the actors and will describe the resources available to Congress and the bureaucracy in those interactions.

In Chapters 4 through 7 we will use a variety of case materials to illustrate congressional–bureaucratic relations in each of the six policy areas identified above. We will focus on the subgovernment phenomemon where it is present. In the absence of a subgovernment, we will describe the broad congressional–executive interactions that do occur. Reality in government and politics is never as simple or clear-cut as analysts and students might wish. The policy categories we use are not perfect, as we have already indicated. We have in Chapters 4 through 7 selected examples that, in our judgment, fit each policy type well. Where individual examples fall into more than one category, we have broken the policy into its appropriate parts.

In Chapter 8 we will summarize our findings about congressional–bureaucratic interactions in the various policy arenas and will make an overall assessment of the substantive impact of the relationship between Congress and the bureaucracy.

CHAPTER TWO

Actors in the Relationship

The interactions between Congress and the bureaucracy are complicated because a number of different groups of participants in both branches of government are involved. These groups of individuals, although within the same branch of government, may behave quite differently from one another. For example, members of authorizing (legislative) committees and appropriations committees in Congress are likely to differ significantly in their behavior. Staff members in the two chambers will also differ in their approaches to legislation. Congressional staff members working for a committee often proceed in ways that would not be used by staff members working in individual members' offices, and vice versa. Presidential appointees in the White House or Office of Management and Budget (OMB) may act quite differently from presidential appointees at the cabinet and subcabinet levels. Civil servants may hold quite incongruent views of the policy world, depending on whether they are in a line-operating position in a program, a staff position—especially one focusing on budgetary matters—or a legislative liaison position. The attitudes and activities of specific groups of civil servants may also depend in part on whether they are assigned to headquarters in the Washington, D.C., area or to a field office.

Differences in behavior not only distinguish groups of actors from the two branches but also have important additional implications. For example, these behavioral differences can influence the relative degrees of conflict and cooperation among the actors involved in policy making. They also help shape the substance, direction, and magnitude of the policy emerging from the relationship.

In this chapter we will begin to make some observations about the nature of the relationships among and between congressional and bureaucratic actors and about the effects of those relationships on policy and policy change. The next two sections of this chapter describe and compare the four major classes of actors in the relationship—members of the House and Senate, congressional staff members, political appointees in the executive branch, and civil servants. We want to depict these four groups of policy makers in ways that show both their similarities and dissimilarities.

These profiles of the individuals involved and of the institutional setting in which each group functions are presented in part to convey basic descriptive information. They are also intended to aid in subsequent analysis of factors that explain the cooperation or conflict in the relationships between the groups and the policies that are influenced by those relationships.

In the concluding section of the present chapter, we assess the impact of specific role orientations on the likelihood of conflict or cooperation in various relationships and on the nature of that conflict or cooperation.

It should be noted that Congress has recently made some institutional changes (often called "reforms"), especially in the first half of the 1970s. The following discussion takes account of those changes if they seem to have had an impact, although in many cases the impact of "reform" has been minimal (Davidson and Oleszek 1977; Dodd and Oppenheimer 1977; Rieselbach 1977, 1986; Welch and Peters 1977.)

In 1978 Congress also passed a civil service reform bill that, theoretically, could have had some impact on the way the bureaucracy conducts business and on the relationships between bureaucrats and other actors, especially their nominal political masters (Cooper 1978). The Reagan administration sought to impose more ideological tests of loyalty on career bureaucrats than had previous administrations. The 1978 act gave the administration more flexibility than it would have had previously in dealing with the most senior career bureaucrats (Goldenberg 1984; Lynn 1984; Moe 1985). The act made no headway in creating a government-wide senior civil service not subject to political domination (Heclo 1984). In short, the 1978 act changed little.

In general, change in both congressional and bureaucratic institutions occurs slowly. New forms and behavior prescribed by statute are often absorbed into customary modes of conducting business with only minor adjustments.

The Individuals Involved

This section presents aggregate profiles of the four major clusters of participants in the relationships between Congress and the bureaucracy: members of Congress, congressional staff members, political appointees in the executive branch, and higher level civil servants.

Geographical Representation

Congress is geographically representative. Since the reapportionment decisions of the federal courts applying to the House of Representatives in the 1960s, rural, urban, and suburban areas are all represented roughly in accordance with their proportion of the total population. If there is any geographical bias in Congress, it may be in the overrepresentation of smaller towns in terms of where members were born and raised. This is true of House leaders, for example (Nelson 1975).

Many congressional staff members, particularly those on personal staffs, come from the state of their first employer. Once established, however, they are likely to work for a member from a different state when their original employer leaves Congress or they leave his or her employ. The most comprehensive study of congressional staff (Fox and Hammond 1977) found that close to two-thirds of personal staff members in the Senate retain a legal residence in the same state as the senator for whom they work. Although reliable figures are scarce, it is reasonable to conclude that staff members in Congress come from all over the United States (and a few from other nations) and are broadly representative in geographical terms. Regardless of their own place of birth and upbringing, some personal staff members have responsibility for tending to the welfare of the geographic constituency of the legislator for whom they work.

Regardless of place of origin, there is good evidence that congressional staff members become identified with the metropolitan Washington, D.C., area (Brady 1981). They tend to get their graduate or professional education there, and many open jobs on the Hill go to individuals already in a staff job there. Some replacements come from Boise, Waco, or Akron; but there is also a large circulating Washington-based body of professional congressional staff members.

Federal political executives—the major appointees in the executive branch—come originally from all over the country in roughly the same proportion as the general population. However, the Washington, D.C., area is heavily overrepresented when place of work immediately prior to political appointment is the criterion for assigning geographical region (Fisher 1987; Stanley, Mann, and Doig 1967).

Members of the policy level of the civil service (also called the higher civil service and defined as either GS 14s and above or GS 15s and above) overrepresent the East and urban backgrounds when compared with the general population. The South is underrepresented (Meier 1987, 182).

Education

All of these groups of policy makers are formally much more well educated than the general population. Between 88 percent and 96 percent of members all four policy-making groups had a minimum of a college degree in the 1970s and 1980s (Fisher 1987, 9; Fox and Hammond 1977, 175; Kessel 1984, 199; Meier 1979, 171). Those in the executive branch were at the high end of this small range. Many (75% of political appointees from 1964 through 1984, for example) had at least one professional or advanced degree. At the same time, less than 20 percent of the general population aged 24 or older had a college degree (1989 *Statistical Abstract*, 133).

Occupation

Reliable comparative figures on occupation of various policy-making groups *before* they attained their present position are difficult to produce, both because the occupation of many is "public service" and because some, especially members of Congress, list several occupations. However, some general statements backed by data can be made.

Backgrounds in law and business are dominant among members of the House and Senate. Education is a distant third. In the Congress that met in 1989–1990, for example, 42 percent of the members of the House were lawyers, about a third had a business background, and just short of 10 percent were educators. In the Senate, 63 percent were lawyers, 28 percent were from a business background, and 11 percent were educators. It is worth noting, however, that long service and the predominance of relatively safe seats mean that many members are actually pursuing careers in congressional service. And, of course, many of them had active careers as elected officials (for example, as state legislators) before coming to Congress, and thus their private occupational backgrounds may in many cases be more a matter of training and limited experience than extensive experience.

Most congressional committee staff members come from other public-service positions, about evenly divided between positions in the executive branch and other positions on congressional staffs, primarily personal staffs of senators and representatives. Only a few come to their committee positions from business or law (Fox and Hammond 1977, 175).

About half of federal political executives are pursuing careers in public service. Of the half whose primary occupation is in the private sector, about one-third come from business, about one-fourth come from law, and about one-fifth come from positions in education (Fisher 1987, 14–21).

Analysis of a sample of higher civil servants in the late 1960s and early 1970s found that most higher civil servants (in this case defined as GS 15s and above and their equivalents in other federal services) began their careers in public service (40%); a large proportion came from business (30%); and a sizable proportion came from education (15%) (U.S. Civil Service Commission, 1976, 35).

A comparative review of what we know about the occupational background of these four policy-making groups underscores a few generalizations. First, regardless of group and regardless of formal training or fairly distant private occupational background, a very large proportion of these people are pursuing careers in public service, both elected and appointed. This is least true for federal political executives, but even for this group the percentage whose primary occupation could be labeled as some form of public service fluctuated between 45 percent and 53 percent when looked at in relation to which president appointed them.

Second, lawyers are much more numerous in percentage terms in Congress than elsewhere, but are well represented throughout the policy-making layers of Congress and the bureaucracy.

Third, individuals with business backgrounds are present in large percentages in all groups.

Fourth, many people in all groups have had experience as educators in public and private schools, colleges, and universities.

The importance of these generalizations is that it is not fanciful to imagine that the concepts, language, and values of the law and business are often predominant in the interactions of these policy-making groups. There is also considerable familiarity with concerns particular to educational institutions. The relatively lower orientation to public service (plus very short tenure in specific jobs, to be discussed later) for federal political executives means that they are the group least likely to be accepted as legitimate by the others (Heclo 1977, 1987).

Age

The average age of the policy-making groups is about the same, with the partial exception of congressional staff members, who are younger. These figures have not varied much over the last several decades. In 1989 the average age of all representatives was 52 and the average age of all senators was almost 56. Between 1965 and 1984 the average age of all federal political executives when appointed was 47 (Fisher 1987, 7). Between 1962 and 1965 the average age of individuals achieving a grade that entitled them to be counted as part of the higher civil service was 49 (Stanley, Mann, and Doig 1967, 28). Professional congressional staff members were found to be about 40 years old in the mid 1970s (Fox and Hammond 1977, 173), but that fact does not put these individuals in a different "generation" (whatever that vague term may mean) than the other policy makers. Whatever difficulties individuals on the Hill and both career and appointed senior members of the executive branch have in communicating with each other do not stem from a "generation gap."

Gender and Race

All of these policy making groups are overwhelmingly composed of white males. The 101st Congress (1989–1990) had 2 women senators out of 100 and 25 women representatives out of 435. It had no black or Hispanic senators; 2 senators of Asian background; 23 black members of the House, 10 Hispanic members of the House; and 4 members of the House of Asian background. All of the Asians were of Japanese ancestry.

There are lots of professional women on congressional staffs, although they are still outnumbered by men. For example, a study done by the office of Republican Representative Lynn Martin from Illinois in 1988 found that of all committee staff members making more than $40,000 a year (a rough indicator of professional status), 32 percent were women and 68 percent were men. No comparable studies identifying black professional staff members are available, but it is safe to say there are relatively few blacks in such positions.

Of all federal political executives appointed between 1964 and 1984, about 8 percent were women and about 5 percent were nonwhite (Fisher 1987, 4–7). The higher civil service is also dominated by white males. In 1974, for example, 96 percent were white and 98 percent were male (Meier 1987, 182). By 1981, despite concerted affirmative action efforts, only 6.6 percent of the Senior Executive Service of about 7,000 of the top-level civil servants were women, and only 5.1 percent were black (Sawyer 1982). These percentages are growing very slowly. Figures for 1987 reported in the 1989 *Statistical Abstract* (p. 318) show 14 percent of GS 13s–15s and about 7 percent of GS 16s–18s to be women. Figures for 1986 from the same source show almost 11 percent of GS 13s, 14s, and 15s to be blacks, Hispanics, Asians, Pacific Islanders, American Indians, or Alaska natives. Close to 7 percent of the Senior Executive Service (generally the equivalent of GS 16s, 17s, and 18s) were from these minority groups.

Previous Governmental and Political Experience

Individuals in the highest positions—senators, representatives, and executive-branch political appointees—are highly experienced both politically and in government service before they reach their high positions. Congressional staff members are less experienced, probably because they are younger when they attain their positions, and high-ranking civil servants gain experience during their careers.

Members of the House and Senate are, generally, experienced public servants before they are elected to Congress. Most have held one or more elected positions at the state or local level. Many senators have also been members of the U.S. House of Representatives. A study of occupation and experience in 1984 showed that two-thirds of the House and three-fourths of the Senate had had "government" as their occupation for at least ten years (Kessel 1984, 201).

Congressional staff members generally have less governmental experience before starting their careers on the Hill, although members of committee staffs are likely to be more experienced than members of personal staffs. Many congressional staff members have considerable political experience, usually through working in political campaigns, often for the individual who appoints them to a position on a congressional staff.

Higher civil servants tend to make a career of the civil service and gain governmental experience as they gain seniority. Civil servants at the management level are quite experienced governmentally.

Federal political executives are often experienced public servants. For example, 63 percent of all appointees between 1933 and 1965 had prior federal administrative exerience. That figure rose to 67 percent for all appointees between 1964 and 1984 (Fisher 1987, 21). A number of these appointees were also politically active in the campaign of the president who appointed them.

Beliefs

Some research characterizes both the beliefs about government and the political ideology of the four groups of policy makers being analyzed here (Aberbach and Rockman 1976, 1977, 1978; Fox and Hammond 1977; Meier 1987; Meier and Nigro 1976; Rothman and Lichter 1983).

Members of Congress, federal political executives, and higher civil servants all tend to believe in the legitimacy of subgovernments. They also generally believe that interest groups should have a high degree of access to both Congress and the bureaucracy (Aberbach and Rockman 1977, 1978). No specific research on the attitudes of congressional staff on these points has been done, but it would be surprising if their views deviated much from the views of the members who appointed them.

Legislators and bureaucrats in the United States deal with each other on a regular basis, much more frequently than in the democracies of Western Europe (Aberbach, Putnam, and Rockman 1981). This fact helps sustain their belief that they *should* deal with each other. Political executives are probably the least supportive of the legitimacy of subgovernments because they are often excluded from those subgovernments.

The political ideology of members of Congress can be expected to change, usually quite slowly, over time. The nature of the change, not surprisingly, is related to public preferences revealed in election results and even public opinion polls. In general, the ideology of members of Congress is similar to that of high-ranking civil servants

(Aberbach and Rockman 1977). High-ranking civil servants hold abstract political beliefs slightly more liberal than those of the general public but very similar to those of the general public on specific issues (Meier 1987, 183; Rothman and Lichter 1983).

The ideology of congressional staff members mirrors closely that of the individuals in Congress for whom they work (Fox and Hammond 1977). The ideology of federal political executives reflects both that of the president who appointed them and of the agency or department in which they work. This dual loyalty can cause problems for both presidents and agencies.

In short, there is widespread agreement among these four groups of policy makers in terms of some central beliefs about the functioning of government. Even in terms of political ideology, there are forces that minimize differences between groups. Partisan considerations can, of course, heighten ideological disagreement.

Table 2-1 summarizes the personal characteristics of these four groups of policy makers.

The Institutional Setting

The institutional settings in which various congressional and bureaucratic actors work help shape their behavior. The settings differ for each of the four principal subgroups of individuals in terms of method of selection, job tenure and orientation, principal loyalties and representativeness, degree of substantive specialization, degree of professionalism, degree of political expertise, and degree of visibility. These factors are relatively unchanging over time, no matter who happens to hold the various positions.

Method of selection means how individuals obtain the positions they hold. The principal methods are election, political appointment, and merit advancement. *Job tenure and orientation* are related to the means of selection and involve the length of service and the nature of career aspirations associated with different clusters of policy makers. *Principal loyalties* involve the individuals' perceptions of the entity to which they feel they owe primary allegiance. *Representativeness* of groups of policy makers varies both in terms of geographic area (national versus local representation) and in terms of the breadth of interests represented (broad-gauged interests versus narrow, special interests). Do actors tend to become experts in a few issues (specialists), or do they tend to have a general understanding of many issues (generalists)? These questions are addressed by the *degree of substantive specialization*. A policy maker's identification with a profession compared with his or her identification with a congressional or bureaucratic unit is the focus of the discussion of the *degree of professionalism*. The *degree of political expertise* inherent in different actors' jobs involves how much political skill is necessary for doing the jobs successfully—skill in bargaining and skill in competing for limited resources. The final institutional factor to be discussed is the *degree of visibility* (or, conversely, anonymity) associated with the different groups of policy makers. How publicly visible are these groups as they perform their daily tasks?

TABLE 2-1
Personal Characteristics of Major Congressional and Bureaucratic Policy Actors

Characteristics	Senators and representatives	Professional congressional staff members	Higher career civil servants	Federal political executives
Geographical representativeness	Broadly representative geographically; over-representative of small towns	Broadly representative geographically	Overrepresentative of the East and urban areas	Broadly representative geographically; over-representative of N.Y. and Washington
Education	Highly educated	Highly educated	Highly educated	Highly educated
Occupation	Heavily in law and business; some educators; many professional politicians	Occupational specialty tied to job; many professional public servants; some generalists	Occupational specialty tied to job; many professional public servants; many with business background; some educators	Heavily in business and law; some educators
Age	Median: about 50 (senators slightly older)	Median: about 40	Median: late 40s	Median: late 40s
Gender and race	Mostly white males	Mostly white males	Mostly white males	Mostly white males
Previous governmental and political experience	High experience in both government and politics	Considerable Hill and political experience; limited executive branch experience	High government experience through civil service career	Moderately high experience in federal service
Beliefs	Believe in subgovernments and interest-group access; ideology shifts with election results	Believe in subgovernments and interest-group access; ideology reflects that of congressional employer	Believe in subgovernments and interest-group access; ideology reflects that of agency	Usually believe in subgovernments and interest-group access, with limits; ideology reflects that of agency and/or president

Method of Selection

Only one of the four groups—members of the House and Senate—is elected, a fact that is enormously important in determining what kinds of considerations are most salient to members of Congress as they deal with policy. Concern for job security nurtures a predisposition for members of Congress to provide the voters back home with sufficient tangible benefits to help ensure reelection. Legislators evaluate a great deal of their behavior in terms of how it affects reelection chances (Mayhew 1974).

Once in Congress, members seek appointment to specific committees and sub-committees for a variety of reasons (Fenno 1973). A number of members consciously seek a specific assignment because of the electoral advantage it can bring them. Even those who pursue memberships primarily because of their policy interests and because of their interest in increasing their influence within their chamber are mindful of opportunities a given assignment might afford them to serve their constituents well. As members become more senior, they are generally less vulnerable to defeat at the polls and can afford to pursue policy views that are particularly congenial to them, especially in the committees and subcommittees on which they sit.

Members of congressional staffs are appointed by members of the House and Senate. Staff members are necessarily also concerned with reelection and constituents' preferences. But since experienced members of congressional staffs can easily work for other members if their own member is defeated, their dependence on the constituents is not nearly so strong as that of the elected members.

Political appointments to high-level executive branch positions are, in theory, made by the president. In practice, the president knows personally only a small fraction of the individuals he appoints. Other high-ranking officials in the administration, themselves political appointees, in fact make most of the appointments.

Higher civil servants and their military and foreign-service equivalents attain their positions on the basis of merit. Political considerations can also play a part, both formal and informal, in filling selected top positions in the civil service.

Job Tenure and Orientation

Job tenure and orientation vary in part with the way in which individuals acquire their position. Personnel turnover in elected positions or appointed positions dependent on elections is more rapid than in civil service positions not dependent on election results. The shortest length of service occurs among political appointees in the executive branch. Median tenure of political executives in specific positions was only a bit more than two years during the entire period from 1933 through 1984 (Fisher 1987, 23; see also Heclo 1977, 104).

Tenure for individual legislators is always uncertain, but seats have become safer in recent years. At present, the average length of service in both the House and Senate is about nine years. For a number of decades, members have increasingly aspired to make Congress a major part of their careers (Huntington 1973; Polsby 1968; Price 1971; Witmer 1964). An increasing proportion of the members have been able to achieve that aspiration.

Many congressional staff members have also become oriente
in legislative staff work (Fox and Hammond 1977, 62–65). In
are able to realize this ambition, for two reasons. First, the long ...
elected members—the appointing authorities—helps them stay in staff positiv....
Second, even if their original patron retires or is defeated, other members of the
House and Senate are always eager to hire experienced staff members. Top staff
members in Congress are likely to be experienced in a variety of congressional staff
positions (Brady 1981).

It is also worth noting that the number of congressional staff members has
expanded dramatically in recent years. Between 1947 and 1986, for example, the
number of personal staff members in the House grew from under 1,500 to close to
8,000. The number of personal staff members in the Senate grew from under 600
to almost 3,800 during the same period. Also during the same period, committee
staff in the House grew from 167 individuals to 1,954. Senate committee staff grew
from 232 to 1,075.

Career orientation among bureaucrats at the policy-making levels is revealed by
the tendency of these individuals to serve with the federal government for a long
time, to spend their entire career in one agency, rarely to change occupational
specialties, and rarely to move between assignment at headquarters (usually in
Washington) and assignment to a field office (Corson and Paul 1966; Stanley 1964;
U.S. Civil Service Commission 1976). Of all of the four groups, the higher civil
servants are the most oriented toward a federal career, although both groups on the
Hill also have a strong orientation toward a career in Congress.

Principal Loyalties and Representativeness

Members of the House and Senate have two major sets of loyalties. One is to their
constituents—or more accurately, to the perception they hold of their various constituencies (Fenno 1978). The other is to their party in the House or Senate. In general,
congressional life is structured so that the two loyalties do not compete head-on.
When they do, members usually choose what they perceive to be in the best interest
of their constituents—or, more to the point, in the best interest of their own reelection.

Congressional staff members are primarily loyal to the individual senator or
representative responsible for having put them in their present jobs. The most
important staff members tend to reflect the orientations and values of their patrons.

In theory, political appointees in the executive branch are primarily loyal to the
president, the president's programs, and the administration as a collective entity. In
practice, political appointees typically also begin to feel loyalty to the agency to which
they are appointed. For example, a secretary of agriculture will try to be responsible
to the president who appointed him to office. But if senior career employees in the
Department of Agriculture think the best interests of the department are at least
partially at odds with the program of the president, they will put pressure on the
secretary to act on the basis of the best interests of the department rather than remain
totally loyal to the program of the president. Political appointees put in this position
of receiving cross pressures will try to find a compromise that will avoid direct

confrontation with the White House but will also avoid the appearance of "selling out" the department. Even during the Reagan administration, which was unusually careful in appointing extremely loyal ultra-conservatives to senior positions in the bureaucracy, some of these individuals turned out to defend agency budgets against severe cuts proposed by the OMB, the loyal budget arm of the institutional presidency.

Civil servants are primarily loyal to the organizations in which they work and in which they are likely to make their career. They are less cross-pressured than the other major groups of policy-making officials. Individual civil servants who also belong to a nationally recognized profession—for example, lawyers, engineers, scientists, doctors—also feel a good deal of loyalty to the standards of their profession (Wilensky 1967).

Members of the House and Senate are concerned with representing the geographical areas from which they are elected. They are also usually concerned with representing a variety of interests they perceive to be important. While the specific meaning of "representation" varies from member to member, they are all concerned with being genuinely representative. For some, this means focusing mainly on helping obtain tangible benefits for their district or state and for the most important organized groups in the district or state. For others, this means thinking more broadly about the needs of the district and about the needs of national interests and groups, both organized and unorganized. For most members, being a good representative is likely to include a broad range of activities that stretches from seeking a new post office for some specific town in a district or state to worrying about the welfare of all poor people or all cotton farmers or all black people or whatever group seems to the individual member to be most important.

Congressional staff members also reflect the attitudes of their patrons as they think about representation. Their interests reflect the views of those patrons.

Executive branch officials are also concerned with representation, but not in the same sense as individuals on the Hill. The geographical ties to a local area on the part of political appointees and senior civil servants are weaker than those of members of Congress and of staff members in Congress. Executive branch officials may retain some ties to the region or area in which they grew up. They may also have some geographical ties linked to a program that has specific regional implications. For example, an official in the U.S. Department of Agriculture working with the program for cotton price supports is, necessarily, going to be most concerned with cotton-growing areas of the South. An official with the Bureau of Reclamation is going to be most concerned with the arid areas of the West. But many programs have no particular regional links.

The great majority (seven-eighths) of federal civil servants are not in Washington, D.C., although a disproportionate share of the higher-level civil servants are. Bureaucrats in various federal field establishments, especially those who stay there for long periods, establish specific regional loyalties and ties.

Executive branch officials are also concerned with representing interests they perceive to be important to their programs and worthy of their attention. In general, political appointees are expected to be supportive of and sympathetic to the programmatic interests of the president and to support those interests in dealing with Congress. They may also be concerned with representing the interests thought to be important to their political party. To survive politically, appointees in departments and agencies are most likely to try to be representative of many of the interests affected by their agency rather than only one or two. An appointeee who advocates only a single interest in a department or agency that deals with many is apt to be controversial and, therefore, apt to become a political liability to the administration.

Political appointees can be representative in the critical sense of allowing competing points of view to be heard in the executive branch on controversial matters before final action is taken. Sometimes policy debates take place almost wholly within the executive branch, and major decisions are made and major bargains are struck before the matter becomes an important item on the congressional agenda. This was the case, for example, with the Communications Satellite Act of 1962 and the Economic Opportunity Act of 1964 (Davidson 1967, 390–393).

Civil servants often become concerned with representing those interests and organized groups they conceive to be important in the substantive fields in which they are working. Sometimes this representational activity takes the form of advocacy by well-placed civil servants on behalf of specific interests and groups. In the other cases, the advocacy of specific interests by a bureaucracy becomes more institutionalized. For example, the advisory committee system used by many bureaucratic agencies is large and growing. In 1984 there were 930 such committees with over 25,000 members. As one study of this phenomenon observed, "Federal advisory committees facilitate the permanent *institutionalization* of linkages between interests and the national executive" (Petracca 1986, 83). In general, many of these committees increase the chances that producer interests will dominate some policy areas (Culhane 1981; Foss 1960; Lowi 1973a; Petracca 1986).

Degree of Substantive Specialization

Members of the House and Senate are both specialists *and* generalists. They are generalists because they are given the constitutional power—which they exercise with considerable, if uneven, vigor—to oversee the entire range of federal governmental activities. They must consider and vote on everything the federal government does, at least in broad outline. Any member has a number of substantive areas in which his or her knowledge is minimal, but most senators and representatives who serve for more than a short time begin to develop familiarity with and some competence in a variety of areas.

At the same time, members also become specialists through their service on standing committees and subcommittees. The committee system developed in large part as the congressional response to a bureaucracy constantly growing in size, specialization, and expertise. Especially in the House—where in the One Hundredth Congress (1987–1988) the average assignments per member were only 1.7 full committees and 3.8 subcommittees—members who serve for more than a short time can become genuine experts in one or a few policy areas. Senators are spread more thinly—with 2.9 full committee assignments and 7.0 subcommittee assignments in 1987–1988 (Ornstein, Mann, and Malbin 1987, 130). But they also tend to become expert in a few areas and have ample staff to cover the other areas for which their committee and subcommittee assignments make them responsible.

The congressional urge to specialize in order to compete with the bureaucrats is reinforced by the staff members in Congress. In both houses, many staff members, especially those who work for committees or subcommittees, have become genuinely expert in bounded portions of the policy universe and are important in the shaping of legislation (Ripley 1988, Chapter 7). Senate staff members are particularly important as specialists. Senators often rely on a staff member to do most of the substantive work in a subcommittee to which the senator is assigned (Ripley 1969a, Chapter 8).

The degree of substantive specialization is very high among higher civil servants. The main reason for the emergence of a large bureaucracy is, after all, to facilitate dealing with technical and complex topics. On the other hand, the degree of specialization among political appointees is very low. These individuals typically have little experience in the subject matter with which they are expected to deal and usually do not stay in office long enough to develop much expertise through on-the-job training.

Degree of Professionalism

Professionalism is used to denote allegiance on the part of individuals to a profession other than that of government employee. For example, chemists employed by the Food and Drug Administration (FDA) may remain most interested in the norms of the chemistry profession, attend meetings of the American Chemical Society, and subscribe to a variety of professional journals. Such individuals are likely to be as concerned with national professional standards and judgments as with the interests of the FDA as a bureaucracy. Most professionalism in this sense resides in the bureaucracy; a number of civil servants are social scientists, natural scientists, engineers, dentists, physicians, and others whose professional identification is high.

The degree of professionalism is much lower in the other policy-making groups we are considering in this chapter. There are many lawyers, particularly in Congress, but they retain little identification with the abstract norms of the profession. For most, law was both a form of academic training and a natural entry route into politics and public service. But few members actively practiced law for long.

Degree of Political Expertise

By definition, senators and representatives are and must be politicians. A member needs the political skill of assessing accurately the mood of his or her constituency. Members also need considerable skill in bargaining over the details of legislation as they pursue their daily legislative tasks. Staff members typically possess many of the same kinds of political skills.

The distribution of political skills among political appointees in the executive branch is uneven. The most effective political appointees have such skills and use them in advancing the interests of the administration and the party of the president in dealing both with Congress and with their own agencies. A few are so skilled politically that they develop their own constituencies and support independent from the president. Such individuals can become a problem for the president if they have policy preferences that vary from his. A classic case of such tension was that between President Franklin Roosevelt and his Secretary of Commerce, Jesse Jones (Fenno 1959, 234–247). Jones's ties with powerful business interests and his excellent relations with Congress allowed him to pursue policy ideas much more conservative than those desired by Roosevelt. Yet the president tolerated Jones's behavior for more than four years because he could not afford to antagonize the interests and individuals who were Jones's strong supporters.

Some political appointees turn out to be quite inept politically. President Eisenhower's secretary of defense, Charles Wilson of General Motors, was usually in hot water with some congressional committee for his seemingly thoughtless remarks ("What's good for the country is good for General Motors, and vice versa") and behavior. Reagan's first secretary of the interior, James Watt, drew constant fire from environmental groups and congressional committees, but received continuous strong support from Reagan. In speaking of members of the cabinet, Fenno (1959, 207–208) concluded that, politically, a skillful secretary "maintains legislative–executive relations in an equilibrium and prevents them from deteriorating to the point where they hurt the President. What the ordinary Cabinet member supplies is a kind of *preventive assistance*. . . . The best that he can ordinarily do is to help the President in small amounts—probably disproportionate to the time he consumes doing it." The same generalization applies to other political appointees in the executive branch in subcabinet jobs.

In theory, civil servants are apolitical. They are barred from most overt partisan activity by federal law. The textbooks proclaim them to be "above politics" and concerned only with rational, economical, and efficient implementation of policy objectives determined by their political superiors in Congress and the executive branch.

The textbook model does not capture reality in the United States, however. Senior civil servants are, of necessity, highly political, although not necessarily in a strict partisan sense. The governmental system is constructed with the expectations that civil servants at the policy-making level will be political actors (Aberbach, Putnam, and Rockman 1981; Heclo 1977; Kaufman 1981; Yates 1982).

The political involvement of the senior levels of the bureaucracy is the result of several factors: grants of administrative discretion to them, congressional reliance on the bureaucracy for decisions that solidify the popularity of members with specific interests in their states and districts, and competition between agencies for budget and other resources. Broad administration discretion to fill in the gaps in basic legislation does not promote "neutral" administration. Bureaucrats' decisions have political repercussions, and bureaucrats experience pressure for and against their administrative decisions. Congress relies on the bureaucracy as a primary source of policy ideas and initiatives as well as for favorable decisions for which the members of Congress can take some credit with their constituents. Senior officials in all agencies continuously maneuver to maximize the interests of their agencies and programs.

Richard Neustadt (1973, 132) has convincingly explained the basic reason for the political nature of our top civil servants: the governmental system puts them in direct competition with other actors and thereby breeds the necessity of developing political skills in order to gain or preserve the resources to perform programmatic tasks effectively.

> We maximize the insecurities of men and agencies alike. Careerists jostle in-and-outers (from the law firms, business, academic life) for the positions of effective influence; their agencies contend with the committees on the Hill, the Office of Management and Budget, other agencies for the prerequisites of institutional survival, *year by year.* Pursuit of programs authorized in law can be a constant struggle to maintain and hold support of influential clients, or the press. And seeking new authority to innovate a program can be very much like coalition warfare. Accordingly, most agencies have need for men of passion and conviction—or at least enormous powers of resistance—near the top. American officialdom may generate no more of these than other systems do, but it rewards them well: they rise toward the top.

Degree of Visibility

Visibility varies from observer to observer. To the interested part of the general public, for example, virtually all of the actors discussed in this chapter, except a few senators and representatives, are anonymous. To most journalists covering Washington, only senators and representatives and a few political appointees in the executive branch are consistently visible. A really skillful reporter will also come to know important congressional staff members and, occasionally, even a civil servant or two. Skillful lobbyists will know individuals in all four clusters of policy makers. Senators and representatives and the major political appointees in the executive branch, such as cabinet members, are the most generally visible individuals. Congressional staff members and civil servants are relatively unknown to a large number of observers.

Table 2–2 summarizes major aspects of the institutional setting for the four major cluster of actors.

Typical Relationships between Congress and the Bureaucracy: The Impact of Role

Thus far in this chapter we have examined the aggregate characteristics of four principal groups of policy makers and the work settings of those groups. Role is a third major factor that can help explain the pattern of cooperation and conflict in the relationship between Congress and the bureaucracy.

As used by sociologists and psychologists, role is a complex concept, but its essential meaning is the "expected pattern of behavior associated with an actor who is in a particular relationship to a social system" (Davidson 1969, 73). The role associated with any particular actor derives from several sources: the actor's individual characteristics and disposition, his or her institutional setting, the cumulative history

TABLE 2–2
The General Institutional Setting for Congressional and Bureaucratic Policy Actors

Characteristic	Members of House and Senate	Congressional staff members	Executive branch political appointees	Civil servants and equivalents
Method of selection	Election	Appointment by senators and representatives	Appointment by president	Competition and merit
Job tenure and orientation	Relatively long service; careerist orientation	Relatively long service; relatively careerist orientation	Short service; noncareer orientation	Long service; career orientation
Principal loyalties	Constituencies and congressional parties	Sponsors (appointing members)	President and agency to which appointed	Agency
Degree of concern with representation	High for geographical constituencies and special interests	Moderately high for geographical constituencies and interests	Low for geographical units; moderately low for special interests	High for special interests; moderate for geographical units among non-Washington-based civil servants; low for geographical units among Washington-based civil servants
Degree of substantive specialization	Moderately high (especially in House)	Moderately high	Low	High
Degree of professionalism	Low	Generally low	Low	High for major subgroups of employees
Degree of political expertise	High	Moderately high	Moderately high	Moderately high (for highest grades)
Degree of visibility	High	Low	Moderately high	Low

of previous behavior in the position (by the current actor and his or her predecessors), and the expectations of others about how an individual in that particular position *should* act. We use "role" to refer to regularities in the behavior of actors in different institutional positions.

Several well-established relationships between Congress and the bureaucracy that are critical to policy making occur among various subgroups of actors: between congressional committees and clusters of bureaucrats; between congressional staff and bureaucrats; between executive branch legislative liaison personnel and Congress; and among the institutional presidency, bureaucrats, and Congress. In the following pages, general descriptions of these types of interactions are presented for two major reasons: first, to illustrate the role—that is, behavioral regularities—of various actors; second, to illustrate the kind of accommodations the actors reach with each other in their interactions. A variety of specific examples of these interactions will also be presented in Chapters 4 through 7.

Bureaucrats and the Appropriations Committees

The interaction between agency bureaucrats and appropriations committee members is of critical importance because appropriations committees allocate some (although not all) of the resources that enable bureaucrats to implement the programs of their agencies. This interaction has been extensively studied (Fenno 1966; Gist 1978; Horn 1970; LeLoup 1980a; Wildavsky 1984, 1988). These studies support several generalizations about the nature of the interaction.

First, there is a great desire on the part of executive branch officials responsible for program operations to build up confidence over time with the members of the subcommittees that have jurisdiction over their appropriations. They believe that longstanding relations of good quality between them and the members will build a solid reputational base for them and will result in larger appropriations. In fact, there is good evidence that the longer individuals in an agency interact with a specific appropriations subcommittee, the better that agency will do in its appropriations, both in terms of the absolute size of appropriations and in terms of the percentage of its requests that are granted (Moreland 1975).

Second, agency bureaucrats seek to reduce uncertainty in the treatment they receive in the appropriations process. They also seek to increase their appropriations in both absolute and relative terms, but they try to pursue those goals in ways that avoid alienating subcommittee members. They seek to reduce uncertainty by being solicitous of subcommittee concerns, by preparing thoroughly for formal hearings, and by maintaining continuing informal contacts so that the subcommittee members always feel fully informed about agency activities.

Third, many members of the House Appropriations Committee take the view that agency budget requests always contain some "fat" and that it is the duty of the committee to trim the fat. But the members typically become agency advocates once the fat is removed, even if the amount is only symbolic. Generally, they do not want to damage the ability of the agencies to function.

Fourth, members of the Senate Appropriations Committee tend to be even friendlier to agencies. This committee generally acts on agency budgets after the House has acted, and therefore the committee becomes an appellate body, in part. Senate subcommittees are more inclined to accept the agency's and administration's views of what an agency needs. This distinction between attitudes in the two appropriations committees became somewhat blurred during the late 1970s and the Reagan years (Schick 1981), although the basic difference remained.

Fifth, neither senators nor representatives on the appropriations committees have much desire to engage in broad-gauged oversight of bureaucratic activities. Their oversight activity is more likely to focus on specific items of expenditure than to pose broader questions about the societal impact of the agencies whose proposals are being considered. Members are disposed, however, to seek membership on subcommittees overseeing agency budgets that are relatively more "controllable" because they are the result of annual appropriations rather than other modes of funding.

Sixth, representatives of interest groups have an impact on appropriations decisions, both directly and through executive branch officials. Lobbyists intervene to preserve advantages—both budgetary and in terms of statutory language—with which their clients are already blessed. Horn (1970, 189–190) provides a classic vignette:

> In 1965, a nationwide automobile rental firm, faced with competition in the Midwest from a small, subsidized airline that also rented cars to its passengers at various airports, successfully secured report language directing the Civil Aeronautics Board's attention to "the practice of certain air carriers to engage in noncarrier activities. . . ." The Senate subcommittee admonished the board to "continue to supervise these activities vigorously to make sure that such non-carrier operations are not being subsidized."

Finally, most of the important actors in the appropriations process desire stability above all else. Fenno (1966, 348) summarizes the relationship between bureaucrats and the House committee succinctly and persuasively. It is a description that would also generally apply to the Senate Appropriations Committee.

> The House Appropriations Committee–executive agency relationship is characterized on the one hand by conflict and uncertainty; it is characterized on the other by a substantial agreement on what should be done and is being done to minimize conflict and uncertainty and, hence, to keep the relationship reasonably stable.
>
> The sources of conflict lie in the difference between the program-oriented goals of the agencies and the combination of economy-oversight goals of the Committee. . . . The existence of conflict helps to promote uncertainty. And the sources of that uncertainty lie in the difference in the political worlds inhabited by the nonelected executive and the elected representative. . . .
>
> Both groups, however, want to stabilize the relationship—want, that is, to keep conflict and uncertainty to a tolerable and predictable level—because it is in their interest to do so. For the agency, a stable relationship is an aid to program planning and implementation. For the Committee, a stable relationship is an aid to adaptation and survival—to its continued ability, that is, to meet House member and Committee member desires.

Early in the Reagan administration, the importance of the appropriations committees in both houses was somewhat diminished because the total budget package went through a reconciliation process in both 1981 and 1982 (Schick 1981). The central purpose of reconciliation is to aggregate decisions. The normal procedure focused on the appropriations committees and especially their subcommittees is highly disaggregated. There was a return to a disaggregated process after 1982. The passage of a statute (known as Gramm–Rudman–Hollings after its sponsors in the Senate) in 1985 (with a revision in 1987 necessitated by a 1986 ruling by the U.S. Supreme Court) mandating a balanced budget within a few years put some extra pressure on Congress to return to aggregated budget decision making. However, the natural centrifugal forces at work in Congress proved too much to overcome consistently, and the appropriations committees remained important in their normal way, although they continued to compete both with authorizing committees and—since 1975—the budget committees in both houses.

Bureaucrats and the Ways and Means Committee

The House Ways and Means Committee has extensive and important jurisdiction: all tax measures; social security, including medicare; welfare policy; and trade policy, including tariffs and import and export quotas.

Executive branch officials working in these areas deal with the committee frequently and closely (Manley 1970). Executive officials are invited to participate in, not just observe, the meetings of the committee at which decisions about the details of legislation that will go to the House floor are made. There is also a great deal of informal interaction between executive branch officials and committee members.

Ways and Means members participate in the details of policy making, a participation that has been broadened since the mid-1970s to include all of the members of the committee instead of just a few (Rudder 1977). The members can, collectively, delay endorsement of major initiatives from the executive branch. The members do not, however, engage in broad-gauged oversight of the agencies and major programs within their jurisdiction. They often make changes in programs without seeking much evidence beyond what executive branch officials tell them about how the present program is working (Pincus 1974).

The desire for stability in policy and in institutional relationships is also a dominant motivation in the interactions between executive branch officials—both political appointees and senior civil servants—and the members of the committee. Major policy changes are typically initiated by the White House since they involve policies with broad implications for society: basic tax law, health insurance coverage, trade relations with the rest of the world, the status of social security. Relations between Ways and Means Committee members and executive branch officials are less stable than the relations between Appropriations Committee members and executive branch officials because of the high visibility of the issues. This means that highly visible and ambitious individuals (the president, the Speaker of the House, the chair of the Ways and Means Committee, well-placed public spokespersons for various major interest groups) will be involved. Both the degree of visibility and the nature of the issues themselves also mean that partisan politics, which also increase the volatility of a debate over policy, will be involved much of the time.

In 1989, for example, all of these ingredients were present in the struggle over whether or not to treat capital gains more favorably than ordinary income by taxing them less heavily, primarily to the benefit of wealthy people. This was a initiative coming from President Bush and pushed vigorously by him and leading members of his administration. The initiative was vigorously opposed by Democratic leaders in the House, including the chair of the Ways and Means Committee, but some Democrats on the committee broke party ranks and helped give the Republicans a victory. Late in the year, the Democratic majority leader in the Senate was successful in scuttling the bill as the price for reaching a general budget accord with the White House. President Bush vowed to try again in 1990.

Bureaucrats and Congressional Staff

Civil servants who are experts on complex subjects and their counterparts on congressional staffs usually work together closely (Fox and Hammond 1977). In general, the congressional staff members need the information the civil servants can provide, and it is usually forthcoming, even when the executive branch and Congress are controlled by different political parties. In such cases, the federal political executives and the majority of various standing committees may have major policy disagreements. Nevertheless, the cooperative relationships between the committee staffs and the agency staffs continue. This has been the case for a long time. For example, in the 80th Congress (1947–1948), when the Democrats controlled the presidency but the Republicans had won control of both houses of Congress, close staff cooperation still marked the relations between the Treasury Department staff and the staff of the Joint Committee on Internal Revenue Taxation, even though tax bills were the subject of major partisan fights between President Truman and Congress (Kofmehl 1977, 157). Regardless of differences in party control, close technical cooperation between staff members often continues unimpaired. Staff members from interest groups may also get involved in the dealings between congressional staff and agency staff. A good example—only one among many—is provided by the three-way staff discussions that resulted in the first federal legislation to contain federal enforcement powers in the realm of air pollution (Ripley 1969b).

In the area of tax policy, a particularly close relationship between relevant committee staff and Treasury Department staff has developed (Manley 1970, 342–346). Staff members from the House Ways and Means Committee, from the Joint Committee on Taxation, and from the Treasury regularly meet and discuss a range of technical details. They form "staff subcommittees" on various topics. The importance of this close relationship is well summarized by John Manley (1970, 344):

> First, the meetings ensure that by the time the Treasury Department sends its tax message the Joint Committee staff is well-versed in the complexities of the proposals and is therefore equipped to explain them to the members. Second, the predictions of Committee response made by the Joint Committee staff have been relayed to the top officials of the Treasury Department and become one more element in

their calculation of what they should propose to Congress. Third, having worked closely together throughout the process the two staffs are better able to draft the necessary language after the Committee makes a decision and to present the issues during the Committee's deliberations on the bill.

Relations between members of appropriations subcommittee staffs in the House and Senate and civil servant technicians are also close. Wildavsky (1984, 55–56) summarizes the nature of this relationship and the reasons for it:

> Many agencies choose to keep subcommittee staff informed months and sometimes years ahead on new developments. This expedient enables the staff to have ready explanations if and when Congressmen make inquiries. . . .
>
> Although it appears that agency personnel are more dependent on committee staff than vice versa, the relationship is by no means a one-way proposition. The staff man knows that he can do a more effective job if he has the cooperation of the budget officer. For much of the staff's work is dependent on securing information from the agency about current programs and the possible effects of various changes. The staff may be blamed for not informing Congressmen of changes in agency plans and expenditures. And when complex problems arise, the agency may actually do the work for the staff. Mutual dependence is the order of the day and both sides generally regard their contacts as prerequisites to doing their best work.

In short, technicians working for both Congress and executive branch agencies have a large stake in maintaining good relations. This means that neither side should spring policy "surprises" on the other.

Executive Branch Congressional Liaison Officials and Members of Congress

Officials throughout the executive branch responsible for liaison with Congress have a particularly large stake in promoting good relations between the two branches (Holtzman 1970). Their job is to sell policy positions favored by the executive branch and to promote a sense of congressional confidence in whatever part of the executive branch they are representing. There are many liaison personnel in the executive branch. White House liaison officials work directly for the president and his legislative priorities. Departmental liaison personnel are presidential appointees and also promote the priorities of the president. At the same time, they are responsive to the legislative priorities of their department. Liaison officials of agencies and bureaus that are subunits of a larger department are concerned primarily with the legislative priorities of their own unit. Liaison officials work with members and staff members in the House and Senate responsible for making decisions important to those liaison officials.

There is, of course, considerable potential for tension when liaison officials interact with members of Congress who disagree with some initiative or position taken by the executive branch. There is also considerable room for tension and confusion within the executive branch liaison operation itself. Promoting the policy priorities of the president, the departments, and the agencies in an integrated and coordinated fashion is a mammoth challenge. Although the president's priorities are, in principle, supposed to be supported by the rest of the executive branch, in practice departments and agencies have their own legislative priorities, and these may or may not be compatible with the president's.

There is a natural tendency for liaison personnel from individual agencies to compromise with committee members and staff members in Congress, whereas the liaison personnel working directly for the White House have a stronger tendency to resist compromise. These opposed tendencies contribute to tension within the executive branch. This tension reached a high point in the Nixon administration. The president and Congress were ideologically at odds on a range of domestic issues, and the White House staff believed that the agency liaison personnel were likely to abandon presidential preferences too quickly in the search for good relations with Congress. The White House, therefore, attempted unsuccessfully to increase the centralization of the entire executive branch liaison operation by making the chief liaison official in each agency and department directly responsible to the White House rather than to the agency head or department secretary.

In contrast to the attempted centralization during the Nixon administration, the first eighteen months of the Carter administration in 1977 and 1978 had a liaison operation marked by low coordination and a proclivity for offending members of Congress (Bonafede 1979; Elder 1978; Light 1979). Even when some of the kinks were worked out, the Carter White House liaison operation was not particularly intent on good relations with Congress, specifically because President Carter had a view of the relations between president and Congress that put the president in an anti-political, trusteeship role (Jones 1988, Chapter 5). Since members of Congress, including the leaders of Carter's own party, did not share that view of executive–legislative relations, liaison was rocky during the Carter years.

The Reagan congressional liaison operation was highly centralized and ran quite efficiently. The White House congressional liaison office received regular reports from the other liaison offices throughout the executive branch. The OMB legislative clearance function—which is supposed to guarantee that departmental initiatives with Congress are in accord with the program of the president—was also used by the White House liaison office to help make sure agency liaison personnel did not free-lance in support of agency objectives that did not meet with White House approval. As the Department of Labor's chief lobbyist put it, in referring to Reagan's first head of White House congressional liaison, "One of the first things Max Friedersdorf said to me is, 'There is no such thing as a departmental position. There is an administration position'" (Keller 1981b, 2392).

The Institutional Presidency, Congress, and Bureaucrats

Individuals working in various parts of the institutional presidency represent, or at least claim to represent, the president in dealing with the rest of the executive branch and with Congress. The heart of the institutional presidency is in the White House, the professional staff of which are all political appointees, and in the OMB, the professional staff of which contains a few political appointees and a much larger number of career civil servants. Despite the predominance of career professionals, however, the OMB has become more political in recent years (Haas 1988). For example, the OMB in the Reagan and Bush years became known for making unreliable public budget projections designed to make the administration look good. The Congressional Budget Office made projections that were widely regarded as more accurate.

The principal role orientation of officials working immediately for the president as they interact with Congress is to create and maintain good relations with that body because any president must have good relations in order to get desired congressional action. At times, however, the programmatic or ideological integrity of policy positions espoused by the president may be viewed as more important than smooth relations, and when this occurs, tension characterizes the relationship. The degree of tension is heightened if different political parties control the presidency and Congress.

If the president confronts a preexisting, entrenched relationship between bureaus and congressional committees and subcommittees, the job of the president and institutional presidency becomes more difficult if they seek policy change. The president and the institutions of the presidency are viewed as outsiders by bureaucrats and members and staff members in Congress who agree on policy they see threatened by presidential preferences. A bureau chief, for example, may prefer the policies agreed on between his agency and the congressional subcommittees that oversee it over the policies being pushed by the president and the department secretary and assistant secretary to which the bureau chief reports.

The Reagan administration made a concerted effort to put and keep the bureaucracy under its thumb and to discourage the normal semiautonomous relations between bureaus, interest groups, and congressional subcommittees that could have resulted in policies and programs opposed by the administration. The top political echelons in the various agencies and departments were kept closely linked to the views of the presidency. A number of the domestic agencies had both their budget and work force cut. Along with the cuts in the work force came massive internal reorganizations and reassignments of personnel in some agencies. These cuts, reorganizations, and reassignments were supplemented by a number of firings and transfers motivated by political and ideological considerations. In some agencies, congressional mandates from the past were ignored, at least in part. The result of these activities in most of the domestic agencies was a combination of widespread demoralization (and the inefficiency that usually accompanies demoralization), acquiescence on the part of most employees to the new situation they faced, quiet resignations by a number of employees, and dramatic protests and resignations on the part of a few employees. From the point of view of the Reagan administration, these actions were all warranted in order to fashion an executive branch responsive to the political and programmatic preferences of the administration. The administration worked to break tight bonds between career civil servants and congressional subcommittees and interest groups if it considered such bonds to support programs not favored by the administration. The administration's efforts met with considerable success. As the Bush presidency began, a number of the domestic agencies were in weakened condition. The revelations of corruption on a massive scale in the Department of Housing and Urban Development (HUD) in early 1989 demonstrated what could happen in an agency run for purely political and ideological reasons, with the best career civil servants either gone or completely dominated by political officials with no expertise. Why the concerned members of Congress did not know how bad the situation in HUD was earlier is unclear.

Despite the impact of the Reagan administration in dominating the bureaucracy at least some of the time, a longer-run view suggests that major forces still push for relatively high degrees of autonomy for bureaucratic agencies and relatively low degrees of central administrative leadership from a departmental secretary and staff loyal to a president. Herbert Kaufman, a leading student of American bureaucratic behavior, summarizes the major forces favoring high degrees of autonomy for individual bureaus: "overextended spans of control, lack of managerial talent among cabinet officers, congressional hostility toward departmental control of bureaus, . . . pressure on the secretaries and their aides to concentrate on responsibilities other than departmental administration. . ." (Kaufman 1981, 189–190).

Even without unusually heavy presidential involvement, the institutional presidency is not viewed sympathetically by most of the bureaucracy, especially those with line-operating responsibilities. The White House and OMB staff necessarily play a centralizing role in the legislative process (Neustadt 1954, 1955). However, this role threatens the stable relations and the stable policy-making processes within agencies and subcommittees.

Bureau chiefs and agency heads complain that the centralizing forces in the executive branch don't understand the political realities that they must face on a day-to-day basis. Comments by two different civil servants in the 1960s are illustrative:

> Sticky problems arise because of the political isolation of the Bureau of the Budget. The Bureau does not have good comprehension of what is in the minds of key congressional committee chairmen and members we have to deal with. They find incomprehensible the political problems we try to explain to them. They see us as being more responsive to Congress than to the President. There may be an element of truth here but they don't understand Congress (Davis and Ripley 1967, 762–763).

> We have to tread a pretty thin line and we're always caught in a cross fire between the Budget Bureau and Congress. I just wish those people over there (in the Budget Bureau) had to carry those requests out—just once. They'd learn what the problems were. . . . The budget is made up over there, but we have to carry the ball. . . . They have no understanding of the climate up there, of the pressures, of the personalities (Fenno 1966, 308).

In early 1985, the head of the Small Business Administration (SBA) (a Reagan appointee) attacked the position of OMB and its director, David Stockman, in wanting to eliminate SBA. The SBA chief said Stockman was "surrounded by fanatics [who] have no real-life experience." OMB officials, in his view, "cannot expect to understand the workings of all the federal agencies. They cannot continue to deal in micromanagement. . . . Continuing to increase the OMB's power is sheer idiocy" (*Washington Post*, April 28, 1985). The SBA had lots of support in Congress and survived.

In general, bureaucrats at the operating level see themselves caught between unrealistic demands and pressures from their executive branch superiors and the pressures and demand from Congress, with which they have more sympathy. Agency officials often talk about their sense of being in the middle between the president and his political appointees on the one hand and Congress on the other. Three statements from such officials illustrate the general point (Fenno 1966, 308–309):

> Sometimes you wonder just who you are working for. I haven't been in too many embarrassing situations. With my relations with the Congress as they are, I may tell them that, frankly, I don't think I ought to tell them—that I have to maintain my loyalty to the department. Sometimes I go against the department.

> Sometimes I'll go over to the Committee and talk about something with them. The first time I went, they told me it was confidential. And I said, "When I came through that door, I started working for the Committee. Whatever goes on in here just didn't happen as far as I'm concerned when I leave here." And I tell them that every time. Sometimes, I'm over here and the Secretary or someone will try to worm it out of me what's going on. But they know I won't tell them.

> I've gone out and tried to develop contacts with congressmen, because that's the way the game is played. But I don't like it. You shouldn't have to lobby for your program. But politics being what it is, I've done a little more of that. . . . Some people higher up in the department object to our having any informal contact with congressmen, but we'll just have to get around that, I guess.

Summary

The five general congressional–bureaucratic interactions discussed here are important ones that occur again and again and deal with a wide variety of substantive matters. Although the individual actors may change depending on the issue under consideration, the general patterns of interaction do not change much. Role expectations produce consistent behavior. Those patterns of behavior have implications for the level of cooperation or conflict between Congress and the bureaucracy in the making of policy.

CHAPTER THREE

Congressional–Bureaucratic Interaction: Occasions and Resources

Interaction between congressional and bureaucratic actors is continuous and occurs in a variety of settings and for a variety of reasons, the most basic of which is that the Constitution created two separate institutions that share powers. It is therefore mandatory that Congress and the bureaucracy interact in order to produce, implement, and assess governmental policy. In this chapter we discuss congressional–bureaucratic interactions during the production of policy by focusing on (1) the motivations of the actors; (2) the resources they have to trade or withhold; (3) the settings for their interactions; and (4) the techniques the actors use in pursuing their interactions.

Some attention has been directed by scholars to congressional–bureaucratic interaction, particularly congressional oversight of bureaucratic activities (Harris 1964; Keefe and Ogul 1985, Chapter 12; Oleszek 1978, Chapter 9). In this book the word *oversight* is used to include the whole array of congressional activities that keeps tabs on what the bureaucracy is doing. We use the term *program oversight* to refer to a specific kind of legislative oversight that systematically reviews and evaluates programs. Program oversight is not as widespread as other varieties of oversight because the rewards it offers legislators are not as enticing as the rewards for other activities.

Motivations and Resources for Interaction

Motivations

Some interactions between bureaucrats and members of Congress are necessitated by the structure of government within which these individuals work. The constitutional allocation discussed in Chapter 1 mandates a considerable amount of interaction. In addition, the history of governmental and programmatic development for almost 200 years has overlaid the rudimentary constitutional necessities with a number of interactions decreed by statutes, other written documents, and custom. This overlay can be used to summarize the motivations of the parties to the interactions.

Both bureaucrats and members of Congress have a variety of motivations for becoming involved in specific ways in policy-related interactions between the two branches. Wilson (1980, 374) offers a suggestive threefold typology of bureaucrats' motivations:

To simplify, government agencies have at least three kinds of employees who can be defined in terms of their motives. The first are *careerists*: employees who identify their careers and rewards with the agency. They do not expect to move on to other jobs outside the agency or otherwise to receive significant rewards from external constituencies. The maintenance of the agency and of their position in it is of paramount concern.

The second are the *politicians*: employees who see themselves as having a future in elective or appointive office outside the agency. They hope to move on to become the vice president for public relations of a large firm, enter the cabinet or subcabinet, or join the campaign staff of a promising presidential contender. The maintenance and enhancement of their careers outside the agency is of paramount importance.

The third are the *professionals*: employees who receive rewards (in status if not in money) from organized members of similar occupations elsewhere. They may hope to move on to better jobs elsewhere, but access to those jobs depends on their display of professionally approved behavior and technical competence. They may also be content to remain in the agency, but they value the continued approval of fellow professionals outside the agency, or the self-respect that comes from behaving in accordance with internalized professional norms. The maintenance of this professional esteem is of major importance to these employees.

In interacting with Congress, a careerist's primary concern is usually for the health and welfare of his or her agency. The careerist seeks to expand the agency's resources and influence or to maintain a low-profile status quo or to fight encroachments on the agency's resources and influence. However, politicians and professionals in the bureaucratic ranks will pursue goals other than agency welfare unless they think agency welfare contributes heavily to the achievement of their personal goals.

Some bureaucrats willingly take positions on issues that diminish or, in a few extreme cases, spell the end of their agency. For example, the last days of the Community Services Administration early in the Reagan presidency were presided over by a longtime career bureaucrat. It is overly simple to portray all bureaucrats as having only the welfare of their agency at heart. Personal welfare in several senses is more important for some. But collective agency welfare is an important motivation for much bureaucratic behavior.

Members of Congress are motivated by two general desires: (1) to survive or advance politically or both, and (2) to pursue policy interests. Political survival and advancement are tied to constituency service and local interests, which in turn are tied to a member's reelection—survival in the most basic sense. Choice of policy interests may also be tied to political advantage. Members may be most interested in policies they believe will help them win reelection or advance to other desirable posts. These two factors influence all congressional activity (Mayhew 1974), including interactions with the bureaucracy, and they are particularly important in explaining congressional exercise of program oversight (Ogul 1973). Because members' schedules are always full and there is insufficient time to do all the things worth doing, these twin desires help them make choices and set priorities. The utility of a particular interaction with some part of the bureaucracy may be assessed in terms of explicit calculations, such as "How will this help me with the folks back home?" or "How does this mesh with my personal policy preferences?"

Resources

Both members of Congress and bureaucrats have a range of formal and informal resources upon which they can draw as they pursue their personal, organizational, and programmatic goals. These resources can be selectively granted and withheld by actors in both branches.

From the congressional perspective, the formal powers of Congress provide a number of resources upon which individual members can draw. These formal powers include, first, the decision about the existence of agencies. Second, Congress provides the jurisdictional and programmatic scope to specific agencies and the limits on that scope both through statutory authority and through money. Third, Congress provides personnel for the executive branch in several senses—through the giving or withholding of statutory authority, personnel money, and confirmation of key appointments. Fourth, Congress influences the specific structure of both programs and agencies through positive statutory action and through action on reorganization plans submitted by the executive branch.

In addition to these formal powers, members of Congress also have less formal, less tangible resources that can be used in dealing with the executive branch. These include the ability to provide or withhold good information on the intentions of other individuals who are working in a specific area of policy, the ability to praise or criticize individual bureaucrats publicly, and the ability to influence the general image and reputation of the agency in general.

From the bureaucratic perspective, the formal powers also provide a number of important potential resources. The bureaucracy makes a number of specific decisions that are important to members of the House and Senate. These include the writing of regulations determining how a program will be implemented; critical personnel decisions on hiring, promotion, and location of individuals both geographically and hierarchically; programmatic and geographic patterns of spending; the timing of spending and other programmatic decisions; decisions about the location of facilities; and the dispositions of the requests of those individuals seeking specific agency rulings.

Bureaucrats also have informal resources to supplement their formal powers. Two stand out: first, the ability of bureaucrats to enhance the personal standing and reputation of senators and representatives through a variety of forms of deference; and, second, the provision of timely and accurate information both about substantive matters and about the intentions of other actors in the policy subsystem.

The Tie between Motivation and Resources

When motivation and resources reinforce each other, the likelihood of action on the part of either members of Congress or high-level bureaucrats increases. For example, a freshman member on the House Committee on the District of Columbia may be highly motivated to criticize the Department of Defense for allegedly sabotaging disarmament talks with the Soviet Union, but he or she can accomplish little because resources are few. However, if the same member of the House becomes concerned about an alleged monopoly on parking in the District of Columbia that results in outrageously high parking fees, then he or she is likely to have some resources in the committee to do something relevant.

Similarly, a bureau chief has the motivation to wish for a large increase in the budget of his agency. However, if that chief cannot point to specific services rendered by the agency to the districts of the members of the House Appropriations Subcommittee with jurisdiction over the agency, a critical resource is missing.

Resources can be present when motivation is absent. A senior member of the Senate Armed Services Committee would have the resources to inquire in an influential way into alleged Defense Department foot dragging on disarmament. But if the senator is not interested in pursuing that line of inquiry, then the resources will not be used. Similarly, if a bureau chief has two major programs and can point to tangible benefits that accrue to key members of the House and the Senate from both, then that chief has resources to pursue budgetary increases in both programs. However, it may be that the chief is motivated to push one program but not the other. Again, the resource created by having a program that benefits important members of Congress will go unused.

A good example in which resources and motivation are closely tied is provided by a long period of policy making dealing with soil conservation (Morgan 1965). From the time that soil conservation districts began to be organized in 1936, a rivalry grew up between the Soil Conservation Service (SCS), representing centralized authority over the program in Washington, and land-grant agricultural colleges and their extension services, which wished to decentralize the program and gain control of it. Some members of the House and Senate with influence in agricultural matters sided with the SCS and favored a centralized program. Others sided with the extension service and land-grant colleges, which were backed strongly by the American Farm Bureau Federation. This conflict was finally settled in favor of the SCS position during the Truman administration.

Constituency interests and interest group support were more important in shaping alliances in this struggle than was party affiliation. For example, a key House Republican supporting the Farm Bureau–extension service position was formerly an employee of the extension service in his home state. An important House Democrat taking the same position came from a state that was a Farm Bureau stronghold. Two of the leading House supporters of the SCS position—one from each party—came from areas of the country that could be expected to benefit greatly from the small-watershed program being designed by the SCS. In addition, the Republican came from a district in which the Farmers Union—the major competing interest group for the Farm Bureau and in conflict with it on this issue—was strong. All of these individuals were fairly senior members of the House Agriculture Committee. Other interested parties in the House were on both the Agriculture Committee and Agriculture Subcommittee of the Appropriations Committee. Important individuals in the Senate held parallel positions, and their views were also closely related to the relative strength of the Farm Bureau or Farmers Union in their states or districts and the relative benefits that would be likely to come to their states or districts from the competing agencies.

Occasions and Techniques for Interaction

Both custom and law create many occasions for interaction between Congress and the bureaucracy. These include budgeting; agency organization or reorganization; creation, amendment, or dissolution of a program or agency; personnel matters; evaluation of program performance; and location of projects. In these interactions, formal routines may be used—for example, a hearing before a committee or subcommittee—and there may be formal outcomes, such as statutes, votes on reorganization plans, confirmation decisions, and committee and agency reports. Equally important, the same issues are also likely to be dealt with in a large number of informal interactions such as phone calls, impromptu visits, lunches, and cocktail parties. During these occasions, a constant two-way flow of information and views on substance, procedure, individuals, and organizations is sustained. Senior bureaucrats may spend more time interacting with Congress than with their nominal supervisors in their own executive branch agency.

No single listing of the occasions and techniques used by the participants in these interactions is likely to be exhaustive. Nor is reality organized as neatly as any set of categories. Nevertheless, it is useful to identify and discuss the major occasions and techniques used by individuals from the Hill and individuals in the bureaucracy. The cases discussed in Chapters 4 through 7 will also offer fuller illustrations of the occasions for interaction and the techniques used in those interactions.

Occasions for Interaction

Budgeting Budgeting is the most regularly recurring occasion for interaction between the bureaucracy and Congress. Budgeting allocates dollars among competing agencies and programs. The lengthy and complex federal budget process has undergone a number of changes beginning in 1974 (LeLoup 1988; Penner and Abramson 1988). It is divided into two major parts: first, the president's preparation of a budget document for the entire executive branch, which constitutes a request to Congress for funds to run the government; and, second, the congressional budget process, which is a response to the president's request. The preparation of the president's budget requires widespread interactions internal to the various parts of the executive branch. Critically, individual agencies negotiate with the presidency (in the form of the OMB). The congressional budget process, which includes the appropriations process, is the scene of extensive interaction between the centralized leadership of Congress and the presidency *and*, simultaneously, between individual parts of the bureaucracy and individual subcommittees in Congress.

In 1974 Congress passed the Congressional Budget and Impoundment Act, a statute designed to rationalize the entire congressional budget process. Before passage of that act, congressional budget decisions were made in a completely disaggregated, piecemeal fashion. Major congressional spending decisions were made primarily by the appropriations committees in the House and Senate. Revenue decisions were made by the House Ways and Means Committee and the Senate Finance Committee. There was neither opportunity nor incentive for comprehensive or integrated assessment of these disaggregated spending and taxing decisions.

The present congressional budget process, created in 1974 and amended significantly in 1985 and again in 1987, differs from the previous one by creating budget committees in both houses that have the mandate to aggregate what were previously separate budget decisions into a single comprehensive budget resolution that specifies the total amount (a "ceiling") for congressionally authorized spending and enumerates spending priorities within that ceiling, before the passage of individual appropriation bills. Table 3–1 summarizes the budget timetable that was in effect beginning in 1986.

The budget process from 1975 through 1980 did not produce substantive policy outcomes that were significantly different from the years before 1975. The new process did, however, provide a more informed decision-making process for congressional budgeting. The relations between individual parts of the bureaucracy and individual committees and subcommittees (especially the appropriations subcommittees) did not alter much from 1975 through 1980 either. In the 1975–1980 period, the new budget committees did not seek large-scale substantive results. Careful analysts of the process in Congress agreed that the main achievements of these first years of the new process were procedural: the process was in place, and it helped Congress make decisions that both balanced a wide variety of interests and did so without allowing conflict to immobilize the process or the ability to arrive at conclusions (Havemann 1978; LeLoup 1980b; Schick 1980).

In 1980 Congress began to experiment with the "reconciliation" option in the budget law, which, until then, had lain dormant. In 1981 it used this option in a major way to respond favorably to the sweeping changes in budget outcomes pushed strongly by the new president, Ronald Reagan. In 1982 Congress again used reconciliation, although not in the same way as in 1981 and with no dramatic substantive changes as a result (Schick 1981; Tate 1982). This process forces the adoption of a single

TABLE 3–1

Congressional Budget Timetable, 1986 and After

Deadline	Action to be completed
Monday after	
January 3	President submits budget
February 15	Congressional Budget Office reports to Budget Committees
February 25	House and Senate authorizing committees submit views and estimates to Budget Committees
April 1	Budget committees submit budget resolution to respective chambers
April 15	Congress passes budget resolution
June 10	House Appropriations Committee reports all bills
June 15	Congress passes budget reconciliation bill
June 30	House passes all appropriation bills
October 1	Fiscal year begins

bottom line in which direct confrontation of priorities and interests must be resolved. A single total dollar figure must be met; a single zero-sum game is created. The strain created by the necessity of resolving all disputes at once made the sweeping use of the process in 1981 unique. It could be pulled off only because of the political strength and skill of Reagan. In 1982 and succeeding years, "normal" pressures returned more strongly and Reagan's impact lessened.

Beginning in 1983 the political warfare between Reagan and Congress, especially the Democratically controlled House, intensified. Under these conditions, the budget process became less important in the sense that the deadlines then in force were routinely missed, and much of the government began to function under continuing resolutions, which simply extended spending at the same level and rate, much as it had in the years immediately before the passage of the 1974 law. In 1984 deficit reduction legislation was approved before the budget resolution and became the vehicle for overall budget policy. Much the same thing happened in 1985.

By 1985 members of both parties in Congress were growing increasingly concerned with the large and growing annual deficits being incurred by the federal government. In that year Congress passed the Gramm–Rudman–Hollings Act that mandated reductions in the deficit and a balanced budget by 1991 and created the procedures and timetables by which those goals were to be met. In 1986 the Supreme Court ruled one procedural detail unconstitutional, and Congress was obliged to amend the law in 1987.

Gramm–Rudman (Hollings's name often gets dropped in accounts of this law) and the political climate that led to the passage of that law (and continued after its passage) produced a number of important effects on the politics of budgeting (in addition to LeLoup 1988, and Penner and Abramson 1988, see Haas 1988a, 1988b, and 1988c; Rapp 1988; and articles by Dan Morgan in the *Washington Post*, May 30, 1989, and June 30, 1989). One of the main effects of Gramm–Rudman has been to elevate the budget negotiations to a level that requires the participation of the president and his chief advisors on the one hand and the party leaders of Congress on the other hand. Once a "treaty" is reached at this high level, then the details are still put into place in disaggregated fashion. But the high-level negotiations produce considerable constraints within which the committees and subcommittees and the two chambers must do their work. In addition, these high-level treaties have come to include agreement on a total figure for defense spending and a total figure for nondefense spending, with the sum of those two, obviously, equal to the overall agreement. This means that the disaggregated budget process that follows the treaty agreement must proceed within the constraints of two zero-sum games—one for defense and one for nondefense. Both Congress and the executive branch have, however, become adroit in using various accounting gimmicks to loosen the constraints.

Other results of living with both the reality of Gramm–Rudman and, more important, the climate that produced it include the relative decrease in power and latitude for the authorizing committees of Congress, the shrinkage in the size of the "goodies" over which the appropriations committees have discretion, the continuing rise of the budget committees in importance, and the continued importance—with considerable autonomy—of the taxing committees, especially the House Ways and

Means Committee. These changes have weakened some of the traditional close links between agencies and key committees of Congress in the sense that it is more difficult for these closely linked groups to get what they want from the federal budget. However, the changes have been incremental and modest. No revolution in the basic nature of congressional–bureaucratic relations has occurred. Political actors— presidents, members of the House and Senate, bureaucrats, interest groups—will work to protect their interests and their alliances no matter what procedures they must use. Procedures can help change the format of debate, but they do not change under-lying political realities. The quest for budget balancing, for example, was not sparked by an abstract concern for rational debate and decision making about spending and taxing priorities. Rather, a large number of members of Congress perceived political danger at the polls if they appeared to ignore the problem of a large deficit. The "solution" in the form of Gramm–Rudman has had some substantive results, but the appearance of action and the perception that that appearance increases electoral safety for incumbent members of Congress of both parties is the most important result of Gramm–Rudman.

Agency programs, organization, and reorganization Proposals to create or dismantle specific programs also stimulate interaction between Congress and the bureaucracy. Such proposals may originate either in the bureaucracy or within Congress, but the decision to implement a new program eventually requires con-sultation with the other branch at minimum to secure statutory authority and funding. Such consultation is also wise because it promotes good relations. Statutory author-ization typically follows hearings before the appropriate congressional committees. These hearings include testimony from interested parties, including those parts of the bureaucracy that believe they are best suited to administer a new program. The decision to terminate a program (fairly rare) follows the same general procedure.

Congress and the bureaucracy also interact on proposals for the organization or reorganization of agencies. Congress does not get formally involved in every change made in the structure of a bureau. But it gets formally involved in most changes made at the departmental level, which are often included in presidential reorganization plans, or within the independent regulatory commissions, which are regarded as arms of Congress. Informally, members of Congress, usually on relevant subcommittees, may get involved in the details of changes deep in the bowels of the bureaucracy.

Program evaluation The evaluation of program performance through oversight is an important form of interaction between the bureaucracy and Congress that occurs when congressional committees examine the performance of programs they have authorized and funded. Responsibility for program oversight is shared: the govern-ment operations committees perform special investigative inquiries, the appropria-tions committees are responsible for fiscal oversight, and the legislative committees are responsible for overseeing the programs they authorize. Oversight activities may take several forms, including special hearings to investigate a program; routine hearings on appropriations or authorizations/reauthorizations; and program monitoring and analyses. In general, Congress has not performed oversight extensively. Much of the oversight that has occurred has been related to appropriations, in which cases the focus is often on small details. Several scholars (Bibby 1966; Davis 1970; Huitt 1966; Ogul 1973; Scher 1963) have studied oversight and the conditions that contribute to it. Their research supports the generalization that personal and political rewards to members for oversight activities are not as great as the rewards for other kinds of behavior, and thus members of Congress tend to shy away from giving much attention to oversight. We will return to the subject of oversight in Chapter 8.

Personnel matters   Personnel matters also provide occasions for interaction between the two branches. The Senate must confirm a number of presidential appointments, including those of agency heads. Congress is involved in setting the pay scales for government employees; lobbying from the executive branch on this matter is often intense. The total amount of money that an agency head has available to pay the salaries and expenses of employees is also determined by Congress. That amount may or may not be enough to allow the agency to fill all of its authorized positions. Congress also gets involved in creating special positions within an agency and in limiting the total size of an agency or the total number of employees in specific civil service grades. Finally, individual members of Congress frequently intervene on behalf of friends who are seeking good jobs or promotions in the bureaucracy.

Other occasions   Decisions about the location of federal projects also stimulate interaction between Congress and the bureaucracy. Because such projects usually entail employment, money, and other benefits for specific localities, legislators are interested in having them in their districts. Bureaucrats are responsible for making decisions about locations of projects. The interaction on this subject occurs in both formal and informal settings. Occasionally, a project may be undesirable (for example, missile sites or a penal facility), and members try to keep such projects out of their districts.

Congress and the bureaucracy are also brought together in dealing with "casework," or the dealings of individuals with various agencies. Many of these interactions involve immigration, social security, medicare, and tax liabilities.

Members of Congress are often solicited to help individuals deal with a bureaucracy. Congressional staff members are the key people in dealing with the bureaucrats on cases.

Congressional Techniques

Personal visits and phone calls   Members of Congress and staff members seek information and desired actions from bureaucrats by keeping in touch with them both in person and on the phone. This kind of personal attention is often sufficient to get the attention of a key bureaucrat, and sometimes it alone is sufficient to obtain a desired result.

The use of third parties   Members often seek to mobilize supporters to reinforce the messages they are delivering to bureaucrats. For example, a member may seek to have interest group representatives, reporters, or well-known "clients" of a bureau approach executive branch officials to support the member's view about some matter.

Release of written materials Individual members of the House or Senate or individual committes and subcommittees can seek to influence bureaucratic decisions by releasing materials such as committee reports, staff studies, and press releases at the most advantageous time.

Hearings Executive branch officials frequently appear before congressional committees and subcommittees as a matter of course. These hearings afford members of the House and Senate recurring opportunities to elicit information about programs and to make their own views known to the bureaucracy.

An excellent example of a routine appropriations hearing being used to underscore a congressional attitude is provided by a former Manpower administrator, Stanley Ruttenberg (Ruttenberg and Gutchess 1970, 77–78). When he became Manpower administrator in 1965, the Department of Labor was urging a reorganization of the Manpower Administration that would have given line authority to regional manpower administrators over all of the operating bureaus, including the Bureau of Employment Security and the Bureau of Apprenticeship and Training, whose directors were both opposed to the reorganization because it would decrease the autonomy of their bureaus. The pressure generated by the proposal's opponents, including several key members of Congress, was strong enough to prevent its implementation. An exchange between Ruttenberg and Representative John Fogarty, a Rhode Island Democrat serving as chairman of the House Appropriations subcommittee responsible for the Department of Labor among other agencies, during the March 1965 hearings on the department's budget proposal, shows Fogarty stating his position succinctly, forcefully, and—as it turned out—successfully:

Mr. Fogarty: I assume you know the feeling of this committee on the proposed reorganization? If you do not, we will spell it out for you later on. . . . I am not going to belabor the point. As far as I am concerned, my mind is made up on the question of this reorganization of your department. Mr. Goodwin (the director of the Bureau of Employment Security) has been here through several administrations and four or five secretaries of labor. The secretaries of labor come and go, but Mr. Goodwin stays on. I think Mr. Murphy (the director of the Bureau of Apprenticeship and Training) will stay on regardless of who is secretary tomorrow or next year, or five years from now.

Mr. Ruttenberg: I think that is unquestionably true.

Mr. Fogarty: The Congress has always supported these two agencies and there is no doubt in my mind as to how the Congress will respond to this proposal. I thought I made it clear yesterday, but I am trying to make it clearer right now. Is that clear?

Mr. Ruttenberg: Mr. Chairman, it was quite clear to me yesterday.

In addition to routine hearings, congressional committees also hold a variety of special investigations to elicit additional information. These investigations may be conducted by standing committees or subcommittees, select committees, special committees, or joint committees. At the hearings, the main congressional–bureaucratic interaction occurs in the preliminary preparation stages between congressional staff and agency members.

A good example of the kinds of impact that a congressional investigation can have, even when it deals with a seemingly minor topic, is provided by the activities of the Senate Small Business Committee in the early 1950s in relation to the controversy over an additive designed to prolong battery life (Lawrence 1965). This issue was complicated and involved conflicting philosophies of regulation of private enterprise, an aggressive marketer of the product, scientists from a range of public and private institutions, three government agencies (the Commerce Department's National Bureau of Standards, the Federal Trade Commission, and the Post Office), and the Senate Small Business Committee. Near the end of the controversy, the Eisenhower administration was trying to fire the head of the National Bureau of Standards. This action precipitated hearings by the Small Business Committee. As the hearings began, a regulatory action initiated by the Post Office against the producer of the additive was still pending. The committee was on the side of the manufacturer and opposed government intervention. By bending to the wishes of the committee, the Post Office removed itself from the dispute. As Lawrence (1965, 70) wrote, "The Post Office Department weathered the storm with little or no damange. Senate Thye (a Minnesota Republican who was chairman of the Small Business Committee) had said at the conclusion of his Small Business Committee's hearing on AD-X2 (the name of the additive), 'Only. . .if the Postmaster General feels the mail fraud order should not be set aside, would it be necessary to find out why the order was ever issued.' " The Post Office quickly bowed to the wishes of the committee in order to avoid an investigation.

Requests for studies by outside sources   Senators and representatives have a number of sources to which they can turn for independent (or at least seemingly independent) studies that can be used to bolster their point of view in a policy controversy. These sources include the General Accounting Office (GAO), the Congressional Research Service (CRS) of the Library of Congress, the Office of Technology Assessment (OTA), the Congressional Budget Office (CBO), the government operations committees in the House and Senate, and respected outsiders such as universities or independent research organizations such as the Brookings Institution.

The GAO is an arm of Congress that in part conducts audits of the expenditure of funds. The GAO also conducts much broader studies, an activity that it has increased in recent years. The reports stemming from these studies can be used by members of Congress. For example, a GAO report on the proposed Cheyenne helicopter was negative, and the House Appropriations Committee used the report to help make its case for terminating the project.

The CRS is a nonpartisan agency but can be asked for information on programs and agencies. That information can then be used by congressional proponents of specific views to buttress their arguments.

The OTA was created by statute in 1972 and began operations in 1974. Its primary function, in the language of the statute, is to provide "early indications of the probable beneficial and adverse impacts of the applications of technology and to develop other coordinate information which may assist the Congress." Subjects for the OTA staff work are decided by requests from congressional committees or by requests from the Technology Assessment Board (six senators, six representatives, and the OTA director) or by the director after consulting with the board.

The CBO was created in 1974 as part of the general congressional budget reform. The professional staff of the CBO reports to Congress on projected short-term and five-year economic consequences of legislation that is proposed or enacted. It develops an annual report on budget alternatives for Congress to consider, with emphasis on fiscal policy and spending priorities. The CBO also responds to requests from the fiscal committees in both houses for special economic and policy studies.

The government operations committees of both houses were empowered by the Legislative Reorganization Act of 1946 to conduct investigations into the operations of government activities at all levels to determine whether programs are being administered efficiently and economically. These committees work closely with the GAO in conducting their investigations.

Statutory changes   Congress can by statute create or dissolve agencies and programs, alter the jurisdiction of agencies, prescribe organizational structure, and intercede in personnel matters such as limits on total number of slots available for specific grades and compensation.

Major statutory initiatives are visible. But there are also more quiet and subtle uses of statutory power by Congress to achieve desired ends. For example, Congress can maximize the responsiveness of agencies to its will through several statutory devices designed to weaken the control of an agency head, as in the Manpower Administration example citied earlier. In that case the field structure was kept decentralized and more responsive to congressional influence than to the administrator of the agency. Similarly, some agencies (usually called commissions) have been given multiple executives (usually called commissioners) by Congress partially to make the agency more responsive to Congress. The Atomic Energy Commission (which later became the Nuclear Regulatory Commission) and all of the independent regulatory agencies illustrate the use of this technique. Congress has often opted to keep the staff assigned to a departmental secretary relatively small as a way of weakening the secretary's control over individual bureaus (Seidman 1980).

In a few cases, Congress can specify that its own members be directly involved in what otherwise would be considered purely the business of the executive branch. Two members of each house were included by statute on the negotiating teams charged with implementing the tariff reduction provisions of the Trade Expansion Act of 1962, for example.

Although appropriations statutes are generally thought of in terms of their fiscal content, they also may have a policy impact beyond the dollars they allocate to agencies and programs. This impact is felt when appropriations statutes contain provisions about how the money must be used or cannot be used. As Horn (1970, 181, 183) noted, these provisions are usually negative (forbidding certain uses of the money) and directed at administrative expenditures such as travel, subscriptions, number of personnel hired, consulting fees, and entertainment. But substantive programmatic matters may also be addressed. For example, a provision in the appropriations statute for the Department of Agriculture in the mid-1950s required that cotton sold abroad be sold competitively, even though the administration argued that this would have a detrimental effect on foreign policy (Kirst 1969, 5). The annual Defense Appropriations Act contains the following programmatic language: "No funds herein appropriated shall be used for the payment of a price differential on contracts hereafter made for the purpose of relieving economic dislocations," and "So far as practicable, all contracts shall be awarded on a formally advertised competitive bid basis to the lowest responsible bidder." That language has "maintained the preeminence of California in defense procurement against large-scale attempts to distribute defense contracts according to the level of unemployment in an area" (Horn 1970, 184).

Language in reports In the technical sense, only statutes have the force of law. However, Congress has also made its will felt in programmatic terms through language contained in committee reports. The executive branch often treats such language as binding.

A good example of language in a report having the effect of law is provided by a 1960 reorganization of the Public Health Service (Carper 1965). The decision by the Department of Health, Education, and Welfare to reorganize the Public Health Service was in direct response to language contained in the 1959 report of the Health Subcommittee of the House Appropriations Committee. A decision not to remove the clinical training programs of the National Institute of Mental Health from that organization was directly responsive to language contained in a Senate Appropriations Committee report in 1960.

In the late 1970s, photocopying machines for public use disappeared from local post offices because of language in reports from two House subcommittees, even though the machines were regarded positively by consumers. The subcommittees were reacting to pressure from a trade association representing office equipment stores.

All committees can use the technique of putting preferences into reports. The appropriations committees are particularly active in using this technique. Not all bureaucrats conform precisely to all such statements of preference, but they go counter to congressional preferences only after weighing the costs of doing so.

Legislative veto Beginning in the 1930s Congress began to develop a technique that has come to be called a "legislative veto," which is a provision in a statute. It can take a number of forms, but the essence of any such provision is a requirement that Congress, or part of it (one or more committees), approve or at least not disapprove an executive branch action before it can become binding, usually within thirty to ninety days (Craig 1983). Between the 1930s and 1983 Congress had put such provisions in about 200 statutes, and the rate of inclusion in new statutes was increasing. In 1983 the U.S. Supreme Court ruled that the legislative veto was unconstitutional (Craig 1988). However, both Congress and the executive branch continued to honor existing provisions, and in addition Congress continued to put such provisions in new statutes after 1983, taking care to use only forms that did not seem to violate a narrow reading of the Court's decision. The legislative veto, therefore, remains a potent tool in the hands of Congress, one the executive branch recognizes as legitimate (Fisher 1985).

Reporting requirements   Congress may require that parts of the bureaucracy make certain information available to it through reporting requirements in statutes. These requirements vary considerably in their form and content. Some are highly visible because they are contained in major statutes and focus on reports from the president. For example, the Congressional Budget and Impoundment Control Act of 1974 requires that the president report annually on the amount of impounded funds and the amount of tax expenditures (defined as the amount of revenue lost lost through various tax loopholes). The War Powers Act of 1973 requires the president to report to Congress on commitments he has made of American military forces.

Less visible reporting requirements are directed at bureaucrats lower in the hierarchy. The kind of information requested can range from details about programs to rationales for decisions. The reporting requirements are all aimed at increasing the amount of information available to Congress and at increasing occasions for consultation between congressional committees and pieces of the bureaucracy.

The Joint Committee on Atomic Energy (JCAE) provides a good example of how a committee can use the reporting technique to extend its influence over an agency (Green and Rosenthal 1963).

An analysis of congressional reporting requirements in the mid-1970s (Johannes 1976) shows that since World War II the number of reports required rose from about 300 to more than 1,000. These requirements fall into three major categories. First, various parts of the executive branch are required to submit "policy-making" reports, such as evaluations of existing programs and recommendations for action. Second, "post facto" reports simply recount actions taken. Third, "advance notification" reports must be filed for a specific period before an action is taken, which gives members of Congress a chance to object, propose changes, or react in other ways. About 90 percent of the reporting requirements are of the first two kinds. A minority (perhaps one in five) of the reports come from or through the president. The rest come directly from individual agencies and departments. About 3,000 reporting requirements are in force governmentwide.

Budget decisions   By virtue of its powers to levy taxes and appropriate funds, Congress is the inevitable focus of attention from bureaucrats requesting and defending their agencies' budgets. The use of budget decisions constitutes a very important congressional technique for influencing programmatic performance in the executive branch. Despite changes in recent years, congressional budget control is not highly centralized. Individual committees and subcommittees are still vital to the budget future of individual agencies and bureaus. Only under conditions of a genuinely comprehensive budget reconciliation bill (as in 1981) are the powers of individual committees reduced significantly. But 1981 remains unique. Other uses of the reconciliation procedure included in the 1974 changes in congressional budgeting have not been comprehensive. Most of the time the procedure is not used at all.

The most visible and familiar noncentralized decision points are the appropriations subcommittees. A steady flow of information is constantly traded between subcommittee members and staff and agency personnel. The annual appearance of the agency head and other top agency staff at the formal hearings is a public highlight, but subcommittees know well the business of the agency before that appearance. The subcommittees have some latitude in deciding on the amount of money that goes to an agency. They can also specify limitations on how the money is spent. Even after appropriations are made, the subcommittees have some continuing influence over the uses of the money. For example, agency reprogramming of funds (shifting money between expenditure categories) often must have at least informal subcommittee approval (Fisher 1974; Horn 1970, 192–195).

Before the appropriations committees can appropriate funds, however, authorizing legislation for the agency or program in question must have been passed. Authorizing legislation gives congressional (and presidential) approval to an activity and often sets a ceiling on the amount of funds that can be made available for the activity. Authorization hearings necessarily focus on questions in addition to money, but important decisions about money are also often made in considering authorizations.

Legislative (authorizing) committees are also involved in budget decisions that have been collectively labeled "backdoor spending." The central feature of the numerous forms of backdoor spending is that a funding pattern is established for some activity by a legislative committee, and funds are available without any input from the appropriations committee and without much program oversight once the pattern is set.

A committee may legislate monetary payments (called entitlements) to certain segments of society and require that money be made available for this purpose in a special trust fund. Social security payments to the retired and disabled are automatically financed in this manner. Sometimes payments to a group such as veterans are tied to the cost of living; money to cover increases in such "indexed" benefits must be provided. A legislative committee may allow an agency to conduct its business through contract obligations, as the Army Corps of Engineers does, for example. Agencies with this authorization can write contracts for services without having the money in hand to pay for them. When the bills come in, Congress must provide the money. Yet another device allows agencies to borrow money from the Treasury to finance their activities without requiring a specific authorization. Legislative committees use all of these techniques to finance agency activities, partly because they are under pressure from agency representatives and their clients and partly because of jurisdictional rivalries with the appropriations committees.

The budget committees offer another locus for making budget decisions. In general, the budget committees try to predict what other players in the budget process are likely to do and, for the most part, adjust their budget resolutions to those perceived preferences. The existence of the budget committees, however, makes congressional budget decision making and congressional–agency interactions additionally complex.

Raising revenue as well as allocating it also requires important budget decisions. Congress, especially in the form of the House Ways and Means Committee and, to a lesser extent, the Senate Finance Committee, is responsible for legislating the federal tax code, which is the complicated mix of rates and exemptions that affects all individuals and corporate entities. A great deal of interaction occurs between the staffs of the tax committees and the executive branch staff dealing with taxation, which is located principally in the Department of the Treasury.

Good relations between members of Congress who sit on the committees that make budget decisions and bureaucrats whose agencies and programs depend on the committees' decisions are important from the bureaucrats' point of view. The members of appropriations subcommittees have special importance for agency administrators (Fenno 1966; Wildavsky 1984, 1988). If a senior member of an appropriations sub-committee expresses a policy view in the course of a hearing, that view is likely to be taken seriously by the bureaucrats as they make subsequent decisions.

Decisions on individual executive branch officials   The Senate has the formal power of confirmation over some critically important executive branch officials, such as department secretaries and assistant secretaries; the director of the OMB; the heads of independent agencies, such as the Federal Power Commission and the Environmental Protection Agency; and the heads of numerous subunits of departments, such as the Bureau of the Census and the FBI. Hearings on nominations to these positions are used to transmit policy preferences of House and Senate members and committees. Occasionally a presidential nomination will be rejected; or defeat will look so likely that a nomination will be withdrawn. In 1981 and 1982, Jesse Helms, a Republican Senator from North Carolina, and his very conservative allies in the Senate forced President Reagan to withdraw a few relatively moderate nominations for positions in the State Department and the Arms Control and Disarmament Agency. Helms did the same thing again with special reference to foreign policy agencies when President Bush began sending nominations to Capitol Hill in 1989.

In 1985 the Senate Judiciary Committee, although controlled by the Republicans, sent a policy message to the Reagan administration about civil rights by rejecting Reagan's nomination of William Bradford Reynolds to be associate attorney general. Reynolds was assistant attorney general for civil rights and was perceived by the majority of the Judiciary Committee to be seriously deficient in his commitment to civil rights. In 1989 the Judiciary Committee, now controlled by Democrats, refused to support President Bush's nomination of William Lucas to become assistant attorney general for civil rights. Lucas's lack of experience was the central issue that led the majority of the committee to conclude that he would not effectively pursue the civil rights policies they favored. Also in 1989 the entire Senate defeated the nomination of John Tower, a former senator, to be secretary of defense, in part because he seemed to be too close to the defense industry.

Even if a nomination is eventually confirmed, it may be that the fight over the nomination will persuade the president to alter the nature of subsequent nominations. For example, Bush's second nominee for secretary of defense was an individual, Congressman Richard Cheney, who had no ties to the defense industry. An earlier example that makes a similar point were nominations to the National Labor Relations Board by President Eisenhower. After one nominee who had had a career in business won confirmation by only three votes in a Republican-controlled Senate, Eisenhower understood that subsequent nominees should not be from management. The Democrats lost the fight over the specific nominee but induced the president to make subsequent nominations more to their liking (Anderson 1970, 373–376).

Occasionally Congress will try to extend the confirmation power to positions not previously requiring action by the Senate. In 1973 Congress and President Nixon battled over the proposal to make the director and deputy director of the Office of Management and Budget subject to Senate confirmation. The president successfully vetoed one bill because it required confirmation of the incumbents. A bill exempting the incumbents and requiring future confirmation was signed by Nixon in early 1974. Similarly, but without controversy, a provision of the 1968 Omnibus Crime Control and Safe Streets Act required that all future directors of the FBI be subject to Senate confirmation.

Congress can make its influence felt on appointments even if formal confirmation is not required. A good case comes from the consumer affairs field (Nadel 1971, 53–55). During the Johnson administration, Betty Furness had held the post of special assistant to the president for consumer affairs and had been a visible advocate of consumer interests within the administration. Early in 1969 President Nixon announced the appointment of a part-time consultant on consumer affairs and chose the director of the Good Housekeeping Institute. Although confirmation was not required for this appointment, this choice was immediately attacked by many in Congress on two grounds. First, the Good Housekeeping Institute itself had been severely criticized by consumer advocates in and out of Congress as a sham. Second, the demotion of the presidential adviser from a special assistant to a part-time consultant signaled to concerned members that the new president planned to downgrade consumer protection programs. The outcry from Congress was so strong that Nixon withdrew his nomination and a few months later appointed another individual as a special assistant for consumer affairs. That person's background and credentials were considerably more legitimate in the eyes of congressional supporters of the consumer movement.

Congressional influence on appointments is felt even after an agency head has been confirmed. Congress can exert pressure on an incumbent that, in effect, forces his or her firing or resignation. This occurred in 1974 when the administrator of the Veterans Administration (VA) was severely criticized for his handling of the organization and its programs both by veterans' groups and by key House and Senate members of committees with jurisidiction over the VA. The administration had virtually no choice but to replace this administrator.

In early 1983 the resignation of Anne Burford as administrator of the Environmental Protection Agency was forced on both her and President Reagan by Reagan's staff, in part because a number of Republican members of Congress had joined the Democrats in calling for her departure. Without such congressional pressure she would have remained in office.

Congress occasionally tries to create a position and name the incumbent simultaneously. In 1978, for example, when Congress was reauthorizing the Comprehensive Employment and Training Act, the Senate tried to create a new assistant secretary in the Department of Labor and make sure that it would be offered to a person already serving in the department as a deputy undersecretary. The Senate language would have waived the normal nomination and confirmation procedures to ensure the promotion without presidential involvement. This individual had worked for the Senate committee with legislative jurisdiction over the Department of Labor for nine years before moving to the department. The House rebelled against the Senate provision, however, and the position vanished from the bill.

Bureaucratic Techniques

The above discussion may make it appear that the bureaucracy can easily be over-whelmed by the rich variety of techniques available to Congress when the two branches interact. This is not the case, however, for two primary reasons. First, the bureaucracy is so vast in terms of individual employees, organizational units, and programs that even a very aggressive set of senators, representatives, and staff members can influence only a relatively small part of the bureaucracy at any given time. Second, the bureaucracy itself possesses techniques that allow it to influence congressional attitudes and behavior. These techniques are not as numerous as those in the hands of Congress, but they can be very effective in achieving the ends desired by the bureaucrats.

Substance of decisions   Bureaucrats can make numerous decisions in the course of administering their programs that are important to members of Congress. This decision making constitutes the bureaucrats' most important technique in interacting with Congress. These decisions cover a broad range of topics and occur in a variety of settings. For example, when a new program is authorized or an old one amended, bureaucrats are required to publish proposed regulations in the *Federal Register* that detail all aspects of program operation. A draft of regulations is circulated for public comment and changes before becoming final. Congressional views during this review and comment period are important in shaping the final regulations.

Many bureaucratic decisions, of course, are not circulated formally in writing but are simply made in the course of implementing programs. For example, a statute may contain ambiguity about eligible recipients of a social welfare program. Some members of Congress are likely to favor a broad interpretation of the eligibility requirements in order to increase the coverage of the program, while others will favor a more restrictive interpretation. The bureaucrats making the decision can calculate the costs and benefits of pleasing one group of legislators and perhaps offending another group.

Bureaucrats also maintain a good deal of control over the use of monies available to them. At one extreme, they may not spend all of the money for any given object—in fact, they may be formally prohibited from doing so by presidential impoundment of funds, although such presidential action was limited by the Budget Act in 1974. More likely, they retain considerable latitude in terms of shifting emphases among expenditures. Various programmatic emphases are pleasing in different degrees to different clusters of members of Congress.

The power that bureaucrats have to determine the geographical location of a number of expenditures and facilities can be used skillfully by them to build supportive coalitions of members of Congress, who are always concerned about such decisions. Who gets contracts, where new federal facilities are located, where facilities such as military installations or federal laboratories or federal field offices are expanded or contracted or even closed are all decisions made by bureaucrats in which senators and representatives take great interest.

A classic case involving closing of field offices and bureaucratic calculation designed to minimize subsequent loss of congressional goodwill and support is provided by the Department of Commerce in 1948 (Arnow 1954). Because of appropriations cuts by the House Appropriations Committee, the department had to close four of its forty-six field offices. Efficiency indicators were developed to measure the workload of each office, the cost of processing the workload, and the population of the city in which the office was located. The fourteen lowest-ranking offices were judged to be candidates for closing. The decision about which four were to be closed during this Democratic administration was made on the basis of explicitly political considerations.

In mid-1985 the new secretary of labor, William Brock (a former senator), announced he was canceling plans to close three of the ten regional offices of the Department of Labor (those in Boston, Kansas City, and Seattle). Senator Lowell Weicker, a fellow Republican, was concerned that service to his constituents in Connecticut would suffer if the Boston office were closed. Weicker chaired the Labor, Health and Human Services, and Education Subcommittee of the Senate Appropriations Committee and was, therefore, influential in the Department of Labor. Simultaneously, a Democratic member of the House Appropriations Committee who came from Seattle indicated he would try to mobilize that committee to block closing the three offices, including the one in his city. Secretary Brock acquiesced, observing that the three offices were "vital to too many citizens." As the *Washington Post* (June 27, 1985) observed, "Everyone on Capitol Hill knew which citizens he meant."

In 1988 the defense bureaucracy supported a bill, which became law, that created an independent Commission on Base Realignment and Closure. The commission made recommendations that closed a few bases, cut back some others, and expanded some in December 1988. In 1989, a few members of Congress whose districts would be most adversely affected attempted to kill the plan but failed. This new method of handling base closings allowed the bureaucracy to make some much-needed savings (which were more cosmetic than sizable in the era of airplanes that cost $500 million each) and, in doing so, they could avoid directly riling influential members of Congress. The commission gave them protective cover and also recommended few enough closings to avoid any serious risk of generating a coalition in Congress that could defeat the entire proposal.

Bureaucrats cannot exercise the power they have over expenditures, location of facilities, or expansion or reduction of services without regard to the political repercussions such exercise of power has in Congress. Successful bureaucrats learn how to balance good programmatic judgment with good political judgment. They learn how to parlay actions that affect the districts and states of individual, well-placed senators and representatives favorably into helping them build supportive coalitions for their agencies. They also learn how to minimize offending influential members with specific decisions.

Timing of decisions   Bureaucrats not only have considerable flexibility in determining the substance of decisions, they also have even more flexibility in determining when those decisions are implemented. Decisions can be timed to give a helpful boost to friendly members of Congress in their reelection campaigns. Decisions can also be timed to magnify the public credit a senator or representative gets for helping create a particular policy outcome. For example, virtually all federal agencies instruct their field offices to refrain from announcing budget allocations for local programs until members of Congress have had a chance to make the first announcement about the federal money coming into their home state or district.

Use of information   Bureaucrats possess a great deal of detailed information. Only rarely is information neutral. The release of important information in a timely fashion by agencies is often used as a persuasive technique. For example, the Department of Commerce opposed cuts in field offices that it was ordered to make even before the 1948 decisions mentioned earlier. The department released a list of thirty-nine offices that might be closed in an effort to get congressional support for overturning or modifying the closings. At least thirty-nine representatives and sixty-eight senators from affected districts and states could be presumed to be interested in the list. Enough money was added by Congress in the appropriations bill to save eight of the thirty-nine offices.

In general, agencies that are managed skillfully will select both the content and timing of the release of various reports and staff studies to maximize the amount of support they generate in Congress for the ends they wish to pursue. Agencies may also be more selective in the release of information and provide it privately only to a few key senators or representatives who can make some use of it in a manner that will redound both to the credit of the member and to the advantage of the agency. Agency personnel often help congressional staff members write speeches for members in which information is used that puts the agency in a favorable light and also makes the member appear highly knowledgeable.

Personal visits and phone calls   Top administrative officials are in constant informal contact with key members of relevant congressional committees and subcommittees. In these relationships the central job of the bureaucrats is to establish personal rapport and trust. The establishment of such a relationship does not mean that all policy and program initiatives will gain congressional approval, but the chances of favorable congressional response are enhanced.

A good example of the elaborate round of personal contacts needed to make a bureaucratic decision is provided by Ruttenberg (Ruttenberg and Gutchess 1970, 80–81) in discussing his tenure as Manpower administrator. In pursuing the notion that there should be regional Manpower administrators (an idea that became feasible once Representative Fogarty had died), Ruttenberg had to establish good working relationships with Fogarty's successor as chairman of the House Appropriations Sub-committee with jurisdiction over the Department of Labor, with the other members of the House Appropriations Committee (including the senior Republicans), and with the chairman and key members of the House Ways and Means Committee, which had jurisdiction over one of the programs that would come under the purview of the new regional Manpower administrators.

The use of third parties   Like members of Congress, executive branch officials can also use supportive third parties to intervene with members of Congress by arguing their case or reinforcing their view. These individuals can include the president or other high-ranking executive officials, newspaper reporters, interest group representatives, and notable clients who also happen to be agency clients. Like Congress, agencies can also commission studies and surveys by outsiders that can be widely disseminated if their conclusions are favorable to the agency and quietly suppressed if the conclusions are not flattering or supportive.

Agency heads must be wary of tapping too often at the doors of higher-ups in the executive branch to engage them as symbolic support for their positions in dealing with Congress. As one close observer of bureaucratic–congressional relations noted (Freeman 1965, 73), "Many committee members do not appreciate bureaucratic attempts to exploit the halo which sometimes attends presidential leadership, especially when the bureau spokesman infers that Congress can be pushed around by a strong President." Bureaucrats are usually better off relying on coalitions that do not rely heavily, if at all, on the top political echelons of the administration.

On the other hand, agency bureaucrats often increase their clout with Congress by mobilizing relevant interest groups to support them. For example, Horn (1970, 197–198) described an instance in 1965 when Secretary of Defense Robert McNamara successfully used representatives of the domestic aircraft industry to obtain approval from the Senate Appropriations Committee to allow British suppliers to bid on planned ship construction projects by the U.S. Navy:

> Most members of the Defense Subcommittee were opposed to the Pentagon posi-
> tion. In a short period before the markup, McNamara personally contacted almost
> all committee members. Representatives of the aircraft industry, coordinating their
> efforts with McNamara's staff, also made known their interest. Potential subcon-
> tractor suppliers of various parts were enlisted in the cause. When the showdown
> came in the full committee, McNamara's personal effort, combined with his skilled
> use of a rival segment of the private economy, paid off.

In addition to mobilizing the support of interested third parties for a specific cause, agency bureaucrats maintain a steady public relations effort to keep Congress and the public informed about the good they and their programs are doing. Agencies also urge their clients to communicate satisfaction with a program to relevant members of Congress.

CHAPTER FOUR

Distributive Policy

In the first three chapters we have made a number of generalizations about the relationship between Congress and the bureaucracy in the making of policy. We have portrayed the relationship in broad strokes in Chapter 1 by discussing its place in the general institutional framework through which national public policy gets made in the United States. In Chapter 2 we focused more concretely on the individuals involved in the relationship and provided some illustrative examples of the relationship in concrete institutional settings. In Chapter 3 we discussed the resources of individuals both on Capitol Hill and in the bureaucracy and the techniques at their disposal for pursuing their diverse goals.

Now we want to get more specific and focus on how Congress and the bureaucracy interact as policy is made in different areas. We are going to focus particularly on the presence and importance of subgovernments within the congressional–bureaucratic relationship. We expect to observe differences in the relationship depending on which of the six policy areas—distributive, protective regulatory, redistributive, structural, strategic, or crisis—is involved. A number of questions are both substantively interesting and important to a systematic analysis of the relationship between Congress and the bureaucracy. How important is the operation of subgovernments in each policy area? With what range of issues does it deal? Do its decisions stand as final, or are they altered before a final decision emerges? Is the relationship between congressional and bureaucratic actors in a policy area characterized chiefly by conflict or by cooperation? If conflict occurs, how is it resolved? Do the policy positions of one branch seem to dominate in the resolution of conflict? In Chapters 4 through 7 we will present empirical material to illustrate and explore these questions in the six different policy areas.

We begin our analysis with some expectations about the nature of the congressional–bureaucratic relationship in the six policy areas. These expectations are summarized in Table 4–1. In this chapter and the three that follow we will first elaborate our expectations about the nature of the congressional–bureaucratic relationship in the policy area or areas under consideration. Second, we will discuss a variety of examples in terms of the analytical questions. Finally, we will summarize our general observations.

TABLE 4-1
Expectations about the Congressional-Bureaucratic Relationship during Policy Formation, by Policy Area

Policy area	Overall importance of subgovernment in policy area	Range of issues decided by subgovernment	Importance of subgovernment in determining final policy actions	Degree of conflict or cooperation between Congress and bureaucracy	Mode and normal locus of conflict resolution	Substance of conflict resolution	Dominant institution when conflict persists
Distributive	High (subgovernment is major decisional locus)	Broad	High	High degree of cooperation—both have primary interest in pleasing clients	Face-to-face negotiations: resolution within the subgovernment	Compromise between initial specific positions	Congress (typically at the subcommittee level)
Protective regulatory	Low (major new decisions are made by Congress)	Narrow	Moderately low on new decisions: moderately high in existing areas of regulation	Potentially high conflict when legislators seek exceptions to general policies	Face-to-face negotiations within the subgovernment or transfer to a higher level	Compromise between initial specific positions; non-resolution; broader compromise at a higher level	Usually Congress at the collective level

(continued)

TABLE 4-1 (continued)

Policy area	Overall importance of subgovernment in policy area	Range of issues decided by subgovernment	Importance of subgovernment in determining final policy actions	Degree of conflict or cooperation between Congress and bureaucracy	Mode and normal locus of conflict resolution	Substance of conflict resolution	Dominant institution when conflict persists
Redistributive	Very low (major decisions are made by executive branch interacting with peak associations)	Very narrow	Low	Potentially high conflict based on partisan and ideological differences; possible cooperation in redefining issue as distributive	No resolution within subgovernment; resolution is transferred to a higher level	Broader compromise at a higher level; redefinition of issues in distributive terms; nonresolution	Depends on relative partisan and ideological strength in Congress
Structural	High (subgovernment is major decisional locus)	Broad	High	High degree of cooperation—both have primary interest in pleasing clients	Face-to-face negotiations; resolution within the relationship	Compromise between initial specific positions	Congress (typically at the subcommittee level)

(continued)

TABLE 4-1 (continued)

Policy area	Overall importance of subgovernment in policy area	Range of issues decided by subgovernment	Importance of subgovernment in determining final policy actions	Degree of conflict or cooperation between Congress and bureaucracy	Mode and normal locus of conflict resolution	Substance of conflict resolution	Dominant institution when conflict persists
Strategic	Low (major decisions are made in executive branch)	Narrow	Low	Some chance for conflict if Congress gets involved	Subgovernment not involved in resolution; resolution occurs at a higher level	Compromise or nonresolution	Executive branch
Crisis	Absent (major decisions are presidential)	None	Absent	Little chance for either cooperation or conflict to develop during decision making; conflict may develop after event	No subgovernment involvement; post hoc legitimation (congressional resolutions, executive orders)	Sham compromise or imposed solution	Executive branch (president)

The Nature of Distributive Policy

The essence of distributive policy is the decentralized award of federal largess to a seemingly unlimited number of recipients—individuals, groups, and corporations. The mechanics of the subsidy arrangement vary. In some issue areas, numerous individual laws may each specify a few beneficiaries. In other cases, a general law may allow numerous similar beneficiaries to collect a subsidy. The duration of the subsidy can also vary, as can its material nature. The reward may take the form of a price-support payment; a contract for procurement, construction, or service; a tax loophole; or a special indemnity award.

The recipients of subsidies usually do not compete directly with each other for them. Rather, each seeks a high level of support without being particularly aware of the other recipients of subsidies and the nature of what they get. The petitioners typically seek direct access to the bureaus in the executive branch and the subcommittees in the House and Senate that are primarily responsible for setting their level of subsidy. Once the level of subsidy is set, the implementation of that subsidy is also delegated to the bureau level of the executive branch—often with close involvement of personnel from the relevant congressional subcommittees.

The interactions of the members of subgovernments are characterized by a low level of public visibility. These interactions are also marked by a high degree of mutually rewarding cooperation (logrolling) that facilitates both perpetuation of the subsidies within the subsystem and its continued low visibility. Logrolling also dominates the relationship between legislative members of the subgovernment and the rest of the House and Senate. Eventutally, most members of Congress want to set up subsidies for groups they support and need cooperation to do so.

The great proliferation of interest groups in the past few decades (Schlozman and Tierney 1986) both reflects the increased number of subsidies and spurs such subsidies. Not all interest groups organize for the exclusive purpose of seeking new subsidies and defending or expanding existing subsidies, but these are strong motivations for many interest groups. The subsidies important to individual groups are often not immediately apparent to them. For example, in 1978 (with revisions and extensions in 1981 and 1982) Congress created an almost invisible provision of the Internal Revenue Code called the Targeted Jobs Tax Credit. Almost invisible, that is, except to enterprising lobbyists for the fast-food industry, who realized that lots of federal dollars would flow to their clients simply for continuing to hire the kind of youths they would hire anyway (Keller 1981a). Congress created the initial program without much pressure from lobbyists, but when renewal of the program was at stake, the lobbyists had seen where their interests lay and were present in force to make sure that the subsidy continued.

Politics and greed coalesce to create a situation in which distributive policy is simultaneously quite popular with potential beneficiaries because of the tangible benefits they receive and also quite popular with members of Congress and bureaucrats because of the plaudits they receive from satisfied constituents and clients who receive the benefits. Distributive policies are therefore numerous.

In foreign and defense policy, as we will discuss in Chapter 7, structural policy is, in effect, the same as distributive policy. Even in the other policy areas—particularly in protective regulatory and redistributive policy—large elements of subsidy can appear. For example, as environmental issues—which began life as protective regulatory measures—have become more attractive, the element of subsidy has increased. A *Wall Street Journal* headline (August 16, 1989) captures the essence of this development: "House and Senate, Recognizing a Pork Barrel When They See One, Warm to the Environment." The text of the article makes the general point succinctly: "Amendments are driven by often-localized interests, and lawmakers vie to bring home parks or to clean up wastes much as they once competed for conventional public works."

The wide-ranging, extremely costly bailout of the savings and loan industry ("thrift" hardly seems the right adjective for the industry since the bailout will cost hundreds of billions of dollars in the next few decades) provides another good example—one that we will discuss further in Chapter 5—of the pressure to include subsidy in policies intended for other purposes. That legislation is theoretically protective regulatory, intended to regulate an industry that had generally been mismanaged and was on the verge of losing vast amounts of savings for depositors. But large dollops of subsidy for a sizable number of people in the industry made the regulation more palatable.

The urge to seek and grant subsidy is seemingly everywhere. When the Postal Service and its congressional overseers and commercial mailers began to ponder creating nine-digit ZIP codes to replace the five-digit codes, for example, the policy makers automatically assumed that business would get "incentive assistance" from the government to make the transition. "Incentive assistance" is, of course, a creative name for a new subsidy. When distribution formulas are designed for allocating federal resources, there is usually pressure to develop criteria that will spread the resources widely. For example, by 1980 the accretion of formulas that surrounded the programs of the Economic Development Administration—which had been created in 1965 and had inherited the programs of the Area Redevelopment Administration, which had itself been created in 1961—made geographical areas containing 85 percent of the population of the country eligible for "special aid" (Rich 1980), even though the programs were supposed to help only areas that were chronically depressed economically.

Subsidy—distributive policy—expands in part to submerge and blur class lines and competition. If the vast portion of the American population that considers itself "middle class" gets its "share" of federal benefits, policy makers benefit politically.

The identity of interest groups, bureaus, and subcommittees within a subgovernment changes slowly over time. The slow nature of the change in the cast of characters helps promote slow change in the nature of distributive policies.

Ronald Reagan and some of his supporters, advisors, and appointees stated that they would attack the "iron triangles"—their favorite name for subgovernments— with their policy decisions. They portrayed the two decades before Reagan became president as a period of unrestrained feeding at the public trough by a plethora of interest groups. By implication, they criticized the administrations of both Republican presidents (Nixon and Ford) and Democratic presidents (Kennedy, Johnson, and Carter) for encouraging this development rather than opposing it. The Reagan administration promised an end to what they viewed as bad policy. When the performance of the Reagan administration is compared with its rhetoric, however, performance falls far short of rhetoric.

The Reagan administration officials defined any program they did not favor that resulted in federal spending as the result of the decisions of "iron triangles." They focused their attack on programs such as welfare and food stamps that were targeted on the less-advantaged classes and groups in society. We think such programs are redistributive and generate political relationships quite different from those typical of distributive policies and programs. But, like officials of any administration, the Reaganites used language and concepts that advanced their political preferences most effectively and did not worry about analytical clarity. They wanted to punish interests in the opposing political coalition and reward interests in their supportive coalition. The Reagan rhetoric about "iron triangles" did not change the fact that a principal goal of the administration was to eliminate or at least cut heavily a number of redistributive programs. Only a few of the Reagan targets were genuinely distributive programs.

What happened in those few distributive policy areas in which the Reagan administration did try to effect cuts? Some modest changes resulted, but these changes amounted to no revolution in the nature of U.S. policy formulation. Incremental change—business as usual—occurred for the most part.

In 1981, *Congressional Quarterly* identified eight programs that, in its view, were in what Budget Director David Stockman once called "the thundering herd of sacred cows." Two of those programs did not fit our description of distributive policies; the other six did. They were the targets of attacks by Reagan, Stockman, and other high-ranking administration officials. What happened to these programs? At the end of 1981 only one of them—Public Health Service hospitals—had apparently been led to slaughter. The other five survived, some unscathed and others with modest cuts (Keller 1981c, 1982). The five survivors were federal aid to schools in areas "impacted" by federal facilities; the Clinch River breeder reactor; support for the Export-Import Bank; a subsidy for Amtrak passenger trains; and the allotment program for peanuts. A survey of a number of distributive programs by the *Washington Post* in early 1982 (January 24, 25, 26, and 27) revealed the same pattern. The headlines summarize what the reporters found: "Despite Budget Cuts, the Hill Finds Dollars to Spread Around at Home"; "Congress' Budget Cutters Protect the Home Folks"; "Budget Knife Only Nicks Road and Harbor Projects"; "Legislative Largesse Puts Energy Firms in a 'No-Lose' Situation."

Early in the Reagan administration a number of statutes simultaneously produced large cuts in federal taxes and large increases in defense spending. These decisions in turn quickly produced enormous and growing deficits in the federal budget. In 1985 Congress created what it hoped would be a formula for reducing the annual deficit to zero within six years and put the formula in the Gramm–Rudman–Hollings

Act. Following a Supreme Court decision declaring part of the process thus created unconstitutional because it blurred the line between executive and legislative responsibilities, Congress tinkered with the act in 1987 to repair the constitutional problem and also to lengthen the timetable by a few years.

Gramm–Rudman–Hollings is part symbol of congressional intent to balance the budget and part rhetoric to convince the citizenry that action is being taken. In fact, attempts to reach the goals are still confused and results are slow in coming. Both Congress and the White House are adroit at inventing fictions to minimize the deficit. For example, in 1989, when both branches tried to figure out how to save the savings and loan industry in the country, they hit on the formula of not counting 60 percent of an eventual cost estimated—probably conservatively—at $300 billion. Exactly why this money should not count as "real" ("on budget," in the jargon of the day) in fiscal terms was not made clear to anyone or by anyone. What was made clear was that the symbolic progress toward Gramm–Rudman–Hollings goals should not be jeopardized by mammoth new spending.

By the end of the first year of the Bush administration, the main impact of Gramm–Rudman–Hollings had been to force the administration and Congress to arrive at sweeping treaties specifying the balance between domestic and defense spending. But within those broad agreements there was still lots of room for maneuver and for creative accounting. *In short, Gramm–Rudman–Hollings did not change in basic ways the politics of program choice we analyze in this book.* Representative Leon Panetta (D–Calif.) summarized the situation succinctly and well in early 1987: "You can build whatever kind of system you want, but the bottom line is still politics and guts" (Rauch 1987, 248). The proper combination of politics and guts was rarely present to wipe out distributive programs. The programs changed in ways and for reasons we will analyze in the rest of this chapter. But they did not change primarily because of the impact of the concern of policy makers in Congress and the executive branch with the federal deficit (LeLoup 1988; Wildavsky 1988).

The Congressional–Bureaucratic Relationship in Distributive Policy

Expectations about the Relationship

We expect the relationship between bureaucrats at the bureau level and individuals on Capitol Hill—both members and staff members at the subcommittee level—to be critically important in distributive policy. As indicated in Chapter 1, it is in this policy area that subgovernments often hold sway. The bureau–subcommittee relationship is at the heart of subgovernments. When subgovernments are in control, they make what amount to final decisions for the entire government on a range of public policy issues. Only occasionally does a subgovernment lose control of part of its policy area and get overruled by other officials such as the full House or Senate, a conference committee, the OMB, the office of the secretary of a department in the executive branch, or the White House.

Ordinarily the relationship between the congressional actors and the bureaucratic actors is marked by a high degree of cooperation. All actors have a major stake in supporting and pleasing the interests of their clients because it is, in part, client satisfaction that produces important political support for both bureaus and subcommittees as they seek to enhance their influence in their respective institutional settings.

Issues that involve differences of opinion are usually resolved by straightforward, face-to-face negotiations between the individuals directly involved in the relationship. There is usually no need to appeal to higher authority because agreement is relatively easy to reach. In fact, both parties have a stake in resolving conflict without involving other parties. If higher authority is invoked, then other substantive matters on which there is agreement at the subgovernment level might also be called into question. That situation could threaten to produce changes in longstanding policies and programs in ways unsatisfactory to both the bureaucratic and congressional members of the subgovernment, as well as to the interest groups in the subgovernment.

The normal resolution of disagreement within a subgovernment is a compromise between two initially contending positions. This compromise is generally satisfying to both the bureaucratic and the congressional members of the subgovernment, although congressional positions are likely to be somewhat more influential than bureaucratic positions.

Although we expect that issues in the distributive arena in general will follow the above pattern, some further distinctions between different types of subgovernment involvement are very important. As suggested in Chapter 1, subgovernments are not always immune to scrutiny from outsiders. The operations of subgovernments can be exposed to a wider view by a number of factors: disagreement among members that cannot be resolved within the confines of the subgovernment; intrusion into subgovernment affairs by outsiders, such as an aggressive president; introduction of a new issue into the subgovernment's jurisdiction; or redefinition of a distributive issue into some other kind of issue. All of these factors increase the visibility of the work of a subgovernment and broaden the number of participants who get involved in that work.

There are four major types of congressional–bureaucratic relationships within the distributive policy area. The most common is *subgovernment dominance.* Two important variations on this type are *major subgovernment adaptation* and *competing subgovernments. Subgovernment distintegration* is the fourth, one that rarely occurs.

Subgovernment dominance is, in many senses, "normal" in cases of distributive policy. Much of the time subgovernments make decisions affecting substantive matters within their purview basically without serious challenge from or involvement with anyone outside the subgovernment except for formal, virtually automatic ratification of subgovernment decisions. From the point of view of the interests they champion, the subgovernments operate at a low level of visibility and at a high level of effectiveness. In those instances in which challenges are made to the government, it prevails with ease, thus retaining its dominance.

In subgovernment dominance, both short-run and long-run policy outcomes favor the interests of those in the subgovernment. No major redefinition of the policy positions by the members of the subgovernment is necessary because challenges can be met without such concessions. The boundaries of the subgovernment's policy fief are, at minimum, stable and, in the case of particularly powerful subgovernments, may even expand. Challenges are relatively infrequent and sporadic and do not pose much threat to the interests of the subgovernment.

Major subgovernment adaptation is required when challenges to a subgovernment become more persistent and powerful. If defeats begin to become frequent and if the subgovernment is being defeated on issues central rather than peripheral to its interests, then often that subgovernment will adapt to the new reality. If the adaptation is successful, the subgovernment will reestablish itself as dominant on the basis of partially new definitions of interests, issues, and positions. If a subgovernment is unwilling to try to adapt or if it is unsuccessful in adapting, then it may disintegrate or be supplanted by a competing set of interests represented in another subgovernment.

When a subgovernment undergoes major adaptation, short-run policy outcomes are likely to be a mix of favorable and unfavorable from the perspective of the subgovernment. If, however, the adaptation is successful, long-run policy outcomes will be favorable. As the subgovernment redefines its policy positions during the process of adaptation, it may be that the scope of the subgovernment's domain may also change. Before and during the process of adaptation, challenges to the subgovernment will be at least moderately strong and relatively frequent.

Competing subgovernments can develop when an issue area is lodged in the governmental decision-making apparatus in a way that allows or even promotes the development of institutionalized competition for dominance. The competition may result in the eventual redefinition of jurisdictions so that one of the competitors becomes dominant, or it may result in replacement of the competing subgovernments by some other mode of decision making, or it may result in continued sharing of the issue-area space by the competitors, with sufficient adjustments to mute conflict enough to allow decisions to be made.

When subgovernments compete, both short-run and long-run policy outcomes typically are mixed from the point of view of either of the competitors. Each of them prevails some of the time. If one of the competitors begins to prevail an overwhelming proportion of the time, competition is likely to vanish. In most competitive situations, members of the competing groups do little redefining of their policy positions. Stability of the domain influenced by each of the competitors is relatively low because competition will ordinarily breed changing patterns of dominance. Challenges to the dominance of any one subgovernment are, by definition, relatively strong and frequent.

Subgovernment disintegration occurs only rarely, but that it occurs at all suggests that some significant procedural and substantive change is at least possible in national policy making. Disintegration may occur because the subgovernment loses jurisdiction over its issues (either because of a reshuffling of congressional or bureaucratic boundaries or because of a redefinition of the issue as nondistributive); because it has been weakened by repeated losses on a series of individually minor challenges; because it has collapsed in the face of a major challenge; or because of key personnel changes in the critical units of the subgovernment.

As a subgovernment approaches disintegration, both short-run and long-run policy outcomes become unfavorable. The subgovernment is not likely to redefine its policy positions. If it would do so, it might be able to adapt to the changed circumstances and survive. The domain in the purview of the subgovernment shrinks until it vanishes. Challenges are strong and frequent and, ultimately, fatal.

Table 4–2 summarizes the four major situations in which subgovernments find themselves as they participate in distributive policy making.

Subgovernment Dominance

Water resources: The classic period   Water resource policy has evolved piecemeal over the years. There is no single comprehensive policy, but rather an aggregation of separate decisions made over time. Administrative responsibility for water policy has been split since 1902 between the Army Corps of Engineers, whose control was concentrated in the eastern United States, and the Bureau of Reclamation in the Department of Interior, which was charged with water development in the western states. For decades, legislating for water projects represented classic pork-barrel politics. Generous benefits were distributed widely to states and localities. Controversy over decisions was quite limited.

The smooth operation of the subgovernment was shaken in the 1970s, and disruptions continued throughout the 1980s. In the remainder of the present section we describe the traditional, smoothly functioning subgovernment surrounding the Corps of Engineers water projects in the golden era of corps autonomy before the mid-1970s. We continue our discussion of water resources since the mid-1970s in the section on subgovernment adaptation later in the chapter.

Rivers and harbors projects have been a traditional form of subsidy throughout our national history, and the principal agency involved in rivers and harbors projects

TABLE 4–2

Four Major Subgovernment Situations in Distributive Policy Making

		Overall subgovernment position		
Major attributes of situation	Dominance	Major adaptation	Competing subgovernments	Disintegration
Short-run policy outcomes	Favorable	Mixed	Mixed	Unfavorable
Long-run policy outcomes	Favorable	Favorable	Mixed	Unfavorable
Degree of redefinition of policy positions by subgovernment	Low	Moderate to high	Low	Low
Stability of subgovernment domain	High; may expand	Low	Low to moderate	Low; then vanishes
Strength and frequency of challenges	Low; sporadic	Moderate to high; frequent	Moderate to high; frequent	High; frequent (ultimately fatal)

has been the Corps of Engineers (Drew 1970; Maass 1950). The responsibility given to the corps for developing the nation's water resources is greater than that of such potentially competing agencies as the Bureau of Reclamation, the Tennessee Valley Authority, and the Soil Conservation Service of the Department of Agriculture. The corps's projects, which have been described by some as a giveaway to local communities, include building dams, levees, and reservoirs; straightening and otherwise rearranging rivers; and building harbors and canals. The purposes served by the projects include flood prevention; creation and improvement of navigable waterways; and provision of hydroelectric power, water supplies, and recreation opportunities.

The water resource programs of the corps operated for decades through a well-established network of ties between individual members of Congress seeking projects for their districts, congressional committees (the House and Senate Committees on Public Works and the House Public Works Appropriations Subcommittee), officials of the Corps of Engineers, representatives of affected local interests; and lobbyists for national interest groups such as the National Rivers and Harbors Congress, the Florida Waterways Association, and the Mississippi Valley Association. A general description of how a project became reality with the support of this network follows.

A project originates at the local level when representatives of concerns that can see profit in a project (for example, industrialists, real estate developers, barge companies) get together with the district engineer from the corps and draw up a proposal for the project. They then enlist the aid of the necessary senators and representatives to sponsor legislation to authorize a feasibility study by the corps. Many proposals never advance beyond this stage, but members of Congress rarely refused to introduce such legislation.

The proposals are referred to the House and Senate Committees on Public Works. These committees make decisions about which of the projects that have received the approval of the corps will be authorized for funding and construction. The appropriations committees in both houses provide the funds for the feasibility studies and for the construction of authorized projects. Once a proposal has received authorization for a feasibility study, professionals in the corps in the area affected conduct the study, which may entail many years and volumes of technical reports. Ultimately, they make their recommendations about the proposal based on the general criterion of whether the benefits are equal to or greater than the costs. Congress has insisted that this criterion remain flexible. Every two years, in an authorization bill, the Public Works Committees identify the projects authorized for feasibility studies and those authorized for construction.

The process of making decisons about whose projects in which districts receive funding is characterized by political negotiation, bargaining, and compromise by the committee members, with a large input from various interest groups, both national and local. Paul Douglas, a Democratic senator from Illinois from 1949 until 1967, offered a good description of the process (Drew 1970, 55): "The [public works] bill is built up out of a whole system of mutual accommodations, in which the favors are widely distributed, with the implicit promise that no one will kick over the apple cart; that if senators do not object to the bill as a whole, they will 'get theirs.' It is a process, if I may use an inelegant expression, of mutual backscratching and mutual logrolling."

The classic water resources subgovernment operated quietly and efficiently. The Corps of Engineers, members of the House and Senate, and local and national interest groups all benefited by supporting each other.

Agricultural policy: The classic period Farm policy has long been synonymous with the dominance of subgovernments (Lowi 1973a; Talbot and Hadwiger 1968; see also Browne 1988). The policies are often controversial, and the subgovernment victories are often ratified by narrow votes on the floor of Congress. It has often been necessary for those dominating agricultural policy to trade their support on other issues for reciprocal support on matters about which they care. The major farm bill passed in late 1985 represented significant adaptive behavior on the part of the coalition of agriculture subgovernments and will be treated separately as an illustration of adaptation. What follows presents the general picture of agricultural policy making for many decades before the mid-1980s. It should be added that this form of decision making is not dead. Elements of it continue even after the changes represented by the 1985 statute, and other elements may reemerge.

Agricultural policy is composed of many separate pieces, around each of which subgovernments form. On some occasions members of the separate subgovernments may form temporary alliances to promote a broad policy, but ordinarily they work independently and focus on narrow policy concerns. A few examples demonstrate how these subgovernments work. First, we will look at two broad areas in which subgovernment success was consistently high over a long period of time: price supports and soil conservation. Then we will observe a case of a subgovernment expanding its domain by opening the federal treasury in a major way to new "disaster" claims by farmers.

Price supports The price-support program is a complex set of laws administered at the national level by two units of the U.S. Department of Agriculture—the Agricultural Stabilization and Conservation Service (ASCS) and Commodity Credit Corporation (CCC)—and at the state and local level by specified state, county, and local committees. The program is designed to protect the incomes of growers of commodities through a combination of acreage allotments (crop quotas), target prices on commodities, government loans and payments to growers, and government purchases of crops.

Subgovernments developed around each major crop or supported item. The basic participants are relevant specialists in the ASCS, the members of the various commodity subcommittees of the House Agriculture Committee, and representatives of the interest groups for various crops and commodities, such as the National Association of Wheat Growers, the National Wool Growers Association, the Soybean Council of America, and the National Milk Producers Federation. Table 4–3 illustrates some of the commodity subgovernments with a partial listing of the institutional locations of some of the principal members.

TABLE 4–3

Composition of Illustrative Commodity Subgovernments

| Commodity | Institutional location of subgovernment members | | |
	Congress	Bureaucracy	Interest groups
Cotton	House Cotton Subcommittee	Agricultural Stabilization and Conservation Service (ASCS) cotton program	National Cotton Council
Oilseeds and rice	House Oilseeds and Rice Subcommittee	ASCS programs for peanuts, rice, tungnuts, flaxseed, soybeans, dry edible beans, and crude pinegum	Soybean Council of America
Tobacco	House Tobacco Subcommittee	ASCS tobacco program	Tobacco Institute
Dairy and poultry products	House Dairy and Poultry Subcommittee	ASCS milk program	National Milk Producers Federation; National Broiler Council
Livestock and grains	House Livestock and Grains Subcommittee	ASCS programs for wheat, corn, barley, oats, grain sorghum, rye, wool, and mohair	National Association of Wheat Growers; National Wool Growers Association

The House Agriculture Subcommittee divided itself into commodity subcommittees in 1955. Over the years these subcommittees have been rearranged and their jurisdictions elided. In the 101st Congress (1989–1990) four subcommittees (Cotton, Rice, and Sugar; Livestock, Dairy, and Poultry; Tobacco and Peanuts; and Wheat, Soybeans, and Feed Grains) retained unalloyed concentrations on specific commodities. A fifth (Forests, Family Farms, and Energy) retained a partial focus on a specific commodity.

In the period of classic subgovernment dominance, the subcommittees drafted the various commodity provisions, which were then stapled together by the full committee and sent to the floor for ratification. A similar process took place in the Senate. As the press secretary for the longtime chairman of the Senate Agriculture Committee, Herman Talmadge, a Georgia Democrat, put it: "Chairman Talmadge would ask every Senator what he wanted for his commodity" (Stokes 1985, 633).

Each commodity subgovernment worked to obtain the most favorable treatment possible for the producers of the commodity in terms of both acreage allotments and target prices. In general, these subgovernments operated without successful challenge in setting the levels of commodity supports, which were then routinely ratified by Congress as a whole and implemented by the Department of Agriculture.

Agricultural policy was built from the bottom up, the result of bargaining and basic cooperation among a collection of subgovernments. Only in the 1980s was this basic way of putting together what passed for national agricultural policy challenged.

Soil conservation   The basic program (or "mission") of the Soil Conservation Service (SCS), a unit of the Department of Agriculture, is development of a national soil and water conservation program. The SCS, however, has never had the only program with this goal. The SCS program focuses on building small dams to help conserve soil, prevent floods, and increase recreational opportunities in rural areas. In addition, the SCS provides technical assistance to landowners, land users, and land developers located in about 3,000 soil conservation districts to assist them in carrying out locally adopted programs.

The local conservation districts have a good deal of muscle and are directly involved in the operations of the soil conservation subgovernment. For example, the watershed projects of the SCS are the result of requests made to the SCS from the local level, usually by the conservation districts. The SCS obtains the necessary authorizations and appropriations from Congress when it wants to respond favorably to requests. The subgovernment that supports and determines the nature of this program includes SCS watershed bureau officials, members of the House and Senate agriculture committees—which handle authorizations of the projects—and members of the House Appropriations Subcommittee on Agriculture, which is instrumental in providing money for the projects. Nongovernmental members of the subgovernment include representatives of organizations such as the National Association of Soil Conservation Districts and the Izaak Walton League of America.

Crop disaster and the Small Business Administration: Subgovernment expansion   In 1977 farmers in Georgia and other southeastern states suffered crop losses because of drought. This triggered events that cost the Treasury of the United States billions of dollars more than it expected to spend (Havemann 1977; Meisol 1978).

The problems in Georgia prompted action by Sam Nunn, one of the senators from the state and a member of the Senate Select Committee on Small Business. He pointed out to both farmers and the Small Business Administration (SBA) that a little-noted provision of a 1975 statute affecting the SBA had made farmers eligible for SBA disaster loans. That amendment had been offered by two senior senators, one of them from a rural state and chairman of the Senate Small Business Committee.

Once Nunn had pushed the SBA into admitting that it could not exclude farmers from disaster loans, the chairman of the House Small Business Committee, Neal Smith, an Iowa Democrat, joined in urging farmers to apply and simultaneously urged the SBA to respond favorably. Iowa farmers had also suffered crop losses in 1977.

The results were costly. In fiscal year 1976 the SBA allowed no disaster loans to farmers. In fiscal year 1977 the agency made only 798 loans to farmers, which represented 4 percent of all of its disaster loans and were for a total of about $40 million. All of these loans to farmers came late in the fiscal year as Nunn and Smith worked to pry open the lid to the public cookie jar for the benefit of their constituents and other farmers. In the first three quarters of fiscal 1978, the lid was gone. SBA disaster loans to farmers in that period amounted to $1.7 billion— 44 percent of all SBA disaster loans in the period and more than 75 percent of the total money allocated to the program.

Even though the usual members of agriculture subgovernments had not instituted this action in the first place, they subsequently rallied to the cause of preserving this gain, despite the existence of a parallel program in the Farmers Home Administration (FHA). That program, however, had tighter eligibility limits and a higher interest rate than the SBA program.

Challenges came from two locations: the White House and the Senate Budget Committee. The challenge from within Congress was to no avail as Congress passed an SBA authorization bill extending the disaster loan program, keeping it open to farmers, and putting no dollar limit on expenditures by authorizing "such sums as are necessary."

White House opposition to the raid on the treasury was only partially effective. After members of Congress had left town in October 1978 and could not vote on overriding a veto, President Carter vetoed the bill for a number of reasons, including the budget implications of the treatment of disaster loans for farmers. He objected to the redundancy of the SBA program with the FHA program when the former was extended to include farmers. He also objected to the very low interest rate of 3 percent and the lack of a limit to the amount that could be spent. His veto had the effect of raising the interest rate on disaster loans to 6.625 percent, still low by commercial standards at the time. The veto did not have the effect of limiting total spending.

In 1980 Congress moved the entire disaster loan program for farmers to the FHA but still made no serious effort to control the cost of the program. In 1981 the program was still operating at record levels: $4 billion in loans in the first half of the year alone.

The Reagan administration proposed severe cuts and limits on the program and also asked that the interest rate be raised to 14 percent. The administration achieved only limited success in that interest rates were capped at 8 percent for borrowers without other sources of credit, which included most of those using the program. This interest rate was established at a time when commercial loans carried an interest rate of about 20 percent. Members of the agricultural subgovernment continued to have reason to smile.

Veterans' benefits Over many decades, the veterans' subgovernment has become and remained powerful, tapping the public purse for enormous benefits (Keisling 1982; Keller 1980; Scott 1977). The natural appeal of helping those who have served their country, sometimes in combat, has produced the third largest bureaucracy in the federal government—the Department of Veterans Affairs, which was the Veterans Administration (VA) until early 1989. Its approximately quarter of a million employees are outnumbered only by those working for the Department of Defense and for the Postal Service. Its annual budget of close to $30 billion is also one of major budgets among federal agencies. Programs that benefit veterans include:

- The largest single hospital system in the country
- Educational assistance
- Compensation to injured veterans, regardless of income
- Special pensions for needy veterans, although the needs do not stem from their time in service
- A large life insurance program for veterans
- Insurance on millions of home loans for veterans

Both the cost of benefits and the nature of benefits have expanded over time. Naturally, the number of veterans and relatives of veterans eligible for benefits also helps determine the actual dollar outlay in any specific year.

The most important support groups for generating these benefits are the department itself; veterans' groups such as the American Legion, the Veterans of Foreign Wars, and the Disabled American Veterans; and the veterans affairs committees of both the House and Senate. (It is worth noting that the House committee has existed for a long time but that the Senate created a separate committee only in 1970, an indication of how powerful the subgovernment had become over the years.)

In 1978 the veterans' subgovernment demonstrated its clout by successfully increasing veterans' benefits in three areas: (1) pensions for those with disabilities *not* connected with service; (2) housing programs; and (3) employment and training. In addition, an attempt by the Carter administration to eliminate "veterans' preference" points added to the results of civil service examinations was quickly killed by Congress.

During the Reagan administration, general domestic budget-cutting efforts avoided tangling with the VA and its programs. The veterans groups gave Reagan important political support, and his administration reciprocated by leaving their special access to the federal budget unthreatened. Even when Congress passed Gramm–Rudman–Hollings in an effort to deal with budget deficits in general, the law explicitly exempted veterans' pensions from any mandatory cuts and severely restricted any cuts in health care programs for veterans. This subgovernment was so strong that most of the debates over spending and deficits that politicians took fairly seriously in the 1980s could simply be ignored as far as veterans' benefits were concerned. Reagan's support for the upgrading of the VA to departmental (and cabinet) status, despite his general attacks on bureaucratic proliferation, was another indication of the influence of this subgovernment.

Tobacco and smoking   Before 1964 the tobacco industry in the United States—including both growers and the manufacturers of finished products such as cigarettes—was protected by an effective subgovernment that subsidized the growers and let the manufacturers alone to advertise their product as they saw fit (Fritschler 1989; Friedman 1975). Fritschler (1989, 4–5) summarized the composition of the subgovernment and its quiet functioning in the period up to 1964:

> The tobacco subsystem included the paid representatives of tobacco growers, marketing organizations, and cigarette manufacturers; congressmen representing tobacco constituencies; the leading members of four subcommittees in Congress—

two appropriations subcommittees and two substantive legislative committees in each house—that handle tobacco legislation and related appropriations; and certain officials within the Department of Agriculture who were involved with the various tobacco programs of that department. This was a small group of people well-known to each other and knowledgeable about all aspects of the tobacco industry and its relationship with the government.

As long as no one objected too loudly, the important and complex tobacco programs, like price supports and export promotion, were conducted without interference from those not included in this subsystem.

But there were objections to the tobacco subgovernment from outsiders, specifically the "health lobby" and the Federal Trade Commission (FTC). Scientific evidence linking smoking and human diseases had been accumulating at least since 1857, accompanied by a very gradual increase in public awareness of the dangers of smoking. An important event in changing the political situation was the publication of the 1964 report of the U.S. surgeon general (the head of the Public Health Service) that placed an official government seal of approval on the evidence linking smoking to disease. Aware of the accumulating body of scientific evidence on smoking, the FTC had been engaged in trying to discourage advertising and sales of cigarettes, but without much effect. The tobacco subgovernment would have preferred to leave the whole issue of governmental treatment of tobacco and cigarettes as a distributive matter. But the challengers to this view wished to shift the debate into the protective regulatory arena.

The objections of the outsiders got loud enough to be disruptive to the subgovernment when the FTC, following the surgeon general's report on smoking and health, published proposed rules in the *Federal Register* that would have severely restricted advertising for smoking and would have required strict health warnings for cigarettes. These regulations were viewed as very threatening by tobacco growers and manufacturers. Congress reacted swiftly to this controversy. The resulting statute, the Cigarette Labeling and Advertising Act of 1965, was an outcome more favorable to tobacco interests than to health interests. The act had two main features. First, the tobacco interests bowed to the inevitability of some regulation because of the degree of public awareness of the hazards of smoking and, allied with advertisers and broadcasters, they lobbied for the weakest regulation possible, which was a labeling requirement limited to packages but exempting advertising. Second, the tobacco interests were also successful in getting a provision in the legislation that placed a four-year ban on FTC rule-making activity in relation to cigarette advertising and prohibited other federal agencies from entering this area. The tobacco interests had fended off any serious challenge to their privileged position, at least for the time being.

In 1970 Congress passed a law that extended the ban on FTC activities for two more years, weakened the wording of the health warning, and required that the FTC give Congress six months' notice of any future rule-making proposals.

Subsequently, more government restrictions on advertising for smoking have emerged, but these additions have come over a number of years and their implementation has generally been relatively gradual. Many of the changes forced on the subgovernment have been largely symbolic. The challenge to the subgovernment has not been consistent or all-out. And, even as limits on advertising in the domestic market grew, the federal government continued to subsidize the production of tobacco and to aid the industry in exporting tobacco products to the rest of the world.

The core of the subgovernment's strength was displayed in the fact that the federal subsidy for the growing of tobacco continued, and efforts to raise excise taxes and totally ban cigarette advertising were repulsed.

But the stability of the subgovernment's power has been shaken. The anti-smoking forces won some important concessions during the 1980s. The surgeon general's reports on smoking and health grew steadily more outspoken about the adverse effects of smoking (Fritschler 1989, 114–115). The 1972 report was the first to draw attention to passive smoke. By 1986, the surgeon general's report documented 2,400 lung cancer deaths per year from inhaling side-stream smoke.

C. Everett Koop, the surgeon general during the Reagan administration, proved to be a powerful advocate of smoking bans and cigarette advertising bans. He pursued these views even though the Reagan administration limited some of his activity. For example, as the *Washington Post* of July 17, 1986, headlined, the White House chief of staff curbed Koop's activity: "Regan Bars Koop's Testimony for Bill to Ban Tobacco Ads." Koop's reports and his policy statements helped to crystallize growing public sentiment against smoking. Local and state government regulation of smoking in public places proliferated in the 1980s. Restaurants, government buildings, even workplaces came under no-smoking rules.

In 1987 smoking was banned on U.S. commercial flights of less than two hours, an action that proved so popular that an extension to all U.S. flights was approved in October 1989, somewhat to the surprise of its legislative sponsors. The tobacco lobby extracted a face-saving exemption for a tiny number of flights to Alaska and Hawaii. The victory for health forces was a significant advance, although some pointed out that smoking had declined more rapidly among those who were economically in a position to fly a great deal than among those who flew infrequently or not at all.

Despite the action that banned smoking on almost all domestic flights, the tobacco industry has not fallen on hard times. The government has not threatened to move against the heart of the tobacco subgovernment, the agricultural subsidy, nor has it seriously declared war against tobacco use as a form of substance abuse. The number of deaths due to smoking grows, as do cigarette advertising budgets and new brands designed to give the satisfaction of nicotine without the dangers. The government also continues to smile on major export activities of the tobacco companies. The days of undoubted, untrammmeled power on the part of the tobacco subgovernment may be over, but the federal policy environment is still more favorable than hostile.

In short, the status quo is being preserved, although its perimeters have been encroached upon over the previous two decades. For the foreseeable future, the core of the system seems secure.

Major Subgovernment Adaptation

Water resources: Adaptation in the 1970s and 1980s No major omnibus water project authorization bill has passed Congress since 1972. Construction has continued on previously authorized projects, but at a slower rate. Fewer dollars have been appropriated for water projects, and the share for new construction has declined relative to the amount for upkeep of existing facilities. Agreements reached in congressional subcommittees have been reopened to heated debate on the floors of the House and Senate.

What happened? Why did the classic period of subgovernment dominance change? Several forces contributed to the change:

1. Growing federal deficits, particularly after 1982, made all spending subject to extra scrutiny.

2. Recognition began to grow that water was not an infinite resource and that various efforts to develop and conserve it must be coordinated and carefully planned.

3. Environmentalists began to be heard as they detailed the environmental costs of various kinds of water development projects.

4. Both Presidents Carter and Reagan challenged the subgovernment, Carter less effectively than Reagan. Both insisted that decision making had to change to take cost-benefit calculations into account. Both urged local cost-sharing on construction projects and outside review of projects before they could proceed. The OMB, a vital presidential agency, also increased its role enormously in reviewing proposals for water development generated in Congress. Congress reacted negatively to this "intrusion," but could not prevent it.

5. Time inevitably produced changes in the members of Congress in key positions to oversee water policy. Some of these individuals did not share the "build water projects at all costs" mentality of their predecessors.

6. Shrinking resources allocated to water development heightened the competition between agencies, their favored regions, and their congressional allies for those resources.

President Carter's challenge to the subgovernment in 1977 was simultaneously vivid and inept. Carter's goals were to eliminate an array of needless and expensive projects from a congressional "wish" list and to make sure that local beneficiaries would begin to pay a fair share of the cost of federally subsidized water. But Carter's staff lacked good political sense, and the "hit list" confrontational style is rarely effective with Congress. In this case, it caused permanent damage to Carter's congressional relationship throughout his entire term. His efforts increased the level of outside attention to water projects in the late 1970s, but failed, in the short run, to change much in the way of outcomes. The subgovernment successfully resisted most of the Carter incursions.

President Reagan, a westerner, was welcomed by the water development forces as more sympathetic to western water interests. In fact, Reagan continued to promote many of the same changes Carter had advocated, especially cost sharing. Reagan's style and approach were less abrasive and more flexible than Carter's, however. In addition, states, localities, and members of Congress had had time to adjust to the idea that cost sharing might be tolerable.

Cost sharing stalled the activities of the subgovernment in the first half of the 1980s. President Reagan, the secretary of the interior, the assistant secretary of the army responsible for the Corps of Engineers, and the OMB director repeatedly stated that the authorization of new projects would be contingent on the provision of some nonfederal financing by state and local beneficiaries. "No cost sharing, no project" was the clear message from the administration, even if it did not agree on the details of the cost-sharing formula in all cases.

At the same time, the Reagan administration was politically expedient in allowing a few projects to move forward without meeting the cost-sharing test. In a 1985 supplemental appropriations bill, for example, the administration allowed funding for forty-five new projects, even though twenty-one of them did not have previous authorization and lacked cost-sharing provisions. Congressional supporters also proceeded cleverly by tying the funding to a foreign aid bill the administration had requested and very much wanted. In 1984 the administration agreed to allow a dam safety bill to be funded entirely with federal money in order not to jeopardize the reelection prospects of western Republicans in Congress.

But on other occasions the administration held fast to its insistence on cost sharing. A major 1984 omnibus bill failed, for example, because individuals within the subgovernment insisted on resisting cost sharing. Fiscally conservative members of Congress who supported the president's views wrangled with these individuals and the bill sank. The president promised to veto the bill if it passed without cost-sharing provisions.

Administratively, the Corps of Engineers and the Bureau of Reclamation have included cost-sharing provisions in projects they recommend. Localities that produce some non-federal financing are favored. Subgovernment members grudgingly began to accept this new reality.

As the 1980s drew to a close, the water subgovernment found itself somewhat bruised but still alive. Its days of smoothly functioning routines and unquestioned influence are a distant memory, however. The political, social, and economic realities of the 1970s and 1980s have altered the rules of water politics. The spectre of growing budget deficits coupled with the implementation of Gramm–Rudman–Hollings balanced budget legislation contributed to a fiscally cautious atmosphere in Congress. Perceptions of water as a finite natural resource sparked competition among contending groups—agriculture, developers, environmentalists, and recreationalists. Public support for protecting the environment grew in the 1980s. Publicity and visibility ensuing from competition over budget allocations and water use introduced new and more numerous actors into the once tidy relationships of the classic water subgovernment.

A significant indication of the change in water politics occurred with the announcement in October 1987 that the Bureau of Reclamation, which had been the engine driving development of western lands through water projects, would dramatically redirect its efforts. Replacing development was a new mission of conserving water and ensuring its quality, protecting the environment, and managing existing projects. The assistant secretary of the interior for water and science, James Ziglar, said, "The bureau largely has accomplished the job for which Congress created it in 1902, namely to reclaim the arid West." Now it would shift its orientation from that of a "construction company to a resource management organization."

Representative George Miller, a California Democrat who chaired the Water and Power Resources Subcommittee of the House Interior Committee, remarked that the reorganization was a recognition by the bureau that its "glory days of pouring concrete" were over (quotations from the *New York Times*, October 2, 1987). The redirection of the Bureau of Reclamation's efforts confirmed its perpetually inferior status relative to the Corps of Engineers (see Clarke and McCool 1985, Chapters 2 and 4).

There has been no sweeping reform of the water project process, nor have appropriations ceased. But potential projects that once would have aroused no interest beyond those favoring them are called into question. Even projects being constructed are questioned. Two recent developments in water policy illustrate the changed environment for water politics. President Bush campaigned in 1988 as a friend of the environment. In August 1989, his claims were given some reality when the Environmental Protection Agency (EPA) vetoed construction of a dam near Denver that had been supported by President Reagan. The EPA cited the significant loss of aquatic and recreational values and the availability of less-damaging alternatives.

Also in August 1989, the Army Corps of Engineers found that its project to drain Mississippi delta land for agriculture was drawing fire from a powerful coalition of state officials, environmentalists, hunters, and local landowners, who claimed the projects aided agriculture at the expense of settled areas and wildlife. The opponents secured court injunctions halting the work and shook up the traditional local alliance of water development and agriculture interests.

The water development subgovernment is not deceased, but it has been forced to adapt to external forces, primarily environmental and economic, that are outside of its influence. These forces have significantly affected the functioning of the subgovernment. Whether the changes are situational (representing temporary conditions likely to change again, perhaps in a way more favorable to water development) or systemic (representing changes permanently hostile to the functioning of the water subgovernment) remains to be seen. The water subgovernment is beginning to adapt to new substantive challenges such as providing water for urban areas, conserving water resources, and increasing the efficiency of agricultural irrigation. These enterprises may not be as "glamorous" as the building of big dams. But they still involve many federal dollars and can enrich interests that successfully obtain federal policy favorable to them. The water subgovernment continues to show resiliency (McCool 1987).

Adaptation in agricultural subgovernments: The 1985 farm bill In 1985 American agricultural policy stood at a crossroads. Existing legislation was expiring. A debate on the shape of the new legislation ground on all year. The Reagan administration and large agribusiness organizations favored a sharp departure from the policies of the preceding fifty years. They wanted to turn to a free-market economy for agriculture, take the federal government out of the business of subsidizing farmers, make American agricultural products more competitive internationally, and help trim the federal deficit.

Traditional farm groups and legislators of both parties from farming areas hesitated to support any changes that would reduce farm income in a period when nearly a quarter of a million farmers were threatened with insolvency. Agricultural subgovernments were under heavy fire throughout 1985. But when the smoke cleared a new law emerged—the Food Security Act of 1985—that demonstrated that although the subgovernments had to compromise on some issues, their core interests were securely protected.

In this discussion we will look at why agricultural decision making was disrupted and at how the subgovernments adapted to accommodate the disruptions while still preserving the aspects of federal agricultural programs about which they cared most.

A changed context   Since the implementation of the Agricultural Adjustment Act of 1933, the federal government has become an active partner in nearly all decisions made by farmers (when to plant, when to harvest, how much to plant, and what kind of crops to plant) through its extensive direct and indirect subsides: price-support loans (mandated loan rates for commodities grown by farmers who can use their crops as collateral and default if the market price is lower than the loan rate); acreage and production controls; mandated target price levels (these generate deficiency income support payments to farmers when market prices fall below target levels); and other mechanisms such as marketing orders, storage facilities, tax breaks, agricultural research and development, and low-interest loans. The normal cloak of anonymity that veiled decision making and implementation of farm policy for many decades was removed in the 1980s as the environment began to undergo seemingly uncontrollable changes. Some of the factors contributing to a new context for agricultural decisionmaking included

- Escalating international competition (declining U.S. exports, overvalued U.S. dollars, cheap imports)
- Overproduction creating surpluses and lowering market prices
- Mounting farm debt (increasing numbers of farm foreclosures as farmers failed to meet loan playments and operating costs exceeded income)
- Hemorrhaging federal expenditures on farm subsidies between 1981 and 1985; these exceeded initial estimates by more than $50 billion
- Increased pressures to trim the soaring federal budget deficit in general

Making a choice   In 1981 the Reagan administration had tried and failed to reduce the power of agricultural lobbies by trimming price-support loan rates and target price levels. Congress, buttressed by affected interest groups, rebuffed these attempts. In early 1985 the admininistration tried again. It presented a package of reforms that nearly every observer agreed was too drastic to stand any chance of adoption. The Reagan package would have quickly removed the crutch of federal subsidies from farmers and would have forced American agriculture to deal with market forces and international competition. The plan represented such a significant change from long-standing agricultural policy that even administration loyalists considered it dead on arrival in Congress. Its doom was sealed by contention within the administration (the director of the OMB and the secretary of agriculture were at odds) and by the lack of President Reagan's personal involvement in pushing the plan.

Supporters of traditional agricultural policy, especially in the House, favored continuing existing programs of price supports and income supplements, with increased aid for fiscally ailing farms. Moderates, particularly in the Senate, looked for some way to bridge the gulf between the traditional views and some of the views of the White House. The struggle was often portrayed in emotional terms by both sides. The status quo supporters spoke of "saving the family farm" in the face of the threat presented by the free market that only the largest operators would survive economically. The debate was often unclear because its participants perceived, although they did not usually articulate very clearly, multiple goals for agricultural policy, some of which conflicted. For example, there was widespread support for increasing sales overseas and keeping prices low for American consumers while simultaneously ensuring stable, high prices paid to farmers for agricultural products. No known policy contortions could produce all of those results at once. In fact, U.S. agricultural policy for the preceding fifty years had not produced clear or prioritized goals. As a result, farmers received a variety of federal payments to produce surplus crops that lowered market prices and tended to push farm income down. That downward pressure was in turn dealt with by increasing the amount and range of payments. A seemingly endless cycle of feckless but costly programs ensued.

So many cooks The large number of participants in agricultural decision making was increased by the heightened interest from many lobbyists not previously active. One observer (Stokes 1985, 634) identified more than 200 agricultural lobbying groups in Washington. Traditional broad-spectrum farm organizations, such as the American Farm Bureau Federation and the National Farmers Organization, and groups representing specific commodities were joined by environmental groups concerned about soil erosion, consumer groups anxious about food prices, and representatives of agriculture-related businesses such as fertilizer, farm equipment, and supermarkets. Unanimity of opinion about the direction of farm policy was notably absent among these diverse groups. In the absence of consensus, the influence of the commodity groups was the greatest. Their aims were clear and narrowly focused. No commodity group directly opposed other commodity groups; at least informally they supported each other. The chief lobbyist for the American Soybean Association summed up his own view in speaking of members of Congress (Rauch 1985, 2535): "They pretty much do what each commodity wants."

The outcome The final bill, hammered out in the closing days of the 1985 congressional session, was a compromise between the House and Senate bills that had been developed in the respective Committees on Agriculture. The committees also had to pay attention to an overall budget ceiling agreed on separately in the congressional budget process. Floor debate in both houses was long and filled with controversy. Both bills were anchored in existing policies, the House bill more than the Senate bill. Neither bill came very close to the administration's preferences as revealed in its proposal. The final compromise exceeded the president's budget target by $2 billion, but Reagan signed the bill anyway. It is fitting that the signing came on Christmas Eve.

The major coup from the point of view of the commodity subgovernments was the preservation of the existing structure of price supports and income payments to farmers. The concesssions to the president were that (1) over the five-year life of the bill the level of price-support loans would be reduced by 10 percent, (2) the level of activity in support of agricultural exports would be increased, and (3) compulsory reductions in corn and wheat acreage and a voluntary dairy herd buyout would help reduce overproduction of those commodities. Both the supporters of the existing agricultural policy and the administration had issues on which they could claim victory. The commodity subgovernments, by prudent adaptation on some peripheral issues, preserved what was essential to them.

Competing Subgovernments

Health research and cancer During the post–World War II period until the late 1960s, the biomedical and health research community created an enviably strong and, from its own point of view, productive subgovernment (Greenberg 1967; Strickland 1972). Tensions were present as the subgovernment developed, but for the last decade and a half of the existence of a dominant single subgovernment (roughly from the mid-1950s to the late 1960s), it could routinely produce all of the funds it could use reasonably well (sums usually greater than those supported by the president and the Bureau of the Budget). There were dominant individuals in this subgovernment in critical institutional positions: the director of the National Institutes of Health, Dr. James Shannon; the chairman of the Senate appropriations subcommittee responsible for this program area, Lister Hill, an Alabama Democrat; the chairman of the House appropriations subcommittee with the same jurisdiction, John Fogarty, a Rhode Island Democrat; and a persistent and skillful lobbyist for health-related biomedical research, Mary Lasker.

The subgovernment was formed to increase federal support for health and medical research as a means to improve the nation's health. The success of the subgovernment in creating a federal health-related, biomedical research system is clear in the existence of the extensive National Institutes of Health (NIH) structure with its separate research institutes. NIH "at its peak in 1967–1968 [supported] more than 67,000 senior research investigators; it sustains academic science programs and research projects in more than 2,000 universities and medical schools, and helps provide advanced science training in basic science and various clinical specialties for more than 35,000 individuals" (Strickland 1972, 236).

Support for the programs of this single subgovernment began to lag in the 1960s in large part because of the economic demands of the Vietnam War during the Johnson and Nixon presidencies and because of the fiscal conservatism that began late in the Johnson administration and accelerated in the Nixon and Ford administrations. As one way of resuscitating the flagging fortunes of federally supported biomedical research, a new coalition formed in the early 1970s around the single goal of conquering cancer. Although the new cancer subgovernment drew some of its key members from the broader and older subgovernment, it also challenged the hegemony of that broader subgovernment and competed vigorously for the same resources.

Not surprisingly, the broader subgovernment and the cancer-specific subgovernment found themselves in disagreement on some matters. The cancer group sought autonomy and wanted direct access to the president in addition to more money to support its research efforts. Scientists from the older subgovernment feared that a special emphasis on one disease would lead to diminished support for other health-related research programs.

The Senate generally allied itself with the cancer subgovernment. The House generally continued to support the broader biomedical research subgovernment. When the 1971 Cancer Act emerged in final form, both of the competitors achieved part of what they wanted and were able to maintain an uneasy alliance. The government-sponsored drive against cancer (a particular favorite of President Nixon's) was officially endorsed with special organizational and budgetary recognition. But the National Cancer Institute remained under the broad umbrella of NIH.

In the years following the 1971 act, the broader biomedical community saw its fears realized as budgets for the cancer program grew while budgets for other NIH research programs remained stable or shrank. In an effort to remedy this situation, the biomedical subgovernment pushed successfully in 1974 for amending the Cancer Act when it was renewed that year to create a special presidential panel to monitor and advise on all federal health-research programs. Top-level officials in the Department of Health, Education, and Welfare opposed the panel, in part because the president had not requested it. Otherwise, the administration supported the bill, which authorized $2.8 billion for cancer research programs over three years. The provision creating the special monitoring panel met no resistance in either the House or the Senate and it became part of the final law. The two subgovernments resumed their competition after the reauthorization of the Cancer Act.

The competition continues. Budget figures suggest that some stability has been achieved, however. For example, the budget share of the Cancer Institute, now one of thirteen institutes under the NIH umbrella, settled consistently during the 1980s at about one quarter of total NIH outlays. This suggests that the cancer subgovernment is well funded but that the competing broader biomedical research advocates have prevented the Cancer Institute from completely dominating all medical research funding.

Employment and training policy: CETA versus JTPA The composition of the employment and training subgovernment has fluctuated since the entry of the federal government into employment and training policy in the early 1960s. This is a policy area with both distributive and redistributive aspects, but in this discussion we focus on the former. The changes in the subgovernment from 1960 to 1982 were primarily in the direction of expanding participation by enlarging the number of programs authorized (Baumer and Van Horn 1984; Franklin and Ripley 1984). The transition from the categorical programs of the 1960s to a decentralized form of special manpower revenue sharing known as CETA (the Comprehensive Employment and Training Act passed in late 1973) in 1974 shook the subgovernment but did not end it. Instead, the transition was the occasion for a major enlargement in the membership of the subgovernment when the representatives of the organizations of local governments responsible for administration of the CETA program were added. This expansion did not reduce the influence of other key members of the subgovernment. Additional groups were added fairly painlessly until the end of CETA in 1982. Members coexisted more or less harmoniously as long as the major operating principle of the program—that CETA could provide something for everyone who was interested— was not challenged.

This operating principle and the subgovernment itself were challenged, disrupted, and dethroned in 1982 when CETA reauthorization was debated. The old employment and training subgovernment was turned out for a number of reasons: (1) the intrusion of nonmembers (such as the new president and his secretary of labor and assistant secretary of labor for employment and training) into the subgovernment's proceedings; (2) the very high visibility of CETA's reauthorization debate because CETA had acquired significant negative national publicity and name recognition following some well-publicized abuses in the public employment part of the program; (3) the redefinition of administrative responsibility proposed by the Reagan administration to increase the role for state governments and private business and greatly decrease the role for the federal government and municipalities; (4) the inability of members of the old subgovernment to coalesce; and (5) a strongly organized opposition to the existing mode of allocating CETA dollars and benefits.

The states and the private sector wanted a greater share of the action in any new or revised program. The Reagan administration's first preference was for no federal program at all, but substantial Republican congressional support for some kind of program got the Reagan administration, as well as the newly Republican Senate, behind a program that would shift more clout to states and private business. The traditional subgovernment's congressional anchor was in the House Subcommittee of the Education and Labor Committee. It included representatives of community-based organizations, the local affiliates of which got contracts from municipalities to run programs; other service deliverers such as state employment security agencies; participants in the programs; local governments; and liberal Democrats in Congress. This subgovernment was perhaps too large to be well organized. In any event, during the 1982 debate over whether to reauthorize CETA, abandon it altogether, or come up with a replacement, the CETA subgovernment was in disarray and could salvage little when its preferences conflicted directly with the new subgovernment. That subgovernment was anchored in Congress in the Senate Committee for Labor and Human Resources and included representatives of state governments and private business organizations. The final congressional decisions in the conference committee, which resulted in the Job Training Partnership Act (JTPA), ratified the programmatic preferences of the new subgovernment.

Early in the Bush administration the old subgovernment began to push for the revival of limited aspects of CETA to replace some pieces of JTPA for which they did not care, such as the prohibition on stipends to needy trainees and a bureaucratic oversight system that offered no inducements to focus on participants most in need rather than those most easily trained and placed. The competition continued.

Subgovernment Distintegration

Occasionally a subgovernment will lose such a major battle that it will disintegrate or change character drastically. The disintegration may, of course, turn out to be temporary.

One way for a subgovernment to disintegrate is to lose permanently to a competing subgovernment. Another way is for the issue area in the subgovernment's purview to be redefined out of the distributive arena into either the protective regulatory or redistributive arenas. For example, the tobacco subgovernment lost some—although far from all—of its clout when health concerns that generated protective regulatory politics replaced a total concern with distributive policy. A similar slippage in the unquestioned power of the subgovernment supporting the water development programs of the Army Corps of Engineers occurred for the same reason: protective regulatory politics stemming from environmental concerns replaced an exclusive focus on subsidy.

Sugar The best recent case of what seemed to be the total collapse of a subgovernment involved sugar. It is also an excellent example of a supposedly dead subgovernment coming back to life, and fairly quickly at that. Putting a stake through the heart of a powerful subgovernment is extremely difficult to do in American politics.

The sugar subgovernment was prototypical of all subgovernments until the passage of the Sugar Act of 1974. It is the example used by Douglas Cater (1964) when he coined the term *subgovernments*. But in 1974 the world of the supposedly invincible sugar subgovernment was turned upside down when the House of Representatives defeated an extension of the Sugar Act by a vote of 209 to 175, an action that undid the basic structure of a series of subsidies to sugar growers and processors that had been in place since 1935.

By the 1980s, however, those growing and refining sugar were once again at the public trough in a big way. Both elements of this story—distintegration and rebirth—are interesting in themselves and also illustrative of how such events can happen in the distributive arena.

The basic reason for the defeat of the Sugar Act in 1974 was that the soaring retail price of sugar in a time of high national inflation made sugar subsidies visible to consumer groups. The visibility was heightened because the timing of the price increases coincided with the expiration of the act. Pressure from consumer groups redefined the traditional subsidy issue into one of regulation to protect consumers. The high prices also provoked opposition to the act from manufacturers of such items as soft drinks and candy, which use large quantities of sugar. An additional element helping defeat the bill was the inclusion in the House of some prolabor amendments that diluted the distributive character of the act by introducing redistributive matters that were jarring to the normal supportive coalition.

The act had many features, central of which was the detailed division of the U.S. sugar market between domestic and foreign producers. Producers were guaranteed a market and, in effect, guaranteed that they would make profits. An excise tax on the production went to support the income of the U.S. sugar growers. Thus, U.S. growers and processors alike worked in a completely managed economy with set quotas for growers on the amount that could be grown and marketed to processors and with quotas for processors on the amount that could be produced and marketed both to other manufacturers and to general consumers. The payoff for accepted total management was a price usually higher than the world market and profits for domestic growers and producers that were stable, high, and virtually guaranteed. Foreign processors lobbied frantically for increased shares of the foreign allotment.

The authorization hearings to extend the Sugar Act beyond 1974 began normally. The House Agriculture Committee—a key institution in the subgovernment—held hearings at which leading members of the committee, representatives from the industry, and officials from the Department of Agriculture praised the bill. The department suggested some major modifications that would have moved the sugar price system toward a freer market, but the Secretary of Agriculture assured the committee of his general support of the bill. The department was probably not much surprised or dismayed when its modest initiatives were largely rejected by the committee.

When the bill came to the House floor in June, the subgovernment was confident of its usual victory. However, it had not counted on the impact that the escalating price of sugar was having on groups such as the National Consumers Congress, the National Consumers League, Consumer Action for Improved Food and Drugs, and the Corporate Accountability Research Group, all of which lobbied against the bill and found members of the House willing to listen.

The world economy, the timing of the decision, and—some would assert—the greed of U.S. processors had at least temporarily redefined the context in which decisions about sugar policy were made. The subgovernment had not had the foresight to realize that this redefinition was taking place. Consequently, the subgovernment suffered a major defeat in 1974. Some observers hailed the death of the sugar subgovernment, but the obituaries were premature. The sugar subgovernment regrouped and began to win some policy battles.

In 1981 President Reagan endorsed sugar price supports as part of an omnibus farm bill in connection with bargaining for congressional votes on his general tax and budget initiatives. Despite controversy in Congress, the sugar lobby rallied general and substantial support, although not for arrangements as lucrative as those prior to 1974.

The basic sugar program in place as the 1990s opened was that adopted in 1981 and continued in the 1985 farm bill (Rauch 1988). The program guaranteed producers a price of 18 cents a pound, about twice the world market price. In 1985 the farm bill prohibited federal purchase of sugar, but the revived subgovernment achieved the same results for itself by generating highly restrictive import quotas that resulted in market pressure being removed from domestic producers. Imports fell by over 60 percent in the following four years. American consumers, of course, ultimately provided the subsidy by paying much higher prices for sugar and for products containing sugar than a competitive international market would have produced.

Conclusions

The material presented in this chapter supports two general conclusions. First, the general picture of the distributive arena drawn at the beginning of the chapter is largely accurate. Second, subgovernments are *not* static in nature, as some of the less careful literature on the subject seems to suggest. Rather, they change and adapt over time in a number of ways. Subgovernments are important in relation to distributive policy. But they represent a complex political phenomenon that requires careful analysis.

The cases of subgovernment dominance lend support to the overview of the distributive arena summarized in the first six columns of Table 4–1. In these cases, virtually all aspects of the issues were decided within the confines of the subgovernment. Rarely were "outsiders" successful in intervening. Normally, the degree of cooperation was high. The few conflicts that occurred were resolved within the confines of the relationship on the basis of face-to-face negotiation, which resulted in compromises that left everyone reasonably happy.

The last column of Table 4–1 asserts that, if conflict persists, the congressional position articulated by the most influential subcommittee is more likely to prevail than the position of the most influential bureaucracy. This generalization was supported in the case of conflict between Congress and the Corps of Engineers over the nature of the proper cost-benefit ratio for the corps to us. It was also supported in 1974 when the House committee rejected the suggestions of the Department of Agriculture that the sugar bill should be modified in the direction of a freer market. The House committee's position is the one that went to the House floor, even though it met defeat there.

Only rarely do outsiders have much impact on the business of a subgovernment, but such can occur. The large commercial users of sugar had this impact in 1974. Presidents Carter and Reagan had limited, but cumulatively important, impact on water resources policy.

The ways in which subgovernments can change are numerous. A "smart" subgovernment—one intent on preserving as many of its policy preferences as possible—will adjust to potentially threatening developments ahead of a public dispute if it can find a way to defuse them. Sometimes a challenge that is defeated will provide the cues for the subgovernment about a marginal policy change it would be wise to make in order to ensure a more secure future. Often a successful challenge will force marginal adjustments that still preserve the most important core of existing policy and subgovernment dominance of that core.

Continuing competition among several subgovernments can also stimulate one or more of them to make adjustments that will preserve substantial portions of their influence. The biomedical lobby, for example, continued to do well after the rise of the cancer-specific subgovernment.

Only rarely does a subgovernment fold altogether. And collapse can be followed by revival, as the sugar case so vividly illustrates.

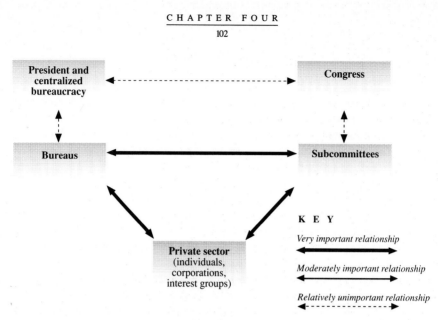

FIGURE 4–1

Relative importance of relationships for determining distributive policy

Subgovernments change. They do not make all policy, even in their principal preserve of distributive issues. They are, however, remarkably persistent and tenacious. Consequently, a logical place to begin the analysis of any distributive policy is to identify one or more subgovernments likely to be very influential, if not completely dominant.

Figure 4–1 displays graphically the typically most important relationships between congressional, executive and bureaucratic, and private sector actors in determining distributive policy. The triangle outlined by the heavy arrows at the bottom of the figure is a pictorial representation of a subgovernment.

CHAPTER FIVE

Protective Regulatory Policy

The Nature of Protective Regulatory Policy

The federal government has regulated private activities for the presumed protection of the general public (or large parts of it) in a major way for a bit over a century. In general, Congress has legislated broad goals and perhaps a few details of how the regulation should proceed. At the same time, Congress has created bureaucratic agencies, including the so-called independent regulatory commissions, to develop and administer the details of the regulation aimed at achieving the broad goals.

In Chapter 1 we discussed the differences between *protective* regulatory policy and *competitive* regulatory policy. In public discussion of regulation, that distinction is often blurred, sometimes inadvertently and sometimes on purpose for political reasons.

One reason for the blurring is that a few regulatory agencies are (or were) concerned much of the time with competitive regulation. The Federal Communications Commission (FCC), for example, decides who gets what television channels and what radio frequencies. Before major statutory changes in the late 1970s, the Interstate Commerce Commission (ICC) decided what trucking companies, barge lines, and pipelines could carry specific goods on different routes. Railroads could not alter their routes through abandonments, mergers, or new construction without ICC approval. The Civil Aeronautics Board (CAB) decided what airlines got to fly what routes.

Agencies with major roles to play in competitive regulation also got involved in protective regulation. The FCC is supposed to make sure that broadcasters serve the public by not broadcasting offensive material either in program content or in advertisements. The ICC has rules designed to protect the consumer who hires a moving company. The CAB, which went out of existence in 1985, made rules designed to protect the lungs of nonsmokers from the pollution created by smokers on airplanes.

Another reason for the blurring of the distinction between competitive regulation and protective regulation stems from the behavior of politicians beginning in the late 1970s. In that period a bipartisan coalition in Washington emerged that favored shrinkage of competitive regulation, a point of view characterized as "deregulation." The supporters of this position succeeded in achieving major deregulation in terms of rates and routes with relation to all forms of transportation (air, rail, highway, barge, pipeline) and some aspects of communication.

When Ronald Reagan became president, he and his supporters—elected officials, bureaucrats, and academics—called for deregulation in the protective arena too. They, of course, used the same word—"deregulation"—to describe what they sought. But they were talking about rolling back regulation in areas such as environmental pollution, banking, and the practices of business with regard to labor relations, affirmative action, and competition. In this debate the two forms of regulation got blurred intellectually. Politically, however, those involved in making decisions could easily distinguish between competitive regulation and protective regulation.

What impact did the strong preference of the Reagan administration for deregulation in the protective arena have? In general, Congress did not pass statutes reducing protective regulatory activity on the part of the federal government. In general, the administrative agencies weakened enforcement in protective regulatory areas in which the administration favored deregulation. One study—which itself blurs the distinction between protective and competitive aspects of regulation—concluded that the growth of spending and staffing in the regulatory agencies during the Reagan years slowed, but did not cease (Warren and Chilton 1989).

Another study (Harris and Milkis 1989) that focused on two agencies—the Federal Trade Commission and the Environmental Protection Agency—concluded that administrative changes at the two agencies in the Reagan years had some of the policy impact desired by Reagan. But Congress was not willing to alter permanently (through legislation) the basic ideas, institutions, and policies (which these authors call "regimes") that buttressed these agencies' efforts to regulate business activities.

In short, the political warfare over protective regulation produced a stalemate. Programmatically, each side scored some victories. The administration and its anti-regulation coalition succeeded in cases in which they had the most administrative discretion. The proregulation forces succeeded in protecting statutes from major alteration in Congress. Budget and staffing patterns showed diminished growth, but—at least in raw numbers—did not indicate a collapse of the federal government's protective regulatory bureaucratic infrastructure.

Although, as Reagan's vice-president, George Bush was in charge of a deregulation effort in that administration, as president in 1989 he demonstrated no particular interest in attacking protective regulation. In fact, at least at the rhetorical level, he sought increased regulation aimed at protecting the environment.

The federal government has become increasingly involved in protective regulation since the late nineteenth century. One persuasive account identifies four waves of new federal regulatory activity, each of which left a residue of bureaucracies that have become permanent (Wilson 1975).

The first wave occurred between 1887 and 1890 and produced the Interstate Commerce Act, which was aimed at regulating railroads, and the Sherman Antitrust Act, which was intended to regulate trusts that had been created to achieve monopolies in the manufacture and distribution of various goods. The second wave came between 1906 and 1915 and produced the Pure Food and Drug Act; the Meat Inspection Act; the Federal Trade Commission Act, which was aimed at preventing unfair business practices such as deceptive advertising; and the Clayton Act, designed to strengthen existing antitrust law. The third wave came during the 1930s and produced the Food, Drug, and Cosmetic Act; the Public Utility Holding Company Act, aimed at preventing the concentration of economic power in the public utility field; the Securities and Exchange Act, designed to regulate the stock market; the Natural Gas Act; and the National Labor Relations Act, intended primarily to prevent unfair labor practices by business. The fourth wave began in the late 1960s and was concerned mainly with protecting consumers and the environment. Major new legislation included the Water Quality Act; the Clean Air Act; the Truth in Lending Act; the National Traffic and Motor Vehicle Safety Act; the Motor Vehicle Pollution Control Act; and amendments to drug control laws.

By the late 1970s the fourth wave had passed. As already indicated, the Reagan years produced a political stalemate that resulted in backward movement in terms of administrative vigor in enforcement, status quo in terms of statutory authority, and modest growth in terms of staff and budget for federal agencies.

Throughout the nineteenth century, Congress oversaw the activities of regulatory agencies with considerable care, and the agencies did not develop a great deal of independent political weight. However, as agencies increased in size and number, they began to develop independent political power. At the same time, Congress began to delegate more authority to the agencies and to pay less attention to how they used that authority. The foundations were laid for what one observer has called "the bureaucratic state" (Wilson 1975). When the scope of the federal government's protective regulatory activity increased dramatically in the 1930s, Congress increased the amount of latitude it gave regulatory agencies through vague delegations of authority that increased the basis for independent bureaucratic power (Lowi 1979).

Decisions about protective regulatory policy are characterized by considerable visibility. As policies are debated, those entities targeted for regulation are very conscious of what they think is at stake. In general, most of those vulnerable to regulation—mining companies, producers of petroleum products, and pharmaceutical companies, for example—would prefer to avoid government regulation. When regulation seems to be inevitable, the companies pursue options designed to make regulation as light as possible. They may also seek governmentally conferred benefits at the same time that new regulation is imposed as the price for cooperating or acquiescing. When new areas of regulatory activity or major changes in existing activity are under debate, however, quiet functioning of subgovernments is not possible. Subgovernments may not be a major feature of the policy landscape in many decisions about creating or altering protective regulatory policy. Subgovernments may reappear, however, when implementation of protective regulatory policy occurs (Ripley and Franklin 1986, Chapter 6).

Coalitions of groups involved in protective regulatory decisions are unstable, depending on what is at stake. Groups contend for the favor of Congress, but usually at the level of the full House and Senate and in conference committees rather than primarily at the committee and subcommittee levels. Subcommittees and committees are involved in decisions, but their preferences are fairly frequently altered by other decision makers. Similarly, in the executive branch, there is generally less autonomy for bureaucratic subunits than in the case of distributive policy. Broader bureaucratic units, such as departments, are likely to have more influence in shaping final policy formulation and legitimation decisions in the protective regulatory arena.

The Congressional–Bureaucratic Relationship in Protective Regulatory Policy

We expect the relationship between bureaucrats (at the bureau level) and individuals in and around Congress (members of and staff members for Senate and House sub-committees) to be only sporadically highly influential in protective regulatory policy. Only some of these issues get full consideration within the confines of the relationship between bureaucratic subunits and congressional subcommittees. Decisions on new protective regulatory efforts or on major statutory changes in existing efforts typically get made by Congress as a whole and its leaders interacting with higher levels of the executive branch, such as individuals from the office of a departmental secretary or the White House. Only in stable areas of regulatory activity—which are quite rare—does the quieter relationship between bureaucratic subunits and congressional subcommittees become dominant and allow the participants to make what amount to final decisions. Even in those few areas, the chances of review by higher authorities is considerably greater than in the case of distributive policies.

Conflict is much more frequent in the regulatory arena than in the distributive arena. When conflict occurs at the bureau–subcommittee level, it often arises because the congressional actors who are seeking exceptions to regulations for favored constituents or clients meet resistance from bureaucrats who oppose those exceptions. Less often, the congressional actors are pushing the bureaucrats for more rigorous enforcement of regulations. Conflict over regulatory policy also occurs at a higher level than the bureau–subcommittee relationship because participants who are dissatisfied with the decisions made at the subcommittee level can appeal those decisions to the full committee, the House or Senate floor, and the conference committee.

Disagreements between subcommittee members and bureaucrats may get resolved within that relationship, but usually the conflict moves to a higher level for resolution, either because the participants appeal to those higher levels or because higher levels intervene on their own initiative.

If resolution of disagreement occurs within the subcommittee–bureau nexus, it is likely to be a compromise between initial specific positions. Some disagreements may also go unresolved for some time. Still others may be made part of a broader compromise (not necessarily at some midpoint) reached at a higher level of institutional actor.

In cases of disputes between the two branches, the congressional position probably prevails more often, especially when the full Congress gets involved.

The protective regulatory arena is not undifferentiated in terms of what is at stake and how the actors behave, however. Behavior might be expected to vary in at least two major kinds of situations. Both will be investigated by looking at several concrete instances of regulatory action or proposed action in recent years.

The first is one in which the focus of debate is over the creation of federal regulatory power that had not previously existed or had existed only in sporadic and scattered form.

The second is one in which major alteration of existing federal regulatory power is the focus of debate. These alterations can be in the direction of more federal power or less federal power.

The Creation of Regulatory Power

Strip mining Strip mining removes coal from the earth quickly and relatively cheaply. Layers of earth are scraped away to expose veins of coal that lie close to the surface. The aftermath of this process can be aesthetically and environmentally disastrous unless the site for the strip mining was initially well chosen and unless postmining reclamation is undertaken. Without safeguards and positive action, land may be permanently scarred, eroded, and made barren; water may be severely polluted. Most states where strip mining occurs had tried to regulate it, but with only limited success and, in some cases, halfheartedly.

Congress first became seriously involved in the question of whether the federal government should regulate strip mining in 1968, when the Senate first held hearings on the subject. In 1971 President Nixon proposed legislation, and in 1972 the House passed a bill, but the Senate did not act.

The place of coal as a desirable source of energy was underscored in 1973 by the Arab oil embargo and the resulting energy crisis in the United States. Coal was suddenly thrust into the forefront in the United States because the country has extensive deposits of it and because many of those deposits could be mined quickly using stripping procedures. These facts increased the intensity of the disagreement between proregulation and antiregulation forces. Those favoring regulation pointed out that more strip mining would occur and therefore safeguards were more essential than ever. Those opposing regulation argued that regulation would cripple the effort to use coal to help the United States become self-sufficient in energy and thereby reduce dependence on Arab oil.

The Senate passed a bill regulating strip mining in 1973. In 1974 the House also passed a bill and went to conference with the Senate on its 1973 bill. After a long conference that almost collapsed several times, Congress passed a bill, only to have President Gerald Ford sign a pocket veto, a form of veto that prevented any attempt by Congress to override it.

By mid-March 1975, both the Senate and House had again passed bills similar to the bill Ford had vetoed a few months earlier and had agreed on the final version through the conference process. Again President Ford vetoed the bill. The attempt to override that veto was delayed because of weakening support for the bill in the House. When the override attempt was finally made in July 1975, it failed by three votes.

In late 1975 attempts were made in the House Interior Committee to revive the bill, but these attempts failed, largely because the bill's supporters calculated that President Ford could again prevent what they wanted by a veto they could not override. Similarly, in 1976 the House Rules Committee forestalled a veto by twice preventing strip mining bills from reaching the House floor. In a related development in 1976, the Department of the Interior promulgated regulations that allowed increased strip mining of coal on federal land in the West.

In 1977 the basic political situation changed dramatically for the contending forces in the debate over federal strip mining regulation because of the assumption of the presidency by Jimmy Carter, who was a supporter of federal regulation in this area. By mid-1977 a new statute had become law.

What follows relates two selected parts of the very complicated story that is outlined above. The first part focuses on the debate and decision making in 1974. The second part concentrates on 1977.

1974 The basic controversy as Congress had pondered federal strip mining regulation had been whether there should be a federal law and, if so, how strong it should be. The administration bills introduced in both 1971 and 1973 were regarded as weak by environmentalists and leading Democratic supporters of strong legislation. Coal producers and most of the electric companies that burn vast quantities of coal to generate electricity wanted no bill at all. Their basic contention was that the coal companies were public-spirited about reclamation and that state regulation was sufficient.

The general position of those opposed to any regulation—or at least to more than a very weak bill—was that the controls proposed in the legislation would reduce the output severely and would also raise the price of coal. Either result would damage the energy self-sufficiency program endorsed by the administration.

The general position of those favoring a strong bill was that strip mining had to be stringently regulated (although virtually no one proposed a ban) in order to avoid the risk that large areas of the country would wind up looking like the worst parts of Appalachia after strip mining. They argued that federal regulation was necessary because the states couldn't or wouldn't act with sufficient force to curb the problem. They disputed the estimates of the other side that strip mining regulation would cut coal production significantly.

A chronology of the process in 1974 sets the scene for an analysis of what happened. In October 1973 the Senate had passed a bill by a vote of 82 to 8 after the Senate Interior and Insular Affairs Committee had reported the bill to the full Senate without any dissenting votes. Two subcommittees of the House Interior and Insular Affairs Committee—one on environment and one on mines and mining—considered the bill jointly. The full House Interior Committee reported the bill favorably on May 30, 1974, by a vote of 26 to 15. The House held an unusually long debate on the bill—six days—before passing it with some amendments on July 25 by a vote of 298 to 81. The conference committee met off and on for eighty-seven hours between August 7 and December 3 before reaching an agreement. Both chambers approved the conference report by voice vote very late in the session, but President Ford refused to sign it, and the bill died as a result.

Several features of the 1974 process deserve special mention. First, detailed drafting of the legislation was accomplished in subcommittees, committees, and the conference committee. However, unlike distributive policy, final decisions were not made at the committee or subcommittee level. Whichever interests believed they had lost most in the decisions made in various committees and subcommittees appealed their case to the full House or full Senate by getting a friendly member to introduce an amendment on the floor that would reverse or alter unfavorable committee decisions. Through this process, the same battles fought before the committee were fought again on the floors of the House and Senate. The same was again true in the conference process. The losers in the conference committee could appeal their case again to the full House or full Senate. In 1974 they did not do so because the compromise worked out in the conference committee had taken so long that Congress was very near adjournment by the time the conference report was ready for floor action. Under these conditions, the majorities in both chambers were in a mood to pass the bill quickly and await presidential action.

Organized groups representing all of the affected interests—environmentalists; coal, steel, and electric companies; the U.S. Chamber of Commerce; and the United Mine Workers (UMW) union—and a large number of officials from the White House, Council on Environmental Quality, Environmental Protection Agency, Department of Commerce, Department of the Interior, and Federal Energy Administration approached both the House subcommittees and committee and the conference committee. Some of the interests—both private and bureaucratic—made some gains at the committee level. As Congressman Morris Udall, chairman of the House Subcommittee on the Environment, said, in speaking of the administration representatives, "We have done all the compromising we are going to do. We accepted a dozen of their amendments in committee, and they just come back for more. The demands are insatiable" (*Washington Post*, July 10, 1974).

Second, the coalitions supporting and opposing regulation of strip mining by the federal government were broad-based but unstable. The legislation was complex and contained numerous features that were separable in the analytical sense. Both coalitions included members who were interested only in narrow features of the bill that affected them directly. On other specific issues, these members would be relatively inactive or would even desert the coalition. For example, the executive board of the UMW narrowly endorsed the bill, but the board's real concern was with an amendment to tax strip-mined coal more heavily than deep-mined coal. Such an amendment would have encouraged exploitation of the coal reserves in the East, a region in which most of the deposits are too deep to be strip mined and in which most of the members of the UMW work. A rival union represented the workers engaged in strip mining in the West. The amendment, offered on the House floor, was defeated.

Another example is provided by Pennsylvanians who supported the bill but whose real concern was that an amendment be added to exempt Pennsylvania's anthracite coal from the provisions of the bill on the grounds that Pennsylvania was already regulating such mining with sufficient laws and vigor. This amendment passed the House and was included in the final bill.

Yet another example: once the conference report passed both houses, some coal companies broke previously united ranks engineered by the National Coal Association and urged the president to sign the bill as a better alternative than a possibly more restrictive bill that would probably be passed in 1975. The same position was taken by the chairman of the board of Bethlehem Steel, a major consumer of coal and owner of its own mines.

Third, the executive branch agencies were badly split in their views of the bill as it progressed through the congressional process. They kept altering their public stances. The Council on Environmental Quality and the Environmental Protection Agency supported both the legislation in general and the details that emerged from the conference committee. The Federal Energy Office, the Commerce Department, and the White House (with support from the OMB and the Department of the Treasury) supported only weak legislation at most. The Interior Department was caught between these conflicting views, and its attitudes kept shifting.

The administration was so divided that key administrators felt safe in making their disagreements public. While the bill was still awaiting floor action in the House, for example, the administrator of the Environmental Protection Agency publicly supported the bill, thereby contradicting the official administration position at the time that the bill was unacceptable because of its alleged impact on coal production and energy self-sufficiency.

Later in the process, when the head of the Federal Energy Administration said that he had recommended a presidential veto, two other officials—one from the Environmental Protection Agency and one from the Interior Department—said they had urged the president to sign it.

The Interior Department constantly changed and modified its position throughout the process. It was widely believed through the spring of 1974 that the department supported a moderately strong bill. But after the House committee had agreed on a bill, the secretary of the interior attacked it on the grounds of projected decreases in coal production. During the summer of 1974, both the Energy Office and the Interior Department advised the president to sign the bill.

The administration was so indecisive at the end of the process that a somewhat unusual—bizarre would be a better word—attempt was made to effect a last-minute compromise that would avoid a veto. While President Ford was still deciding whether to sign or veto the bill, communications between the chairman of the Senate Interior Committee and the administration led the administration to think that somehow Congress could pass another strip mining bill in the few days left in its session. This bill could be signed along with the original bill. Presumably this additional bill would contain amendments that would make the two bills together palatable enough to gain Ford's signature. Congress, of course, can rarely act with such speed, short of a genuine national emergency. And the spectacle of a president signing a bill and amendments to weaken it before it had been law for more than a day or two made such a happening unlikely. Nothing along these lines happened. The president used the amendments he had requested in late 1974 as the basis for the administration bill sent to Congress in early 1975.

Fourth, the critical decisions on the substance of the legislation were made on the House floor or in conference committee in the form of acceptance or rejection of amendments. The House subcommittees and full committee had set the agenda for House floor action—as is the case for virtually every piece of legislation in all policy areas—but a broad range of options was presented, debated, and decided on the House floor. Likewise, enough differences remained between the House version passed in July 1974 and the Senate version passed in October 1973 that a range of options also received consideration in the lengthy proceedings of the conference committee.

The quiet, stable politics of distribution were nowhere to be seen in the maneuvering and decision making that marked this proposal for a major new federal regulatory endeavor. Instability and public proceedings were much more characteristic than were the stability, predictability, and privacy that usually are the hallmarks of a distributive issue. Furthermore, resolution of the conflicts was transferred all the way to the highest level—the president—where the outcome was a decision to have no regulation at all. This pattern of visibility, conflict, and presidential resolution to have no legislation was repeated again in 1975.

1977 In 1977 the proponents of strong federal legislation had to retreat from some of the positions they had taken in 1974 and 1975 to get a bill through Congress. Now, however, the president wanted a bill with some teeth in it.

The first compromise decision made by the proponents of a bill was to limit the bill almost exclusively to coal mining. Earlier bills had covered other kinds of mining, such as copper, but the possibility of a negative coalition being formed by a number of the interests targeted for regulation led to the focus on coal alone.

As in 1974, issues were not settled quietly and definitively in subcommittee and committee. Rather, decisions made in those settings were reexamined, debated, and extensively amended on the floors of both the House and the Senate. Some issues also remained to be resolved in the conference committee.

The House committee produced a moderately strong bill in late April. The House passed it a week later and strengthened it even more during floor action. A different outcome occurred in the Senate. The committee reported a moderately strong bill in early May, but a few weeks later the bill was weakened considerably on the Senate floor by expanding the allowable mining in alluvial valley floors in the West, withdrawing the requirement that the owners of the surface approve the mining of federally owned coal under their land, exempting small miners from some of the environmental standards set in the bill, and watering down the provision that the original contours of the land had to be restored at the conclusion of mining.

The conference committee bill, reported in July, was predictably somewhere between the two versions presented to it. The principal concessions to the mining interests were in the areas of minining alluvial valley floors, a twenty-four-month exemption from environmental standards for smaller operators, variances allowed in restoring original contours, and allowance of the removal of mountain tops as an acceptable mining method. Both houses passed the bill, and the president signed it in early August.

As in 1974, the final decisions were made on the floor and in conference. Those affected by the regulations prevailed on some issues. The supporters of federal regulation made an early decision to focus only on coal in order to keep a broader opposing coalition from forming. Copper mine owners could, for example, be expected to show little interest in the bill if they were not directly involved.

The coal companies did not give up their fight, and in a sequel typical of protective regulatory policy, they shifted their pressure from Congress to the bureaucracy responsible for implementing the legislation and to the courts. The implementation stage now became the battlefield (Ripley and Franklin 1986, 156–163). The Carter administration tried to administer the law with some vigor; the Reagan administration weakened and slowed implementation. No new legislation was forthcoming either to encourage or to impede enforcement of the 1977 act.

Pesticides Government regulation of pesticides began with passage of the Federal Insecticide, Fungicide, and Rodenticide Act (FIFRA) of 1947. Emerging from a close relationship among Agriculture Committee chairmen, U.S. Department of Agriculture (USDA) bureaucrats, and chemical industry interests, the law was focused on product efficacy—did the chemicals kill the pests that the manufacturers claimed would be killed? The primary beneficiaries were American farmers, who were seeking to expand crop production, and the chemical interests, which could make a good deal of money in producing the pesticides.

The workings of this classic distributive subgovernment were disrupted in the 1960s as concerns about environment, health, and safety arose (Bosso 1987, Chapters 6–8). Federal policies on pesticides became a matter of protective regulation. FIFRA was revised in 1972 and required that new chemical pesticides be tested for toxicity. Pesticides introduced prior to 1972 were left on the market until they could be tested. The implementing agency was the Environmental Protection Agency (EPA). No longer did USDA have jurisdiction. But the EPA had to judge test results against competing criteria of economic costs and benefits versus potential health threats. Hampered by insufficient funding and requirements to pay manufacturers for withdrawing chemicals ("indemnification"), the EPA's testing program proceeded at a snail's pace. By late 1988 only 2 percent of the pre-1972 pesticides had been retested.

As public concern about birth defects, cancer, and groundwater pollution from pesticide runoff mounted, there was wide recognition, even among agricultural interests, that the current law was inadequate. A solution in the form of acceptable public policy, however, remained elusive. Various proposals were considered, debated, and abandoned in Congress. Environmental issues in general and pesticides in particular were frozen in legislative deadlock in the 1970s and early 1980s (Bosso 1987, 213).

In the spring of 1986 a unique and temporary coalition of producers, environmentalists, and consumer groups acted on their own to develop a bill overhauling the 1972 act. They presented it to Congress, which initially seemed to react favorably. Deadlock in the final days of the 99th Congress in 1987 prevented passage, however, as the coalition disagreed over details.

In 1988, phoenix-like, the pesticide reform bill was back. The Senate passed a tough bill that looked just like the 1986 version. Moving more slowly, the House passed a "core" bill, essentially a stripped-down version that eliminated the most controversial parts of the legislation. In September, the House version prevailed, passing the Senate by unanimous consent without a recorded vote and passing the House by voice vote. FIFRA of 1988 represented an important advance over the 1972 version. It eliminated government indemnification of manufacturers; it required producers to pay for the cost of testing, removing, and storing pesticides; and it required the EPA to finish retesting old pesticides (pre-1972) within nine years. Critics lambasted the new act for failing to address contamination of groundwater by pesticides, for exempting certain chemicals, and for not allowing states to set standards more stringent than the federal standards.

FIFRA of 1988 has shifted federal policy firmly away from the mission of seeking efficacious pesticides for farmers to reducing environmental pollution and health hazards. The number of participants in the development of the 1988 legislation was vast in comparison with the 1947 version. Interest groups for environmental, public interest, health, and consumer issues joined chemical and agriculture interests in the maneuvering. Within Congress, environmental panels in the House and Senate are pressing the Agriculture Committees for shared access and oversight on pesticide legislation. Increasing technical complexity of pesticide testing and regulation means that few in or out of Congress will be able to grasp policy content and implications fully.

In the end, a revised FIFRA emerged not because a powerful new coalition formed but only because the most controversial issues were deferred. The politics of instability that surround protective regulatory decisions permitted only partial answers to identified problems.

The chairman of the House Agriculture Committee said that "the bill reflects the art of the possible." A spokesperson for the National Resources Defense Council called the legislation "an important environmental victory." Another public interest group spokesperson castigated the bill for leaving "the majority of pesticide issues to be addressed in future Congresses." Oddly enough, all of these seemingly conflicting assessments were true in part. In protective regulatory policy making, compromise is essential and avoidance of the painful is common. The saga will continue as future Congresses confront additional aspects of pesticide pollution, such as that of groundwater.

The Alteration of Existing Regulatory Power

The savings and loan industry: Bailout in 1989 Since the Great Depression of the 1930s, the federal government has regulated the banking industry and, at the same time, guaranteed deposits held by banks and other financial institutions, including "thrifts," as savings and loan associations are called. This federal activity was aimed at preventing the disaster that overtook these institutions in the Depression and, more important, the personal disaster facing large numbers of citizens who had lost their savings in large part because of shoddy management of banks and bank-like institutions.

For many decades savers felt secure. The assumption was that the government's protective regulation was sound and careful and prevented most losses. The few collapses that occurred were easily covered by various earmarked federal insurance funds.

All of this optimism and the assumption that things were well run in both the government agencies dealing with banking and thrifts and in the banking and thrift industry itself turned to grief in the mid-1980s. Widespread, severe problems in the thrift industry began to come to light. In 1987 Congress passed a bandaid bill that allowed the Federal Savings and Loan Insurance Corporation (FSLIC) to borrow $10.8 billion in additional funds. This bill was aimed at restoring the confidence of savers in these institutions and was largely in accord with the wishes of the savings and loan industry itself, which had an influential lobby in Washington. Even though the FSLIC insurance fund had dwindled to only $1.4 billion to insure over $900 billion in deposits at more than 3,000 thrift institutions nationwide, the thrift lobby opposed larger borrowing authority because the institutions were required to pay the interest on the funds thus borrowed. Congress and the administration bought the thrift industry's view of matters. "Protective regulation" was still largely "self-regulation." The fecklessness of this effort became all too apparent very quickly. Simultaneously, the competence and honesty of key governmental officials—both bureaucratic and legislative—began to be seriously questioned.

In 1989 the debate followed an erratic and unpredictable course. The president, the relevant committees in the House and Senate, and even the lobby for the discredited thrift industry all played important roles. Elaborate compromises were needed at every step in order to produce an extraordinarily complicated law that was over 1,000 pages in length. No one in the process was completely satisfied. Perhaps happiest was George Bush, who, in the words of an analyst of the industry, said, "In 1989 the president asked for just half a loaf...and that is all that Congress gave him" (*Congressional Quarterly Weekly Report,* August 12, 1989, 2113). At the signing ceremony in early August, Bush expressed great pleasure at what had been achieved: "This legislation comes to grips with the problems facing our savings and loan industry. It'll safeguard and stabilize America's financial system and put in place permanent reforms so these problems will never happen again." By December 1989, Bush publicly admitted what virtually all other observers had known even before the bill passed: it was insufficient and would be vastly more costly (although no one knew how much) than the $50 billion allocated in the bill for the first three years. Most estimates ran to hundreds of billions of dollars for the life of the bailout.

In crude terms, no one in the decision process seemed to know very much about what they were doing. Members of both parties in Congress, as well as the president, were eager above all to avoid having blame attached to their own political party. At the same time, they all had a stake in appearing to do something larger than what had been done in 1987. The chief federal savings and loan regulator, a Republican and former Senate staff member named M. Danny Wall, had no credibility with most members of Congress. He insisted throughout 1988 that the thrift industry did not present a problem requiring government action. Throughout 1989, as the magnitude of mismanagement, stupidity, and fraud became at least partially apparent, many members of Congress involved in trying to find a legislative solution to the problems of the industry joined in blaming Wall for many problems. Whether he was a scapegoat or genuinely incompetent and blameworthy made little difference. Politically he was dead, and he finally acquiesced to this fact by resigning in early December 1989.

In the gaps left by the political and policy struggle among forces that seemed to have little comprehensive grasp of the enormity of what they were facing, lobbyists for at least portions of the industry got some favorable provisions in the bill— provisions only an informed and interested few could find in a thousand pages of technical language.

The three most major thrusts of the bill were, first, to allocate $50 billion for three years to close insolvent savings and loans; second, to require thrifts to maintain larger cash reserves; and third, to require thrifts to put less of their money in risky ventures and more in the home mortgage market. Critics found all three provisions lacking. Most agreed quickly that $50 billion was insufficient to cover insolvent thrifts for three years. Within four months of declaring all problems solved, President Bush also agreed. Many deemed the cash reserve provisions too loose. And, ironically, many pointed out that home mortgages are only marginally profitable at best and well-managed thrifts (which still exist in large numbers) would suffer most by being restricted from making more profitable investments.

In this morass of complicated decision making, it is perhaps fitting that when the final decision about the bill was being made in the congressional Conference Committee in late July and early August 1989, the main debate within Congress and between Congress and the administration focused on how the $50 billion would be charged, or not charged, against the budget and how this expenditure would be squared with the restrictions of the Gramm–Rudman–Hollings bill that, theoretically, was to force the government to balance the federal budget in the next few years. In this kind of political and symbolic debate, without real policy consequences for the state of thrifts and the safety of deposits, members of Congress and the administration were on familiar ground. They could deal with this issue much more convincingly and resolutely than they could deal with the complicated issues of finance presented by the savings and loan disaster itself.

As a nice political coda to the 1989 activity, five senators (four Democrats and one Republican) were accused in the fall of 1989 of, in effect, taking political payoffs from the head of one of the most spectacularly insolvent and costly savings and loans. Again, both the accusers and accused were at home in playing this political game of charge and countercharge. Meanwhile, the prospect of uncovered bills mounted. The taxpayer and the consumer had little reason for satisfaction with this exercise of protective regulatory policy making.

Limits on a protective regulatory agency: The case of the Federal Trade Commission Congress created the Federal Trade Commission (FTC) in 1914 and gave it a number of powers to prohibit unfair business practices and, in effect, to protect consumers. A complicated series of legislative amendments, regulations, and court decisions over the years expanded the power. However, in recent times the FTC has come under particularly careful scrutiny by business and has been subject to many charges that it proceeds against businesses unfairly or without just cause. The period since 1977 provides a good case of a protective regulatory agency under attack, an attack that inevitably involved congressional use of its legislative powers.

In this case, the attack on the agency led Congress to narrow and restrict some of the powers of the FTC. The whole of Congress got involved, as we would expect in a protective regulatory matter. Likewise, a great number of interest groups—both from different areas of business and from consumer interests—got involved. Strong presidential involvement was generally missing, which helps explain why some limits could make it through the legislative process. The limits, however, were incremental and not fatal to the basic mission of the agency. Incrementalism and nonresolution of basic issues characterized the outcomes. Such outcomes are common in the highly charged atmosphere surrounding protective regulatory issues.

Before 1977 the FTC kept a relatively low profile in choosing the cases it decided to pursue. It did not anger a wide range of businesses (and their congressional supporters) at any one time (Katzmann 1980). But in 1977 a new and aggressive FTC chairman was named. The agency initiated a series of actions that were widely interpreted to be pro-consumer and antibusiness. The businesses affected complained vociferously. They and their representatives descended on Congress in droves and demanded restrictions.

A sizable portion of Congress responded to these complaints and began to question the FTC's utility and performance and even its legitimacy. For four years, from 1977 through 1980, Congress quite deliberately did not renew the FTC's basic authorizing statute. The agency could not get regular funding through the appropriations process and ran on money provided through continuing resolutions. Symbolically, Congress forced the agency to close its doors for three days during the spring of 1980.

When Congress finally passed a new three-year authorizing statute in the spring of 1980, that statute contained a major new use of the legislative veto. Congress gave to itself a new formal role in overseeing the agency. It enacted a number of limits, the most important of which was the power to veto any FTC rules that displeased it. Such a veto would come about if both the House and Senate passed a resolution of disapproval. The president played no role in the process that was established and did not have to sign the resolution of disapproval for it to have the force of law. Only involvement by President Carter in 1980 kept the anti-FTC forces from enacting even more severe restrictions on the agency's power. Beginning in 1977, the howling of the business oxen who perceived they were being gored produced a reduction in the power of the FTC. Congress put the agency on notice that it would be closely overseeing—and second-guessing—its work.

In 1981–1983, congressional concern about the FTC continued. In 1982 Congress made its first use of the new legislative veto provisions in the 1980 authorization statute. By lopsided votes, the two houses disapproved an FTC rule—which had been ten years in the making—requiring used car dealers to disclose the defects in the vehicles they sold. The used-car lobby opposed this rule and prevailed. The president remained silent on the matter, although most observers believed that Reagan's generally negative attitude toward governmental regulation of business would lead him to side with the car dealers.

In late 1982 Congress again became mired in an attempt to reauthorize the FTC for another three years. A major fight broke out over the attempt of the American Medical Association and some other professional associations to get a provision in the law exempting doctors, lawyers, and other professionals from FTC jurisdiction over anticompetitive business practices. The House passed a bill with an exemption favored by the lobbyists for the professional associations in December 1982. The Senate, however, did not act on the authorization bill. The compromise that allowed the FTC to retain this jurisdiction over the behavior of professionals was saved, at least temporarily, by finessing the need for a final decision on the exemption by dropping the authorization bill altogether. This also meant that Congress would not provide regular appropriations for the agency, which once again got its operating money through a continuing resolution.

In 1983 both the House and Senate passed authorization bills for agency. But the differences between the two versions of the bill were too great to allow the conference committee to produce a final compromise.

Agitation surrounding the FTC subsided in 1984 and 1985, primarily because of diminished complaints from business interests. Reagan appointees now dominated the agency (four of the five commissioners had been named by Reagan). The new chairman of the commission, James Miller, was both sympathetic to and acceptable to business. He believed deregulation and the free market were the best safeguards for consumers and the most conducive to a healthy climate for business.

Under the policy guidance of the Reagan commissioners, the FTC reined in its rule-making activity, thus giving business less reason to complain and Congress less incentive to curb the agency further by statute. Congress, however, made it clear that it would be vigilant in monitoring future FTC activity. An activist FTC could again expect legislative problems from that quarter. Neither chamber acted on an authorization bill in 1984. In passing the Fiscal Year 1985 appropriations for the FTC, both houses agreed to curb FTC power to investigate monopolistic activities of municipalities. The provision in the appropriations bill did not remove FTC authority to investigate matters pertaining to *allegations* of such activities, but it did prevent FTC action until an authorization bill specifically approved it.

Miller, who left his FTC position in 1985, was unsuccessful in inducing Congress to pass major permanent legislation restricting the FTC and reducing the scope of its activities. Congress remained wary of the agency but did not adopt the Reaganite views that favored major permanent reduction of FTC power (Harris and Milkis 1989, Chapter 5).

In 1985 both houses of Congress passed versions of a three-year reauthorization bill. Once again, however, the conference committee was unable to reach agreement. Both versions of the bill were silent on FTC regulation of professionals, the issue that had blocked reauthorization for the preceding years. One issue that the conference committee could not reconcile involved a Senate provision that prevented the FTC from initiating industrywide rules to regulate advertising alleged to represent an unfair business practice. The House conferees objected to this provision. Also, the Senate permitted Congress to enact joint resolutions, which had to be signed by the president, to disallow specific rules promulgated by both the FTC and by the Consumer Product Safety Commission. The House wanted such a provision only for the FTC.

The next (and most recent, as of this writing in early 1990) effort to agree on an authorization bill came in 1987. Again both houses passed a bill. Again the conference committee was unable to reach agreement. The same bars to final success appeared again: the FTC role in preventing "unfair" advertising and the specific provisions for disallowing agency rules.

As of the early 1990s the FTC is still without permanent authorization (as it has been since the 1980 bill expired in 1983). Congress gives it operating money through the appropriations process. Those appropriations bills contain continuations of most of the curbs on FTC activity contained in previous authorization bills.

The congressional attitude toward legislating for the FTC is ambivalent. Congress does not trust the agency. It remains sensitive to business complaints. But it also remains wary of wholesale "deregulation" in this protective regulatory arena. The activist commissioner Michael Pertschuk, who was instrumental in getting the agency in hot water with business and the congressional supporters of the business view beginning in 1977, sums up the congressional attitude succinctly and graphically: "Congress wants an active FTC as long as it does not bite anyone's ass too hard" (quoted in Harris and Milkis, 216).

Conclusions

We can now enrich the very broad picture of the protective regulatory arena we presented in the opening pages of this chapter and summarized in Table 4–1. In general, the patterns described are accurate, especially in cases involving the creation of new regulatory powers. But the distinction between the creation of regulatory power and alteration of existing power also allows us to make some amendments and refinements to the initial statements. It should also be noted that creation and alteration of regulatory power are interrelated. For example, the creation of powers is usually followed by continuing dispute over proposed alterations of powers, both by those who think the initial powers too broad and sweeping and by those who think them too pallid in comparison with the problems they are supposed to address.

In the cases in the foregoing pages, the smallest organizational units— subcommittees in Congress and bureaus in the executive branch—discussed the full range of issues both internally and with each other. However, in broad questions such as the creation or alteration of regulatory powers, virtually no final decisions were made at these lower levels. Inevitably the issues were moved to higher organizational levels for continuing debate and possible resolution, although such movement does not mean that a final decision will be reached. Many regulatory issues are debated over and over in much the same terms for many years.

Protective regulatory issues all contain the seeds of considerable conflict. The conflict does not merely stem from aggressive agencies being challenged by legislators representing regulated clients. In some cases the senators and representatives involved are more aggressive in asking for regulatory action than the regulatory agencies. Administrations are often reluctant to pursue aggressive regulatory policies. Some members of the House and the Senate fight against regulation, but there are also leaders in the effort to extend regulation—individuals such as Udall, in the case of strip mining.

The potential for conflict in most regulatory areas also means that often the coalitions supportive of and opposed to some specific power or its use are not unified or stable. Members of Congress, executive branch agencies, and interest groups all have been shown to have varying degrees of commitment to general questions, depending on what specific, more focused question is at stake. In a sense, regulatory issues are also separable, just as distributive issues are. But the nature of the regulatory issues means that volatility rather than relative stability and quiet will characterize the regulatory arena.

Conflict resolution generally occurs above the level of the bureau–subcommittee interaction when resolution occurs at all. But resolution often is not reached; conflict continues. Many important regulatory issues seem to be almost permanently on the agenda of the federal government before solutions are reached. Even when legislative solutions are reached, the conflict is likely to continue, and the legislation may be amended later.

One way in which regulatory issues become less volatile is for them to begin to be turned into distributive issues. Arguments have been made that, over a long period of time, regulatory agencies will be "captured" by the regulated interests. When such capture occurs—and there is good evidence that capture is not universal or inevitable—regulatory issues are treated as distributive. A good deal of the presumed regulation will be left in the hands of the interests themselves, which amounts to self-regulation with governmental blessing.

Over time, if Congress is persistent, it probably will possess the potential to be more important in making protective regulatory decisions than the executive branch. However, the element of persistence is critical, particularly for the supporters of regulation. The foes of regulation have an advantage in that they are more likely to have more powerful private interests supporting their position. The private interests

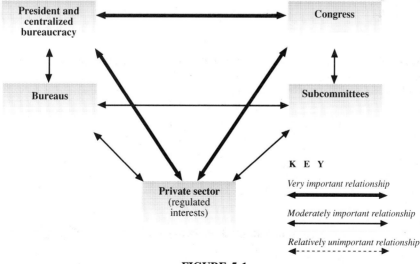

FIGURE 5-1

Relative importance of relationships for determining protective regulatory policy

supporting regulation (except for competitors) are usually not numerous or at least not very politically sophisticated or powerful.

Figure 5-1 summarizes the most important relationships between executive, legislative, and private sector actors in formulating and legitimating protective regulatory policy.

CHAPTER SIX

Redistributive Policy

The Nature of Redistributive Policy

Long periods of time required to arrive at decisions and a high degree of ideological content to the debate over decisions characterize the process of arriving at redistributive policy decisions. Who wins at whose expense is the central substantive question posed by redistributive policy decisions.

Many groups and individuals get involved in the debate over redistributive issues even if they don't have a direct, tangible stake in the outcome. Logically, many different positions are often possible in relation to a specific redistributive issue. In practice, however, the debates are conducted between two grand coalitions, usually designated as liberal (the side favoring extension of what Americans think of as redistributive policy) and conservative (the side favoring no extension or perhaps contraction of redistributive policy). Redistributive issues tend to produce similar coalitions on a wide range of specific matters. "Liberal" and "conservative" are neither precise nor analytically useful labels, but they are meaningful politically in the arena of American national policy.

The executive branch—particularly at the presidential level—is an important actor in redistributive policy formulation and legitimation. The president and his closest advisors and appointees negotiate with representatives of the "peak associations"— best characterized as holding companies of interest groups—that get involved in most redistributive controversies.

Ideological controversy characterizes redistributive policy debates because such policies seek to reallocate valuable goods and symbols among different economic classes and racial groupings. In redistributive policy, as it is defined in practice in the United States, less-privileged economic and racial groupings are the intended beneficiaries, at the perceived expense of more-privileged groups. Many programs in fact reallocate goods and symbols of value from the less well-off to the more well-off, but because such programs and the policies from which they stem are not *perceived* as redistributive they therefore do not generate the politics that are typical of debates over redistributive policies. In this chapter we focus on redistributive policies that define the less well-off as beneficiaries, although we also treat at some length the common situation in which redistributive policy is redefined as distributive in whole or in part.

The Reagan years and the early Bush years provided an emphatic reaffirmation of the view that policy is treated as redistributive only if aimed at benefiting relatively underprivileged classes and races. If it is aimed at benefiting the already well-positioned—as much policy favored by the Reagan and Bush administrations did—then it is not thought of as redistributive.

In 1981, for example, President Reagan could say with a straight face that the tax system was not the proper vehicle to use for the achievement of redistribution. What he meant was that he did not think the tax system should be redistributive in favor of the disadvantaged. While denying that the tax system should be used to achieve redistributive ends, he was simultaneously proposing major changes in the tax code that redistributed in the other direction. But in American political practice, few label a policy that benefits the already well-off at the expense of the less well-off as redistributive. Such policies are generally perceived and treated as if they were distributive.

Efforts to aid the disadvantaged virtually always set off major political rows. Efforts to aid the advantaged rarely do so. In 1989, for example, the Bush administration's proposal to lower the tax on capital gains for a period of a few years—a proposal that would have provided a very large windfall for the richest Americans—passed in the Democratically controlled House of Representatives because the minority Republicans had only one defector and the Democrats had sixty-four spread out across the country. The Democratic leaders in the House tried to make a major political statement. They roused neither a united party in the House nor much interest in the population at large.

From 1933, when Franklin Roosevelt became president, until 1981, when Ronald Reagan assumed that office, presidents of both parties initiated and supported at least some redistributive policy aimed at aiding the disadvantaged. Democratic presidents were more inclined to do so than Republicans, but Eisenhower, Nixon, and Ford also all led selected efforts to enact, sustain, or expand redistributive policy. All presidents in the period between 1933 and 1981 also presided over a federal bureaucracy that, in many domestic agencies, leaned toward promoting redistributive policy.

Ronald Reagan's "revolution," in terms of the role of the president, was to dismiss the 1933–1981 period of presidential and bureaucratic commitment and activity in the realm of domestic policy as wrongheaded. He returned the administration and, as quickly as he could, the bureaucracy to the policy commitments of Republican leaders of the 1920s. He wanted to halt federal support of redistribution to the less well-off. He took major legislative and administrative initiatives to cut that support in virtually all areas and to reverse the trend in many of those same areas. His administration did all it could in this direction without asking for new legislation. But it was unafraid to tackle a Congress that always had at least one chamber controlled by the Democrats to ask for legislative blessing for the new directions. The major Reagan legislative initiatives aimed at reversing five decades of policy commitments came in major tax and budget bills. The Reagan administration had considerable success in reducing the federal commitment to the disadvantaged and extending additional benefits to the advantaged (Page 1983; Palmer and Sawhill 1982, 1984; Pechman 1983).

From its own point of view, the greatest successes of the Reagan administration along these lines came in the combination of administrative action and broad-gauged budget and tax bills. Initiatives to attack specific programs legislatively did not get as far.

Redistributive Policy and the
Congressional–Bureaucratic Relationship

We expect the importance of subgovernments to be minimal in relation to final decisions about redistributive policy, both (1) because only parts of some redistributive issues are likely to be considered in the deliberations within a subgovernment, and (2) because final decisions are almost always made at levels higher than those represented by the members of a subgovernment.

The potential for conflict between various combinations of congressional and bureaucratic actors on redistributive issues is high because there are usually ideological and partisan differences. If general agreement on these differences can be reached, the conflict potential can be reduced considerably. If these differences are not muted and if redistributive issues are not redefined in some way, then the debate and final decisions may take a long time. Five substantive areas—the war on poverty, medicare, civil rights, voting rights, and tax policy—illustrate the congressional–bureaucratic relationship in reaching decisions on redistributive policy and also illustrate the factors that impede or facilitate reaching those decisions.

Even when conflict based on partisan and ideological differences is present, however, the contending parties in the two governmental branches may be able to reach agreement by casting the issue in distributive terms either in whole or in part rather than continuing to debate it wholly in redistributive terms. Four substantive areas illustrate the dynamics when distributive considerations are substituted for all or many redistributive considerations: model cities, employment and training programs for the hard to employ, aid to education, and housing.

When conflict exists, usually there is no final resolution at the level of executive branch bureau and congressional subcommittee. If resolution is achieved, it comes at a higher level, usually in negotiations between the president, his top appointees and advisors, and the full Congress, often represented by the party leaders and relevant chairs of full committees. If conflict is resolved at this higher level, it is either in terms of a broad compromise or in terms of a redefinition of issues in distributive terms. Many times, however, resolution of the conflict evades the actors, sometimes for many years and sometimes forever. When resolution of conflict does occur, the prevailing view depends largely on the relative strength of competing ideologies in Congress at the time, the ties of those ideologies to the political parties in Congress, and the relative strength of the parties and of the major ideological factions of the parties in Congress.

Some of the examples of the action on redistributive policy we have chosen for this chapter come from the 1960s for the simple reason that the 1960s represent the last concentrated burst of redistributive policy making in the United States. Interest in such policy waned in the 1970s and especially in the 1980s, although we have used selected examples from those decades too.

Reaching Basic Decisions about Redistributive Issues

The war on poverty The creation, alteration, and eventual dismemberment of the war on poverty between 1964 and 1974 exhibit a number of patterns common to redistributive policy. Individual members of the House and Senate, particularly those in strategic committee posts, were important in helping make decisions, as were individuals scattered throughout the administration and relevant executive branch agencies. However, these individuals could not make binding decisions by themselves. A much broader set of decision makers got involved in all key decisions, including all senators and representatives (through floor action that did not rubberstamp decisions made in subcommittees and committees), the president and his top advisors, and a variety of interest groups. Programs avowedly redistributive along class and/or racial lines were continuously controversial. Our intent is not to tell the entire story of the war on poverty, but rather to explore a few aspects that illustrate the nature of redistributive politics with particular clarity. (For discussions of the politics surrounding the entire war on poverty, see Donovan 1973; Levitan 1969; Loftus 1970; and Sundquist 1968, Chapter 4.) The episodes on which we will focus in the following pages include the 1967 Green amendment to the Economic Opportunity Act of 1967, the Job Corps, the Legal Services Corporation, and the end of the Office of Economic Opportunity (OEO) as a separate organizational entity in the federal government.

The Green amendment The original Economic Opportunity Act that passed in 1964 authorized the program until 1967. In 1967 the program required renewal. The program seemed to be in serious trouble (see Loftus 1970 for a fuller account of what follows). There had been complaints about the administration of the program and about its alleged involvement in stirring up the urban riots that had torn the country apart for the previous three summers. In the 1966 congressional elections, liberal Democrats—who provided the core of support for the war on poverty—suffered heavy losses in races for the House. Congress convened in 1967 amidst widespread expectations that the conservative coalition of Republicans and conservative southern Democrats could kill the entire poverty program during the reauthorization debate.

As it turned out, the program survived, largely because the House adopted an amendment sponsored by Representative Edith Green, an Oregon Democrat who had been critical of the OEO and its programs. The amendment was designed to mollify two groups: conservative southern Democrats and some northern urban Democrats from cities whose mayors had had poor relations with the OEO and its community action program. Centrally, the Green amendment gave mayors and other locally elected officials the means to gain substantial control over community action agencies.

The negotiations that produced the amendment were carried on by Green on the one hand and the director and staff of the OEO and members of the White House staff on the other, through the mediation of five Democratic supporters of the war on poverty who served with Green on the House Education and Labor Committee. Green did not want to admit that she was willing to help save the program. The Johnson administration was not able politically to admit it was willing to pay the price of accepting the Green amendment in order to save the program. The public stances of the two groups of individuals negotiating, therefore, remained in conflict. But the intermediaries, who realized that to save the program they favored they would have to acquiesce to the adoption of the Green amendment, promoted compromise for which neither of the contesting parties had to take public responsibility. These relatively quiet third-person negotiations illustrate that even in the midst of loud public discord over redistributive policy, some features of subgovernment activity can appear and have an impact. This was not a consensual "poverty subgovernment" at work. But private negotiations and compromises could, even in the realm of redistributive policy, produce results with which both ideologically contesting groups could live, at least privately.

Job Corps The Job Corps, one of the original programs in the war on poverty, was aimed at preparing disadvantaged teenage youths for the labor market by offering them residential training and experience in centers in both urban and rural areas. The central premise was that young persons from extremely deprived backgrounds needed to be removed from "the culture of poverty" in order to develop adequate reading ability, job-related skills, and appropriate attitudes about work and holding a job. (For discussions of the politics of decision making about the Job Corps from 1964 through 1971 see Ripley 1972, Chapter 3, on which some of the following discussion is based.)

Controversy surrounded the Job Corps from its inception. It received negative coverage in the press during its first year of operation. Many incidents that reflected poorly on the program received national attention out of proportion to their real importance. In addition, the program was expensive. Even with the support of the Johnson administration, the Job Corps had trouble holding its own in Congress in its early years. Although the initial goal of the program was for 100,000 enrollees, the target was soon revised downward. The program leveled off at between 35,000 and 40,000 enrollees, with an annual budget of about $280 million.

When the Nixon administration took office in early 1969, it cut the Job Corps quickly and deeply. Nixon had promised such action in the 1968 presidential campaign and lost no time keeping his pledge. The administration took the Job Corps away from the OEO and put it in the more traditionally oriented Department of Labor. The administration also cut both the budget and the number of enrollees in half. The residential centers that remained open—all in or near urban areas—drew enrollees from the local area rather than nationally.

The Job Corps survived, but only in a form that made it seem relatively non-threatening and relatively minor in terms of its actual and potential redistributive impact. Unlike the OEO and the Green amendment, no private negotiations saved the original concept and bureaucratic location of the Job Corps. It apparently was so vulnerable that continued existence—even under dramatically altered circumstances—was about the best its supporters could hope for.

It still retained enough Democratic supporters to be continued as a categorical employment and training program in 1973, however, even though most other employment and training programs (called manpower programs at the time) were included under the Comprehensive Employment and Training Act (CETA), a special revenue-sharing program created in 1973. The fortunes of the Jobs Corps revived somewhat in the Carter administration.

The Job Corps was one of the few redistributive programs that caught the imagination and therefore generated the support of some conservative members of Congress. This support helped it survive—at a very modest level of funding—when CETA was reauthorized in 1978 and also when the Job Training Partnership Act replaced CETA in 1982. Orrin Hatch of Utah, the very conservative chair of the Labor and Human Resources Committee in the Republican-controlled Senate from 1981 until 1987, was a particularly important supporter of the Job Corps. It remained as a small, categorical program aimed at helping the poor and survived the general onslaught against such programs in the Reagan years.

Legal Services Corporation   The final form in which a Legal Services Corporation (LSC) was permanently established in 1974 again illustrates compromise between individual members of the House and Senate (in this case, mostly members of a conference committee) and representatives of the administration. This compromise resulted in breaking a three-year deadlock over a program perceived to have considerable redistributive potential, at least by the opponents of the program. The dispute over the LSC was highly visible. One side in the dispute was committed to the provision of legal services to the poor by the federal government. This side argued that such a program would redistribute the outcomes of the legal system more equally. The side opposed to the proposed program felt it would be disruptive to social order. As with the Green amendment, final resolution of the conflict was achieved because some relatively private negotiations took place among the most concerned individuals at the last minute. These negotiations avoided a direct confrontation between supporters of the program and President Nixon, whose veto of the program (if he chose to exercise it) could not be overridden. Proponents of the program were also motivated to negotiate and arrive at a compromise because they were aware that the OEO itself was unlikely to survive beyond 1974. That year represented a last chance to create some kind of legal services program.

Congress had passed a bill establishing an LSC in 1971, but President Nixon had successfully vetoed it, primarily because the bill did not give the president the power of appointing all of the directors of the corporation. In 1972 a conference committee eliminated an amendment to the bill reauthorizing the OEO programs that would have created an LSC because it feared the inclusion of such an amendment would have provoked a successful presidential veto of the entire bill. In 1973 President Nixon submitted his own proposal for an LSC. The House passed a bill that was even more conservative and restrictive than what Nixon had requested. Opponents of the creation of any LSC, no matter how constrained, filibustered against the bill in the Senate in late 1973 and early 1974. The Senate stopped the filibuster on the third vote on cloture and passed a bill that was far less restrictive of the activities of the corporation and its professional staff than the either the president's original bill or the House-passed version.

The conference committee reached a series of agreements that both chambers approved in the spring of 1974. One provision of the bill continued to generate trouble, however. Conservatives in the House were opposed to a provision in the bill that authorized the creation of so-called backup centers (LSC-funded poverty-law research centers), and they narrowly missed sending the bill back to conference with instructions to delete these centers. Even though the Senate solidly supported the centers, Senate conferees realized that Nixon would probably veto a bill allowing them and that the House would certainly sustain such a veto. Therefore, in a series of last-minute negotiations outside of the formal, visible conference committee meeting, supporters of the creation of an LSC met privately and agreed to delete the research centers as the price they had to pay to get a corporation at all.

Other restrictions added to the bill indicate additional prices that liberals had to pay in this case. The president was given the power to appoint all directors of the corporation. Attorneys employed by the corporation were severely restricted in terms of their political activities, even those undertaken on their own time. LSC-sponsored lawsuits aimed at school desegregation or obtaining nontherapeutic abortions were forbidden. And lawyers for the LSC could not become involved in draft cases or criminal cases. President Nixon signed this very conservative bill even though some congressional conservatives urged that he veto even this version because they simply wanted no program at all.

The Reagan administration launched an all-out assault on the LSC, hoping for its elimination. When that did not seem to be possible politically, the administration instead slashed both budget and staff at the LSC. It also put new appointees on the board unsympathetic to the program. Some of those appointees got into trouble by taking fat consulting fees and by declaring meetings to be secret even though such secrecy was probably illegal (Drew 1982; Kristof 1982). President Reagan and the Senate engaged in a long-running battle over board appointees in 1984 and 1985.

The fight between liberals and conservatives over an LSC spilled over into the early Bush years. The archconservative board barred suits involving redistricting, prisoners' rights, and, in some cases, aliens. It also agreed that the agency's structure was unconstitutional. In late 1989, the board remained in the hands of a conservative majority. President Bush and Congress continued to engage in partisan warfare over this remnant of the war on poverty.

The end of the OEO   The flagging fortunes of the OEO once the Democrats lost the White House in the 1968 election and its eventual dismantling suggest how critically important presidential support is to the creation and maintenance of redistributive policy and how devastating presidential opposition to such policy can be. The OEO was established in the poverty-conscious political climate of the mid-1960s with President Lyndon Johnson's strong support. Although its community action program had been amended in 1967, funding support did not begin to diminish until Richard Nixon became president in 1969. Nixon had never been enthusiastic about the poverty program. Although he made no mention of the OEO during the

1968 campaign, a 1969 message to Congress expressed skepticism about the agency and its programs. In 1973 he began a full-scale attempt to kill the agency and cut off federal funding for its community action programs, which provided a variety of services to the poor.

The OEO had been created as an independent operating agency at the insistence of its first director, Sargent Shriver. When Nixon assumed office, his administration began to remove programs from the OEO and to cut its budget in order to reduce its operating role. In 1973 Nixon appointed an acting director of the OEO (an appointment that he did not submit for Senate confirmation) with a specific mandate to dismantle the agency and to transfer its programs to other agencies. However, in his budget for Fiscal Year 1974, no money was requested for the OEO as an agency, even though its existence was authorized by statute through June 1974. The budget proposed placing the OEO's legal services in a separate corporation, transferring a variety of the OEO programs to other agencies (the Departments of Health, Education and Welfare; Labor; and Commerce), and allowing the community action programs to expire. This executive action sent threatened community action agencies and employee unions to the courts, where a judge ruled that no budget message could overrule a previous legislative authorization. The judge declared the actions of the acting director of the OEO void and also declared his appointment to be illegal.

The court decision forced Nixon to name another acting director and submit his nomination to the Senate for confirmation. The Senate confirmed this appointment by an 88-to-3 vote, in part because the nominee said he was in favor of continuing the OEO. Nixon later fired this individual for acting on that view. Nixon continued to move programs out of the OEO and into other agencies by administrative action. By declaring that a program was being "delegated" by the OEO to another agency, Nixon's actions required no congressional approval. By the end of 1973, only three programs were left in the OEO: legal services, community action, and community economic development. Moving any of these required congressional action.

Despite Nixon's wish to let the community action programs expire in 1974, support in Congress was still strong for their continuation. In addition, support came from a number of mayors and governors who in earlier years had opposed the poverty programs. They feared that the loss of the services provided by these programs would put local communities in a bad position. The rising national unemployment rate sharply emphasized the need for programs for the poor. Members of Congress who thought that a bill continuing community action programs was likely to pass could reflect that a bill passed in 1974 would very likely be less liberal than one passed in 1975, when the new Congress would almost surely be more heavily Democratic because of the Watergate disaster that had befallen President Nixon.

Because of support both inside and outside Congress and because the new president, Gerald Ford, did not oppose the poverty program, a bill continuing community action emerged late in the 1974 congressional session. Conference committee members negotiating among themselves and in touch with the Ford administration produced a winning compromise that continued a number of poverty programs and created an agency to succeed the OEO; but it simultaneously reduced the redistributive potential of both the programs and the agency.

The Community Services Act of 1974 was a victory for supporters of the poverty programs in the sense that the programs were authorized through Fiscal Year 1977. The OEO as an independent agency ceased to exist, however. Its programs were lodged in a new independent agency: the Community Services Administration (CSA). The new law gave the president the option of reorganizing the CSA and its programs. The total federal commitment to the programs in terms of money was small: Ford requested only $363 million for the CSA for Fiscal Year 1976, a far cry from the $2 billion OEO budget for Fiscal Year 1969. The federal share of funding for community action programs was cut back to 60 percent over the following three years.

President Ford did not exercise the option to reorganize or transfer the CSA, but the agency's impact was seriously curtailed by the decreased level of funding. Although between Fiscal Years 1975 and 1978 Congress routinely provide appropriations much larger than the president requested, the size of the appropriations was still much lower than in the pre-CSA days. The CSA budget expanded only at roughly the level of inflation.

In 1978 the CSA and other antipoverty programs were reauthorized through 1981. The CSA emerged from the authorization process with no deletions from and no additions to its programs. The federal formula for sharing program costs was again altered, with the 60 percent federal share increased to 80 percent. However, Congress continued to provide only minimal budgets in the late 1970s and into the 1980s.

In 1981 President Reagan sought the elimination of the CSA altogether in his comprehensive budget reconciliation proposal. The agency and its programs succumbed with little notice, and this institutionally based redistributive policy passed into history.

Medicare   The notion of government-sponsored health insurance to assist citizens in meeting the cost of their medical care has been on the national agenda since 1935. Only in 1965, after the first three decades of debate, did a major piece of health insurance legislation emerge: the medicare program created under the social security system. No extension of federal health insurance to other parts of the population has been enacted since that time, although the debate has continued. The one effort to expand medicare itself in 1988 met with political disaster and was repealed in 1989. In the following discussion we focus on the creation of medicare in 1965. We add a short discussion on the short-lived extension of medicare to include special provisions to cover catastrophic illness in 1988 and 1989.

During the debate that eventually led to the adoption of medicare, two ideological positions emerged that were espoused by the large coalitions that stood in opposition on this issue. The debate was largely static in terms of the content of the rhetoric and the arguments: the same actors repeated the same arguments year after year. In procedural terms the debate was also static. The opponents of creating any kind of national health insurance found the numerous levers in Congress that can be used to obstruct action and, with only minor exceptions, were successful until 1965 in doing just that.

The side favoring action, although that action was now limited to health insurance for the elderly, finally won in 1965 because of the emergence of an aggressive new political majority in Congress supported by a skillful and committed president, Lyndon Johnson. Even in 1965 the final floor votes in Congress could accurately be interpreted as logical outcomes of twenty years of conflict between two coalitions holding wholly predictable views. The reason that the losers for so many years suddenly became winners in 1965 was that the election of 1964 had altered the liberal–conservative balance in Congress and had also swept Lyndon Johnson into office with an impressive victory. Even under these generally favorable political conditions, however, the final creation of medicare was achieved only through considerable bargaining and compromise among those members of the House and Senate who held differing viewpoints and among people in Congress and high-level members of the Johnson administration. In large part because of the 1964 election returns, Congress played a more creative role in shaping the 1965 legislation than might be expected in the case of a redistributive policy.

Proponents and opponents of various forms of national health insurance had held and expressed their diverging views with great intensity for many years before 1965. Two basic positions were adopted by the core coalitions. Proponents of health care (which included the AFL–CIO and other labor unions, a variety of public welfare organizations, the National Medical Association [a group representing black physicians], the National Council of Senior Citizens, and many northern Democrats in Congress) supported full federal sponsorship of medical insurance. They believed that private insurance companies could not handle national medical insurance, that their premiums would be too high for many people, especially the elderly, and that state action would be insufficient in several respects.

Opponents of national medical insurance (a coalition that included the American Medical Association, the insurance industry, business groups such as the U.S. Chamber of Commerce, and most Republicans and southern Democrats in Congress) favored only a very narrow federal role in this area, one that would be limited to encouraging private and state efforts and that would provide federal health-care insurance assistance only to welfare cases. Opponents were especially fearful of government interference in private medical practice and warned against the dangers of "socialized medicine."

A close observer (Marmor 1973, 108–109) commented on the explicitly redistributive nature of the debate over medicare:

> Debate [was]...cast in terms of class conflict.... The leading adversaries...brought into the opposing camps a large number of groups whose interests were not directly affected by the Medicare outcome.... [I]deological charges and counter-charges dominated public discussion, and each side seemed to regard compromise as unacceptable. In the end, the electoral changes of 1965 reallocated power in such a way that the opponents were overruled. Compromise was involved in the detailed features of the Medicare program, but the enactment itself did not constitute a compromise outcome for the adversaries.

The debate over medical insurance that had proceeded sporadically since the Roosevelt administration first pondered including a national health insurance program in its original social security proposals (although it did not do so) was cast in terms of universal coverage. A major step in narrowing the debate was taken in

1957 when the liberal supporters of the idea focused exclusively on the elderly. The following eight years witnessed continuing fierce fighting between the pro (liberal) and anti (conservative) forces. The lobbying efforts on both sides were notable for their intensity. They were aimed not just at members of the House and Senate but also at the general public in order to influence mass opinion. In the end, the static and largely unchanging substantive debate was resolved with a compromise that included considerable input from conservatives and Republicans that blurred some of the redistributive focus of the final program. Republican contributions to the final act included coverage of almost 3 million people who were not covered by the Old Age and Survivors Insurance provisions of social security, the separation of medicare funds from old-age pension funds, the authorization of the use of private, nonprofit organizations to deal with hospitals, and the addition of a subsidy to cover surgery and doctors' fees. The last two features in particular were distributive provisions that resulted in less fierce opposition to the final bill from the professional health community.

Medicare, therefore, like social security in general, is not purely redistributive. The criteria for eligibility cut across class and income lines. The middle class has a very large stake in making sure that both medicare and the broader social security program are solvent and that benefits are generous. The modest redistributive features (the elderly poor are subsidized) in medicare may well be hostage to the political forces most interested in the distributive features (everybody is subsidized, regardless of how well-off they are).

The events surrounding the overwhelming adoption of catastrophic insurance added to medicare in 1988 and the rapid and overwhelming repeal of that provision in 1989 demonstrate that Congress has little sustained interest in making medicare even faintly more redistributive. The information also adds to our understanding of the relationship between political coalitions among Washington policy makers and their relations with coalitions with a more public base (Haas 1989; Rovner 1989a, 1989b, 1989c; Tolchin 1989).

In mid-1988 the Democratically controlled Congress and the Reagan White House agreed to provide new benefits to the elderly under medicare for what they called medical catastrophes. The new provisions put ceilings on medical bills and expanded payments for care in nursing homes and prescription drugs, among other things. Many Democrats in Congress liked this agreement because they thought they were meeting real needs and would, therefore, get political credit. Reagan also liked the new program for political reasons. He thought it was good insurance against the charge that Republicans (especially both Reagan himself and George Bush, who was his vice-president and would be running for president in 1988) were insensitive to the needs of the elderly. As part of the compromise—at the insistence of Reagan—a small surtax to pay for the program was added to the charges already assessed for medicare coverage. Reagan's ideology led him to want the elderly to have to pay something for these new benefits. The Democrats' ideology led them to make the surtax mildly progressive (that is, the more affluent elderly would pay more than the poorer elderly).

As soon as they realized they would have to pay for something many of them already had under their pensions or private insurance plans and that the surtax was even mildly progressive, the more affluent of the elderly organized. The most potent new organization dedicated to killing catastrophic coverage was known as the National Committee to Preserve Social Security and Medicare. It enlisted widespread and vociferous support for the campaign to repeal the program. By the autumn of 1989 this campaign led to overwhelming repeal of the program in Congress. No groups spoke up for the impoverished elderly, who really needed the coverage. Those among the elderly who resented subsidizing the medically indigent through the surtax had their way virtually unchallenged.

The main lesson for those in Congress who want to expand redistributive programs is that it is foolish to do so without organizing a strong supportive coalition outside of the government. This was policy making in which the presumed beneficiaries were not involved. They were simply told what was good for them, both in terms of benefits and in terms of funding arrangements. Although Congress had some programmatic commitments when it enacted the program, it acted primarily for political reasons. President Reagan had almost exclusively political motives for buying the compromise in 1988. Thus, when a firestorm of criticism from the more well-off elderly arose, there was no preexisting coalition to counter that criticism and fight for retention of the program.

The original medicare program took decades to enact. But once it was in place it was unlikely that an opposition coalition could dismantle it, because the supportive coalition is large and active and politically potent. In the case of catastrophic insurance tacked onto medicare, "success" came quickly. But since no publicly supportive coalition had been built in the process of achieving "success," "failure" was just as rapid once the more affluent oldsters set their mind to it. The congressional retreat was ignominious. Repeal came just as quickly and relatively thoughtlessly, as had enactment. Politics was virtually the only driving force behind both actions. Ultimately, the public-based politics of repeal was stronger than the politics of enactment, which had been almost exclusively a game among Washington insiders.

The Civil Rights Act of 1964   Civil rights for racial and ethnic minorities (understood and debated almost exclusively in terms of civil rights for black Americans from the 1930s through the 1960s) had a long and complex, and often heartbreaking, history from the end of the Civil War up to the passage of the first postreconstruction civil rights legislation of much substance in 1964. This history was both legislative (characterized largely by inaction) and judicial (characterized by sporadic, faltering, and often negative action until 1954 and by a quickening tempo of positive action after that). Recounting that history easily fills a large book (see Kluger 1976 for one excellent summary).

In this section we will focus on one important part of civil rights history, the passage of the Civil Rights Act of 1964, to illustrate the kinds of political forces that are generated when the matter for decision is a redistributive measure that deals with questions of racial justice. As with other redistributive policies, this story features a combination of highly visible and emotion-filled debate, both in Congress and in other public arenas, and private negotiation of compromises that allowed forward movement at critical junctures. The private negotiations were conducted by key individuals in both the executive branch and Congress. (Principal sources for our discussion are *Congressional Quarterly Almanac, 1965*: 1615–1641; Kluger 1976; Lytle 1966; Sundquist 1968, Chapter 6.)

When John F. Kennedy became president in 1961, he raised the hopes of leaders in the civil rights movement that some federal civil rights legislation might be forthcoming if he chose to play a leadership role. Instead, he chose to proceed very cautiously in this area, primarily to protect other parts of his domestic program from being defeated in Congress because of well-placed southerners in both houses who would be angered by a civil rights initiative from the White House. Critics said Kennedy was not proceeding on civil rights at all.

However, as the activity of the civil rights movement at the local level increased, that activity inevitably generated opposition. Peaceful pro-civil rights demonstrations, boycotts, and sit-ins resulted in violent opposition in some instances. The administration felt compelled to act. In February 1963 President Kennedy announced that legislative proposals would be forthcoming, but only a few minor proposals followed in May. Major action still did not seem imminent.

However, in May and June 1963 the attention of the nation was drawn suddenly to Birmingham, Alabama, where a particularly evil manifestation of officially sanctioned violence in support of blatant racial discrimination was being challenged by civil rights leaders and a large number of followers. Additional public drama was created when the governor of Alabama, George Wallace, took his stand in "the schoolhouse door" to prevent two black students from registering at the University of Alabama. He gave up in a few hours when President Kennedy called the Alabama National Guard into federal service. Television transmitted to the public all of these events as they happened.

President Kennedy, energized by his own reading of these events, by congressional supporters of civil rights, and by a host of interest groups and coalitions of groups supporting civil rights, submitted a moderately strong civil rights bill to Congress in mid-June. More important, he committed himself personally to the fight to get legislation passed and immediately became involved in a number of meetings to work on strategy with groups supporting the legislation. These included a variety of black-led groups (for example, the National Association for the Advancement of Colored People, the National Urban League, the Congress of Racial Equality, and the Southern Christian Leadership Conference), a number of labor unions (especially the industrial unions from the old Congress of Industrial Organizations), a large number of church groups, and the Leadership Conference on Civil Rights—a "holding company" for seventy-nine groups supporting civil rights, including all of the above plus many more. The president also began meeting with pro-civil rights Democrats and Republicans in Congress and with officials from the White House and the Justice Department, which was headed by his brother Robert Kennedy.

A subcommittee of the House Judiciary Committee held hearings in the summer of 1963 and moved to strengthen in a number of ways the bill proposed by the president. The White House feared that the bill had been strengthened so much that it would never pass the Senate. The administration calculated that the votes of a number of western Democrats and moderate Republicans were essential for passage, particularly in the Senate. The administration further calculated that only a bill of moderate strength could win the necessary support from these moderate groups. In order to gauge what could pass even the House, Attorney General Kennedy entered directly into negotiations with two key Republicans—the ranking Republican on the Judiciary Committee and the minority leader. When the bill went into the full Judiciary Committee, the southern Democrats worked to report the strongest possible bill, believing that defeat of such a bill on the floor of the House was more likely than if the bill were more moderate. The administration intervened both publicly and privately to get the majority Democrats to weaken the bill so that it could pass the full House. Attorney General Kennedy publicly asked for moderating amendments in full committee hearings and was also active in private negotiations. The administration was successful in its efforts: the House Judiciary Committee reported a moderate bill that most observers agreed would pass the House easily.

In 1963 the Senate Judiciary Committee, chaired by one of the most reactionary of the southern Democrats, had predictably buried the parts of the bill referred to it. One major part of the total package—that guaranteeing nondiscriminatory access to public accommodations such as hotels and restaurants—had gone to the Senate Commerce Committee and had been approved, although for strategic reasons it had not been formally reported by the end of the session.

The next year, 1964, began with a new president, Lyndon Johnson, in office because John Kennedy had been assassinated in November 1963. Johnson quickly and effectively made his total commitment to a strong civil rights law public and worked closely with friendly lobbyists, members of Congress, and individuals in the White House and Justice Department to develop a strategy and generate compromises that would attract enough moderate votes to pass the whole package.

Pressured by northern Democratic and Republican support, the House Rules Committee, although chaired by an archconservative Virginian, proved to be no major stumbling block to the progress of the bill in early 1964. The full House debated the bill for ten days and passed it by a large margin (290 to 130) on February 10. The bill's managers acquiesced in accepting a few amendments on the floor restricting the scope of the bill. On the whole, however, the bill the House passed was very close in content to the bill that had been hammered out in the bipartisan negotiations in the Judiciary Committee in the autumn of 1963. Two amendments even strengthened the bill a bit.

The first critical action in the Senate occurred when the whole Senate voted simply to place the House-passed bill on its calendar for floor consideration rather than referring it to the Judiciary Committee, where it no doubt would have died. The Senate debated the bill from early March until mid-June 1964. The key figure in the Senate turned out to be the minority leader, Everett Dirksen of Illinois. If he could be convinced of the fairness of the bill, he would vote for closing off a filibuster the southern opposition to the bill had mounted and would also vote for the bill itself. Most important, his position on both votes would be imitated by a number of moderate Republicans. The vote on the filibuster would be the most important because two-thirds of those present and voting had to vote "yes." This meant that 67 votes were required because all one hundred senators were present. Attorney General Robert

Kennedy and the leading Senate Democrat during floor debate, Hubert Humphrey of Minnesota, negotiated details of the bill with Dirksen over a period of several months. Eventually this trio reached compromises that weakened the bill somewhat but that got the all-important votes of Dirksen and those who took their cues from him. Victory came in votes of 71 to 29 on cloture and 73 to 27 on the bill itself.

The majority of the House Rules Committee again overrode its conservative chair to guarantee that the House could vote directly on the Senate-passed bill without sending the bill to a conference committee, where it once again might die. The House easily approved the Senate bill 289 to 126 on July 2. Later the same day, President Johnson signed the bill into law on live national television.

Despite the numerous compromises that had been necessary to achieve passage of the bill at several sticky points in both houses, it was not toothless legislation. In fact, the long process produced a bill that was stronger than the one initially proposed by President Kennedy. It had provisions dealing with voting rights, public accommodations, desegregation of public facilities, desegregation of public education, extending the life of the Civil Rights Commission, nondiscrimination in programs assisted with federal dollars, equal employment opportunity, registration and voting statistics, and the creation of a Community Relations Service in the Commerce Department.

The passage of the 1964 Civil Rights Act was characterized by lengthy debate that was highly emotional and very visible. There was no quiet subgovernment at work in this policy area. The benefits to be conferred by the legislation—equal treatment under the law—created distinct classes of perceived winners and losers. Successful passage of the legislation required the forceful personal involvement of many key actors, most notably the president, and a willingness to compromise on the part of the supporters of government action. The passage of the act alone did not guarantee implementation of its provisions, but it was an important step toward the provision of simple justice to all Americans.

Voting Rights Act renewal, 1982   In 1965 Congress continued innovative activity in civil rights by passing the Voting Rights Act. This law rapidly brought about a large increase in the number of blacks who registered and voted in federal, state, and local elections. Many observers point to it as the most effective of all national civil rights laws. Some sections of the 1965 law were permanent and required no reauthorization. Enforcement provisions of the original law, however, required reauthorization if they were not to expire. These provisions required affected states to obtain federal permission or "preclearance" before making changes in their election laws. They also prescribed the conditions under which suits could be brought charging voting discrimination. The most recent renewal of the enforcement provisions—for a period of twenty-five years—occurred in 1982, when they were scheduled to expire.

Congressional passage of the Voting Rights Act extension in 1982 contrasted sharply with the turbulence surrounding enactment of the 1964 Civil Rights Act. In 1982 the redistributive effects of the legislation enjoyed widespread bipartisan support in both houses of Congress. The law's effectiveness in increasing registration and voter participation was undisputed. Even among southern members of Congress, support for passage was widespread, in large part because of the effectiveness of the 1965 law in producing large numbers of black voters.

The enactment of the 1982 extension, however, was not entirely free from controversy. Everyone knew the law would be extended; the issues involved the length of the extension and the details of the enforcement provisions.

The House and Senate debated two significant issues in 1982 in addition to the length of the extension. The first addressed the standard of proof to be used in settling suits alleging voter discrimination. Senate conservatives and the Reagan Department of Justice wanted to insert language requiring that the *intent* to discriminate must be proved instead of simply allowing suits to rest on the argument that the *result* of a voting law was discriminatory, even if inadvertently. The second issue affected the preclearance requirement of the statute. The specific dispute was how states could be exempted from coverage of the act if they complied consistently with federal rules and did not discriminate in their election laws. How stringent should this test for compliance be? What criteria would allow a state to be released from preclearance provisions?

The Reagan administration did not exhibit leadership in urging extension of the law. Despite pressure from civil rights groups, the president withheld endorsement of the bill and took no personal role in promoting its passage. The attorney general and the head of the Civil Rights Division in the Department of Justice favored a narrow "intent" standard of proof provision and a fairly short extension of the act. No one from the administration testified at the House hearings in 1981.

Passage of the bill in the House was overwhelming: 389 to 24 on the final vote. Debate and passage took only one day on the floor. The House Judiciary Committee had worked for many months to find a winning compromise on the question of criteria for release of states from preclearance (called "bailout"). By large margins the House defeated any amendment that seemed to dilute the bill.

The Senate presented more problems. Passage was never in doubt; some details were. The chair of the Senate Judiciary Committee, Republican Strom Thurmond of South Carolina, was a longtime opponent of the act. The chair of the relevant subcommittee of the Judiciary Committee, Republican Orrin Hatch of Utah, opposed use of the "results" standard of proof for suits and wanted extension of the act limited to ten years. The committee was divided on the standard of proof issue but after two months accepted the "results" criterion that the House had adopted. Opponents of that standard were somewhat mollified by a clause that proportional representation for minorities on local governing bodies was not guaranteed or intended by the act. Republican Senator Jesse Helms of North Carolina waged a dispirited filibuster for nine days before giving up. The Senate then passed the extension 85 to 8. Supporters of the committee bill easily defeated amendments on the floor aimed at diluting the bill.

Tax policy, 1986 Tax policy always presents an occasion for policy makers to confront head-on the issues of distribution and redistribution. In 1986 Congress and the president produced a major overhaul of the internal revenue code in the form of a new, comprehensive tax act (*Congressional Quarterly Almanac, 1986*, 491–524;

Kettl 1988, Chapter 4; Pechman 1987). It was widely touted by its supporters as fairer, simpler, and more generous to the poorest Americans and aimed at taxing the richest Americans more heavily in line with their ability to pay. In fact, it did not turn out to be simpler. It did achieve some modest redistributive ends in terms of exempting some of the poorest people from income tax and removing or restricting some of the largest loopholes for the wealthiest taxpayers. Perhaps the most concentrated benefits went to the lower and middle sections of the middle economic class. Those hit the hardest in redistributive terms were the upper middle class, not the most wealthy.

The complicated story of the passage of the Tax Reform Act of 1986 is too long and involved to tell here, but the important analytical points can be made briefly. First, an unusual set of political actors supported "tax reform" for a variety of different political reasons. The major actors meant different things by "reform" and had a mix of motivations for working toward what became the final bill. Second, the substantive compromises needed to produce the final bill resulted in quite moderate redistribution and, as always, left the way open for future adjustments that might reduce the redistribution that survived the political process in the first place.

What key actors and perceptions helped produce the final result? President Ronald Reagan was important, as a president almost surely has to be if redistributive policy is to result. Reagan's values led him to believe strongly in simpler and lower tax rates. At the same time, he was willing to remove some of the poorest people from taxable status altogether as a way of promoting his simpler, lower rates. He was also willing to countenance higher corporate taxes for the same purpose. His general position got support, for different reasons, from various "citizens' lobbies" pushing for "fairness." The most important organization was the Citizens for Tax Justice. It served as a rallying point for the relatively "simple" goals of simpler, lower, fairer rates. By contrast, the lobbies working actively for their own special tax breaks were not united and were all concentrating on the few provisions in the elaborate tax code that applied to them individually. Facing a president and a united lobby of citizens' groups, and—critically—some key members of Congress, these special lobbies lost in 1986. Naturally, in the years immediately following this defeat, they began to press for revisions of the 1986 law.

The heart of the negotiations over details came in long sessions within the Treasury Department, the House Ways and Means Committee, the Senate Finance Committee, and—ultimately—among representatives of these institutions. Narrow partisanship was abandoned at critical points as a Republican White House, the professionals in the Treasury Department, the Democratically controlled House Ways and Means Committee, and the Republican-controlled Senate Finance Committee labored to produce a bill with which they could all be reasonably pleased. At the final critical stage of the conference committee, the House chairman, Dan Rostenkowski, an Illinois Democrat, and the Senate chairman, Robert Packwood, an Oregon Republican, met at length privately and produced a final product they could sell both to their respective committees and the White House. At some point, all parties decided they could not stand the political heat if they appeared to be the ones to kill tax "reform." Even though the element of "reform" was modest, "fairness" was not self-evident (as it never can be in any tax scheme, no matter its nature), and "simplicity" vanished along the way, the players were, at some point, caught in a momentum that made the likelihood of a final compromise very high.

In terms of popular support, the strategy was to focus on relief for the "middle class," an elastic concept. One analysis of the class basis drive for a bill (Kettl 1988, 78) summarizes the situation succinctly:

> ...tax reform was to benefit principally the *middle class*. The underlying populist motivation for tax reform was the perceived injustice of the tax system: the poor had little income on which to pay taxes, the rich had tax shelters, corporations were paying less and less tax, and the middle class was stuck with the bill. Though the definition of the middle class was imprecise, the underlying political energy behind tax reform was to give a break to middle-class taxpayers.

During the negotiations and debates that produced the final bill, the definition of middle class kept changing. The decision makers were able to be particularly flexible in their definition of middle class on any particular day because such a high proportion of Americans think of themselves as middle class. Ironically, the final product did not produce much tax relief for the middle class, no matter how that term is defined. In addition, it seems that President Bush's adamant pledge of "no new taxes" in the 1988 campaign and during his first year in office is a tacit recognition that new taxes would almost surely hit the "middle class" hardest. If the tax code had, indeed, been permanently reformed in favor of the middle class, then new taxes would presumably fall more heavily on wealthier individual taxpayers and on corporations. But such was not the case.

Inevitably, tax policy shapes economic behavior in society. Sometimes those who make the policy predict correctly what behavior will be generated by different provisions. Other times, they mispredict badly. The tax code not only sets rates but also creates categories of income, expenditures, and investments for special treatment. Some people call these various provisions "loopholes." A more neutral term is "tax expenditures"—that is, the tax code forgoes the collection of certain revenues, which can be viewed as expenditures. The debate over the 1986 Tax Act had complicated outcomes. The redistributive impact, although mild, was preserved because some of the poorest citizens were removed from being liable for income tax. Beyond that stratum of society, however, the results were more uneven and specific (Kettl 1988, 91):

> There were losers in the tax reform battle, especially individuals and corporations who had taken advantage of tax shelters to avoid—quite legally—their fair share of taxes. Industries such as real estate, steel, and banking saw themselves as big losers. Yet there were also winners. Some industries—including oil, electronics, publishing, and retailing—either kept their threatened tax breaks or improved their position because of the lower tax rates. Middle-class taxpayers, especially homeowners, also benefit. The 1986 tax bill did not end tax expenditures; rather, it redistributed the costs and benefits contained in the tax code.

A few years after this modestly redistributive tax act became law, organized interests that yearned for the good old days of numerous special tax breaks were becoming increasingly active in seeking to nibble at the changes that had been made. The most powerful effort was made to restore special tax treatment of capital gains—

taxing those gains at a lower rate than regular income. Virtually all of the tax benefit of such a provision would go to the most wealthy individuals in the country (99% of the benefits would go to the top 1% of the population in terms of their economic standing). This initiative came close to succeeding in 1989 because it became a major priority of President George Bush. In elaborate negotiations over a final budget compromise in the autumn of 1989, Bush agreed not to push for inclusion of this provision until 1990. But he made it clear that it remained a top priority for him. He had considerable congressional support. Even what remained of redistribution in the 1986 act was in danger from this effort. If it succeeds, others may follow.

Redistributive Issues Redefined as Distributive

The redefinition of a redistributive issue as distributive is sometimes the price for allowing any redistribution at all to emerge. The redefinition can take place in several ways. Arguments can shift to focus on distributive aspects of the policy being considered rather than on clearly redistributive aspects. The policy itself may become more distributive and abandon many or all of its redistributive purposes. In most cases, a mix of rhetorical change and real change occurs. Such changes continually reveal the relative ease policy makers have in dealing with distributive issues and the relative difficulty they have in facing redistributive issues head-on.

In some of the cases already discussed, the pressure to mute redistribution with more distribution was evident. The retention of community action programs and the retention of legal services for the poor were both bought at the cost of severely limiting their redistributive potential through large budget cuts, in the case of community action programs, and strict limitations on the services that could be provided, in the case of legal services. In the case of medicare, success was achieved in part because subsidies went to hospitals and doctors. Some procedural changes were added to mute the redistributive potential of the 1964 Civil Rights Act.

Redefinition of redistributive issues into a more distributive mode can occur during the initial formulation of a policy. It can also occur over time both during implementation (with which we do not deal in this book) and as policy is reformulated by subsequent legislative amendments and reauthorizations. The following examples deal both with initial authorization and with amendment and reauthorization.

Model cities The history of the model cities program runs from its germination in a presidentially appointed Task Force on Urban Problems in 1965, its initial statutory authorization in 1966 until its replacement by a special revenue-sharing program in 1974, and its organizational termination in 1975. That history is characterized by a short initial period of redistributive rhetoric about helping poor people, followed by the reality of a distributive program. The primary orientation of the program became simply distributing federal dollars to cities. Revisions in the program over time also increased the autonomy given to city governments as they made spending decisions for model cities money. Improving relations between the federal government and the cities became another goal of the program (Ripley 1972, Chapter 5).

Congressional attitudes and reactions in the early days of the program set these changes in motion. Through informal contacts with high-ranking officials in the Model Cities Administration, the Department of Housing and Urban Development, and the White House, and through formal legislative actions on authorization and appropriations bills, members of the House and Senate helped alter the nature of the program from centrally redistributive to centrally distributive, despite the clearly redistributive thrust initially preferred by President Johnson and the liberal Democratic supporters of the program in Congress.

The original supporters of the model cities proposal saw the program as one that would deliberately manipulate social conditions in favor of the poorest residents of city slums. Supporters sold the program in two different ways, however, in putting together a winning coalition in Congress. When they sought to convince liberals, they advocated the program on the grounds of its redistributive effects. When they approached moderates and conservatives, they portrayed the proposal as focused on subsidies for city governments.

Achieving congressional passage of the Johnson administration's redistributive vision was difficult from the outset. Significant opposition to the proposal developed in Congress, especially among Republicans, including those sitting on the committees that had jurisdiction over the initial bill authorizing the program. Compromise was necessary to produce winning coalitions for the bill in 1966. These compromises reduced the redistributive nature of the program that was authorized. For example, provisions requiring model cities to have racial integration as a goal were dropped as a requirement for funding. Subsidy to city governments and autonomy for those governments were stressed by changes to the original proposal that increased the number of eligible cities, dropped the requirement that a city must establish a separate administrative agency in order to receive funding, and eliminated a federal coordinator who was to be stationed in each funded model city.

Because of these early congressional statutory decisions and also because of continuing informal pressure from Congress, the stress during administration of the program quickly focused on process rather than on outcomes. The administrations themselves came to prefer these goals. The increasingly distributive nature of the program became apparent late in the Johnson administration, although some redistributive aspects remained.

Early in the Nixon administration (1969 and 1970) the dominant themes of the program moved almost exlusively to those of underscoring autonomy in local governments and creating a distributive rather than a redistributive image for the program. Congress and the administration joined in stressing federal responsiveness to the priorities of local governments; mayoral authority; deemphasis of citizen participation in the program; the inclusion of entire cities instead of only the poorest neighborhoods; reducing expenditures; less rhetoric about societal results; and administrative consistency.

From 1971 until the end of the program, virtually all vestiges of redistribution disappeared. HUD officials announced their desire to give city governments virtually complete control of the federal resources under the program. Federal oversight was reduced to auditing rather than focusing on programmatic achievements. President

Nixon began his drive in 1971 to eliminate the program altogether by folding it into a broader special revenue-sharing program that would encompass a number of community development and housing programs. Liberals in Congress prevented this change for several years, but in 1974 Congress acquiesced by passing the Housing and Community Development Act, which spelled the end of model cities as a separate effort.

Employment and training Between 1966 and 1975, Congress and the president generated five major special revenue-sharing programs that sent federal funds to states and localities for use in prescribed substantive areas but with fewer strings and restrictions than existed in previously existing "categorical" grant programs. One of the five programs—the Comprehensive Employment and Training Act of 1973 (CETA)—focused on employment and training for the hard to employ.

In general, CETA and the other four special revenue-sharing programs (the Partnership for Health Act of 1966; the Omnibus Crime and Safe Streets Act of 1968; the Housing and Community Development Act of 1974; and Title XX [social services] of the Social Security Act of 1975) replaced categorical programs that had considerable redistributive potential. The special revenue-sharing programs, including CETA specifically, emphasized distribution. The immediate "clients" of special revenue-sharing programs are governmental units—states, cities, and counties—rather than a class of persons, such as the economically disadvantaged. The choices about who gets what at the expense of whom—the essential question in any redistributive program—are obscured by the use of a formula to allocate funds and by the stress on local control.

In the case of CETA, neither most local governments with responsibility for the program nor the federal bureaucrats in the U.S. Department of Labor—who had relatively weak and loose oversight over the program—addressed redistributive questions directly. They acted in accord with the intentions of Congress and President Nixon when they created the program. Most local and federal bureaucrats were inexperienced in dealing with redistribution, and few were interested in it anyway. CETA, like the other special revenue-sharing programs, was defined essentially as a distributive program in practice. The focus of most bureaucrats at all levels, most interest groups, and members of Congress who were interested, was on questions of jurisdiction and dollar allocations to geographically defined units rather than on who benefits to what effect in terms of individuals grouped in socioeconomic categories. Redistribution sank even further from view when CETA was replaced in 1982 by the Job Training Partnership Act (JTPA).

The initial replacement of categorical employment and training programs (which themselves had proliferated after the first major effort in the Manpower Development and Training Act of 1962) with a special revenue-sharing program involved a lengthy battle (Davidson 1972, 1975). It took five years for the Nixon administration to obtain a comprehensive manpower bill (note that "manpower" was the term used until it was replaced by "employment and training" in the mid-1970s). The package that emerged in 1973 contained only part of the preferences of the Nixon administration and only part of the preferences of the congressional supporters of preexisting categorical manpower programs. The five-year debate over authorizing what became CETA focused on three major aspects of the Nixon proposal: decategorization, decentralization, and public service employment.

The categorical programs represented a piecemeal approach to redistributive employment and training policy. Although those programs were established in part because of their redistributive potential (a focus on training unemployed and disadvantaged workers to improve their job skills and, ultimately, their economic well-being), in practice they emphasized distribution. Numerous subgovernments sprang up around each categorical grant program. These subgovernments fought hard to resist revenue sharing, fearing it would mean the end of the privileged access to resources they each had because of the welter of categorical programs. The proposals debated from 1969 to 1973 gave discretion to local governmental units to decide which categorical programs might be continued. None of them, with the final exception of the Job Corps, had a guaranteed future.

Decentralization was also an issue. States, cities, and counties (at least those with large populations) competed to become the chief administrative unit in any special revenue-sharing effort in employment and training. Cities were especially fearful that they and their problems would be slighted if responsibility were given to the states, which historically had not been sensitive to urban problems. Populous counties were most concerned with suburban areas and their problems, which are also quite different from those of central cities.

Debate about how to consolidate and reorganize employment and training programs was complicated further by the inclusion of the public employment issue—the historically divisive, ideologically based question of the proper role of the federal government in creating subsidized jobs for the unemployed. Liberals traditionally favored a strong federal role, and conservatives opposed it. President Nixon strongly resisted the inclusion of a public employment title in a comprehensive manpower bill. Ultimately, he lost on this issue.

The final compromise that passed in 1973 combined the competing points of view in a way that did not fully satisfy anyone but allowed a majority that could pass a bill to emerge. The administration got its basic mandate for decentralization and decategorization along with a much-diminished federal administrative role in making final program choices, which was delegated primarily to the local level. Liberals retained a few categorical programs, most notably the Jobs Corps, and also got some categorical references in the statute that would presumably nudge local governments to continue the programs. The liberals also got a sizable permanent public service program included in the statute, a program vastly increased in late 1974 by the addition of another title to CETA in response to a severe national economic recession.

As enacted in 1973, the central features of CETA were

1. Basic responsibility for deciding how to spend money for employment and training purposes was given to "prime sponsors," which were, with only a few exceptions, cities or counties with more than 100,000 people, consortia of cities and counties, and states.

2. The great bulk of manpower money was allocated to the prime sponsorships by formulas based on various weightings for unemployment, number of low-income people, and previous federal manpower spending.

3. Several forms of advisory council were mandated by the statute and the regulations issued by the Department of Labor. Most important were the planning councils that were required in each prime sponsorship.

4. The regional offices of the Department of Labor retained a variety of supervisory duties and responsibilities, although in general they were primarily to offer "technical assistance" to prime sponsors.

5. In pre-CETA manpower operations, the standard model of service delivery to individual clients was for the regional or national office of the Manpower Administration of the Department of Labor to contract directly with deliverers. Under CETA the prime sponsors wrote and monitored the performance of those contracts.

The experience under CETA underscores the generalizations made earlier about revenue-sharing programs in general (see Franklin and Ripley 1984 for a detailed analysis). A focus on redistribution faded. In the aggregate, localities were happier politically serving the relatively more well-off parts of the eligible population: the near-poor rather than the poorest. Many were also happier politically not focusing on racial minorities with special needs. Community action agencies—likely to be the most redistributively oriented of local institutions that might deliver services— lost their role as service deliverers in a number of prime sponsorships. "Work experience" for youth—including large numbers of black youths—was given greater stress under CETA than in pre-CETA days. This shift represented a relatively cheap way of "serving" large numbers of clients who were both black and among the most disadvantaged part of the eligible population. Elected officials in prime sponsorships could use their work experience programs as protective coloration against charges from politically hostile groups that the program was shortchanging such clients. In some jurisdictions the advisory councils were relatively effective in representing officials, service deliverers, or high-status individuals. The advisory councils were not, however, constructed to provide access to decision making for actual or potential clients.

When Congress reauthorized CETA in 1978, it attempted to insert a bit more redistributive potential into the program by tightening some eligibility requirements. But Congress spent much more effort on considering the public service employment program in terms of both size and how to prevent abuses. Considerations of size were distributive: how much subsidy should CETA generate for local units of government?

In 1982, when Congress replaced CETA with JTPA, it again mixed elements of distribution and redistribution. The new prescriptions for funneling program money through states and to and through local businesses were distributive elements that made the new program salable, ultimately, to a conservative Congress and a very conservative president. JTPA was also nominally redistributive in that 90 percent of the individuals trained had to come from economically disadvantaged groups, with definitions adopted from the 1978 CETA revisions. The redistributive emphasis was muted because allowances to trainees during the period of training were, for the most part, prohibited. This prohibition made it unclear whether genuinely disadvantaged individuals could afford to enter JTPA-supported training unless they were receiving welfare.

The issues of the relative strength of the claims of a distributive focus and a redistributive focus surfaced with regard to JTPA in 1989 early in the Bush administration.

The secretary of labor, Elizabeth Dole, proposed legislative changes that would force JTPA to focus more of its resources on the neediest part of the eligible population. These proposals were in accord with a number of fruitless Democratic initiatives during the Reagan administration after it became clear that the focus of JTPA was more diffuse. Others at both the national and local levels indicated that they thought JTPA should not be changed. Once again the individuals making policy began to debate issues almost three decades old.

Aid to education   The history of federal aid to education in the United States since World War II is complex and tangled (Bendiner 1964; Eidenberg and Morey 1969; Munger and Fenno 1962; Sundquist 1968, Chapter 5). The federal government began to give increasing amounts of special-purpose aid to both elementary and secondary education and to higher education during the early part of the period. But a logjam developed on the question of broad general aid—especially to elementary and secondary schools. That logjam was broken only by changing the nature of general-purpose aid. Educational aid measures that were perceived as providing benefits to many special segments of the population or to specially defined geographic areas—measures essentially distributive in character—were much easier to enact than broad general-purpose aid measures that were perceived as shifting benefits from one racial or religious group to another racial or religious group.

The final breakthrough that allowed a form of general-purpose aid in 1965 was possible only because of two simultaneous developments: the redistributive focus was shifted away from race and religion to poverty; and distributive features were emphasized.

Throughout all of the debates, members of the House and Senate and a few individuals in the hierarchy of both the Department of Health, Education and Welfare (HEW) and the White House were important in framing initiatives, attempting compromises, and—usually—shifting the grounds of debate until the most threatening aspects of redistribution were removed. These individuals were usually senior members of the relevant Senate and House subcommittees and individuals in HEW at the level of assistant secretary or above. Agreement at this level was never simply ratified by others in the process, however. Many were involved, and the issues were often contentious. Inevitably, major interest groups such as the National Education Association, civil rights organizations, and both Catholic and Protestant organizations also got involved. The highest echelons of the executive branch—usually including the president personally—also participated.

All of this visibility and political volatility made most members of the House and Senate feel that they had a personal stake in outcomes, even though their own committee assignments might be quite remote from education. But congressional decision making tended to get moved from quiet committee settings onto the floors of the two chambers, where everyone could get involved. The perception that these policies were redistributive helped lead to intense philosophical and partisan dispute. That perception also increased both the number and formal rank of important participants in decision making. Members of relevant committees in Congress and bureaucrats in HEW and the Office of Education even up to the level of assistant secretary and commissioner of education were only moderately important rather than dominant in influencing final decisions.

Federal aid to education provided between 1940 and 1965 was distributive, a fact that explains the relative ease with which these various aid programs were established. Table 6–1 summarizes the most important programs created during this period. In all cases except the 1965 Elementary and Secondary Education Act, the statutes provided subsidies for students or institutions such as colleges or school districts in a nonredistributive way.

Proposals for general federal aid to local school districts failed throughout the same period because of hostility to federal "control" of a traditionally local function, because of the perception after 1954 that federal aid would be used as a lever to force racial integration in public schools, and because of the issue of whether private schools, especially those run by the Roman Catholic Church, would or would not receive benefits. Various combinations of these issues—with the racial question being the most explicitly redistributive in nature—repeatedly led Congress to kill various proposed general aid programs. Presidents were unable or unwilling to find a way around this impasse. Two careful students of the politics of this issue summarize the history of failure to achieve a winning compromise (Eidenberg and Morey 1969, 23–24):

> In searching for school aid stumbling blocks, one is quickly led to the House of Representatives. Starting in 1948 the Senate passed each bill that reached the floor—1948, 1949, 1960, and 1961. On the other hand, in the House three bills were killed on the floor (1956, 1957, and 1961) and another (1960) was passed but subsequently held in the Rules Committee on the way to conference.
>
> From 1943 to 1955 the prime obstacle in the House was the Education and Labor Committee. During this period, hearings were held on seven bills, but not one was reported. In 1955 the opposition bloc finally crumbled when 15 non-Southern Democrats aligned with 7 Republicans to approve a bill for the first time in recent history. By 1959 federal aid supporters had a solid majority on the committee. . . .
>
> As the complexion of the Education and Labor Committee changed in the mid-1950s, the antifederal aid bloc in the Rules Committee was solidified. This committee was the principal obstacle to school aid bills in 1955, 1959, 1960, and 1961 through 1964.

The breaking of the logjam in 1965 came for several reasons. One was that liberal Democrats made sweeping gains in the House of Representatives in the 1964 election at the same time that President Lyndon Johnson was winning a landslide victory. Even more important, the effort to achieve general-purpose aid was set aside in favor of a special-purpose approach. As Sundquist (1968, 206) described the situation, both proponents and opponents of general purpose aid finally decided that some aid was better than none:

> The sudden turnabout reflects, perhaps most of all, a simple fact: people *do* learn from experience. First, both sides of the religious controversy had learned. The NEA and its public school allies now knew that an all-or-nothing attitude would mean, for the public schools, nothing. Likewise, Catholic leaders now understood that an equal-treatment-or-nothing position would mean, for the Catholic schools, nothing.

TABLE 6–1

Federal Aid to Education, 1940–1965

Program	Benefits	Recipients
Higher education		
1944 G.I. Bill of Rights	Living expenses, books, tuition	World War II veterans (later Korean, Cold War, and Vietnam veterans)
1950 National Science Foundation	Support for science research and education	Colleges, universities
1950 Housing Act of 1950	Low-interest loans for dormitory construction	Colleges, universities
1958 National Defense Education Act	Loans; training in science, math, languages; equipment purchases	Students, teachers, colleges, universities
1963 Classroom construction	Grants for classroom construction	Public and private colleges
1965 Higher Education Act	Scholarships, library support, construction grants	Colleges, universities
Elementary and secondary education		
1940 Lanham Act	Financial aid	School districts impacted by war-related personnel dislocation
1946 National School Lunch Act	Aid for providing school lunches	School districts
1950 Impacted areas aid	Financial aid	School districts impacted with federal personnel
1954 Agricultural Act	Aid for providing school milk	School districts
1958 National Defense Education act	Matching grants for equipment and classrooms; aid for foreign-language training institutes, testing, guidance, counseling	States
1965 Elementary and Secondary Education Act	Aid for equipment, classrooms, staff, construction; aid for library resources; matching aid for supplemental education centers; aid for education research; aid for state departments of education	School districts with concentrations of poor and unemployed persons; state departments of education; local education agencies; colleges, universities, states

SOURCE: Adapted from E. Eidenberg and R. D. Morey, *An Act of Congress* (New York: W. W. Norton, 1969), 16–18, 247–248.

For each side the question was whether it preferred to maintain the purity of its ideological position or receive some tangible benefits for its schools. The Washington representatives of organizations on both sides were, with a few exceptions, cautiously on the side of accommodation. . . . Accommodation was supported by public opinion polls, which showed that a majority of Americans no longer opposed aid to parochial schools. Second, the tacticians had learned. The National Defense Education Act had shown that special-purpose aid, carefully designed, could be enacted at a time when general-purpose aid could not be.

In our terms, the passage of the 1965 act came because the proponents of a redistributive school aid policy packaged their program in a way that emphasized distributive features and combined a number of those distributive ("special purpose") features in one bill. The new special purpose was "the education of children of needy families and children living in areas of substantial unemployment." As Sundquist observed (1968, 210), "Congress had, after all, acknowledged a federal responsibility for assistance to families on welfare and for aid to depressed areas. Assistance to school districts 'impacted' by federal activities was also long-established; would not it be as logical to assist 'poverty-impacted' districts?"

A change in the general political climate was also important in establishing the partially redistributive emphasis on disadvantaged children in the 1965 aid to education bill. The changed climate included the rediscovery of poverty by the federal government a few years earlier, a commitment by the liberal portion of the Democratic party to attack poverty in a number of ways, and the dominance of the national government by an aggressive liberal Democratic president and large, liberal Democratic majorities in the House and Senate.

Housing policy, 1987   Federal housing programs have long been in the middle of partisan dispute. Ever since the federal government began debating a role for itself in housing—a role first created by a major piece of legislation in 1937—liberal and moderate Democrats on the one hand and conservative Republicans on the other have agreed on little.

In 1980 the Democratic president Jimmy Carter and the Democratically controlled Congress agreed on a housing authorization bill. However, as soon as Ronald Reagan became president and a conservative Republican majority took control of the Senate, partisan warfare once again became intense. Initiatives coming from the liberal Democrats in the House went nowhere.

In 1987, with the Senate newly restored to Democratic control, a greater chance of passing a housing bill was again created, although it was clear that Congress would still have to deal with the possibility of a Reagan veto if it went too far beyond the conservative predilections of the administration.

Both houses passed legislation fairly early in the year by healthy margins (71 to 27 in the Senate and 285 to 120 in the House). The conference committee produced a generally moderate bill, with some redistributive aspects, in the autumn. It passed the House by a vote of 391 to 1 in early November. However, the bill was still too liberal and redistributive for the taste of the Reagan administration. The Senate, considerably more conservative in composition than the House in 1987, defeated the conference report on several procedural votes, and it appeared as if Congress would once again fail to produce a housing authorization bill in 1987.

However, intense year-end negotiation and compromise—which moved the bill much more toward providing distributive benefits—proved to be sufficient to obtain a presidential pledge to sign the final bill, which Reagan did in early 1988 after both houses passed a final conference report. The core group that produced the winning compromise included four senators (the Democratic chairman of the Housing and Urban Affairs Subcommittee of the Senate Banking, Housing, and Urban Affairs Committee; the two ranking Republicans on that subcommittee—who were simultaneously the two ranking Republicans on the subcommittee of the Senate Appropriations Committee responsible for the budget of the Department of Housing and Urban Development—and the third-ranking Republican on the appropriations subcommittee on HUD) and staff members responsible to them. This group produced a little something for everyone.

Central to approval by all concerned was the provision that the Federal Housing Administration (FHA) would be extended permanently. FHA mortgage guarantees represent a very large subsidy to middle-class homeowners. A few new programs to benefit the poorer classes also survived, although in more constricted form than originally envisioned by liberals and with shorter life spans. In addition, some existing redistributive programs were also given new, shorter life spans. The most redistributive programs were a program of interest-free loans in targeted (poor) areas, benefits for households displaced by community development projects that had received federal aid, and an increased regulatory effort to remove lead-based paint from federally aided older housing. The Reaganites also got additional emphasis on vouchers, the administration's preferred method for dealing with housing, among other areas.

Conclusions

The generalizations made at the beginning of this chapter (and also summarized in Table 4–1) about the redistributive arena, including the specific characterization of bureaucratic–congressional relations, appear to be broadly accurate. We can, however, add a few important points to that picture.

First, initiative for redistributive policy can come from within Congress and, occasionally, from the higher levels of the career bureaucracy. But more often the initiative for such policy comes from the White House. Active presidential participation is always helpful and usually essential for those wanting to create redistributive policy.

To the extent that the president is either opposed to the proposed redistribution or active only verbally, sporadically, unenthusiastically, or ineffectively, the chances increase that either nothing will happen and a long-standing stalemate will persist or that the issue will be redefined, at least in part, as distributive. Congress often instinctively seeks compromise through the latter redefining process. Lack of presidential initiative or, even more dramatically, presidential initiatives opposed to redistribution to the less well-off, almost foreordain that even mild redistribution will not be ratified legislatively. In some cases, past redistributive decisions may be severely altered or repealed.

Second, Congress often has an important role in generating redistributive policy at those critical moments in the development of a long-running debate over a redistributive proposal when the political situation seems to have produced an unbreakable stalemate. Important congressional figures, often working with technical experts from the bureaucracy, can engage in relatively quiet bargaining and negotiation that are essential to breaking the stalemate. These negotiations usually limit the redistributive potential of the original proposal, but they do not eliminate potential redistributive impact altogether.

Third, in general, the successful creation of at least partially redistributive policy is often achieved by diluting its redistributive impact with some visible distributive features. Programs that are purely redistributive are almost impossible to enact. Program proposals that have a mix of redistributive and distributive elements broaden the base of support by camouflaging in part and reducing in part the most controversial redistributive features. The pressures to redefine controversial redistributive programs as more distributive continue after the original creation of a program. Both during implementation and in subsequent legislative consideration of the program, "natural" pressures push toward broadening the number or type of beneficiaries

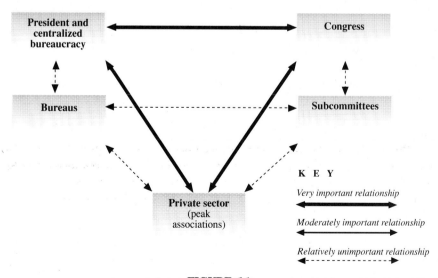

FIGURE 6-1

Relative importance of relationships for determining redistributive policy beyond the most disadvantaged. These pressures mean that the actual cumulative impact of redistributive federal policies is mild. That impact is constrained by the bargains necessary to have any redistribution at all.

Figure 6–1 summarizes the most important relationships between executive, legislative, and private sector actors in formulating and legitimating redistributive policy.

CHAPTER SEVEN

Foreign and Defense Policy

The Nature of Foreign and Defense Policy

Congress has the potential to be heavily involved in many aspects of foreign and defense policy. It actively used this power during the 1970s and 1980s. The major changes throughout the world, especially in the Soviet Union and Warsaw Pact nations of Eastern Europe occurring in the late 1980s and into the 1990s, guarantee that Congress will have the chance to address a great variety of vital issues in this realm in the 1990s. It will surely continue to play an active part in making important decisions for the nation. The relatively quiescent stance of Congress on foreign and defense policy in the late 1950s and early 1960s was deceptively atypical. Congressional activism is the normal state of affairs. (On the changing role of Congress in foreign and defense policies in general see Carroll 1966; Destler 1980, 1985; Franck and Weisband 1979; Frye 1975; Kolodziej 1966, 1975; Lanoutte 1978; Manley 1971; Moe and Teel 1970; and Pastor 1980.)

Unfortunately, most of the literature on the involvement of Congress in foreign and defense policy—and on the relationship between Congress, the president, the military bureaucracy, the civilian bureaucracy, and interest groups—treats foreign and defense policy as a single undifferentiated area. We argue, however, that three kinds of foreign and defense policy are distinguishable by the kinds of politics surrounding each. Tables 1–3 and 4–1 and the discussion of those tables summarize our view of the nature of these three policy areas.

The characteristics of *structural policy* are virtually the same as those of domestic distributive policy. Subgovernments composed of participants from bureaus, subcommittees, and small units in the private sector (influential individuals, corporations, a variety of interest groups that includes some relatively small ones) dominate policy making on the basis of mutual noninterference and logrolling. The relationship among the actors in these subgovernments is stable. Their decisions are implemented in a decentralized fashion, usually at the bureau level.

In *strategic* policy the pattern is somewhat similar to domestic protective regulatory policy. The major difference is that interest groups and especially bureaus and subcommittees have a smaller role in strategic policy than they do in protective regulatory policy. The major decisions are made in those upper reaches of the executive branch, particularly the office of the president, which deal with the whole Congress.

151

In *crisis policy* the basic decision-making structure is very simple: it is the president and whomever he chooses to consult. Usually he will consult only a few of his top advisors. Sometimes he will bring in leading individual members of Congress. Occasionally he will consult leaders of very large ("peak association") interest groups. In these consultations the issues are defined quickly, discussed in private, and decided swiftly. Presidential action and presidential decision are dominant in these cases. Once announced, the presidential decisions about how to react to crises may provide considerable broader public debate.

As in the case of domestic policies, the different types of foreign and defense policies are interwoven in two senses. First, some specific policies do not fall neatly into one category. Any specific policy may incorporate aspects of both strategic and structural policy. Or the relative emphasis of a specific policy may vary between different weights accorded to strategic ends and structural ends over time. What may begin as a crisis may last long enough to move into the realm of strategic policy.

Second, decisions in one area have implications for decisions in one or both of the other areas. Decisions made in a crisis help determine the options identified and the final choices in later strategic decision making. Decisions made on strategic matters help limit some of the options with regard to subsequent structural decisions. For example, the perceived need for certain kinds of weapons geared to put pressure on the Soviet Union or to be ready for specific kinds of "brushfire" (strategic) operations will help determine the kinds of requirements and specifications that go into later procurement (structural) decisions. The influence can also run from prior structural decisions that push certain kinds of strategic options forward and eliminate others. For example, a decision to help get rid of American agricultural surpluses makes decision makers create programs such as Public Law 480 ("Food for Peace," discussed later) or expanded grain sales to the Soviet Union. These latter programs have important strategic implications for general foreign relations between the United States and other nations.

The Congressional–Bureaucratic Relationship in Foreign and Defense Policy

The relationship between members of the executive branch at the bureau level and individuals in Congress at the subcommittee level vary depending on the kind of foreign and defense policy. In the case of structural policy, we expect that the subgovernment relationship will be the most important source of decisions. We further expect that those decisions will not be altered in subsequent stages of the formal legislative process. The subgovernments will deal definitively with many aspects of the issues within their jurisdiction. There is a high degree of cooperation between bureaucrats and legislators because each is motivated to serve clients. If there are differences of opinion, they will generally be resolved by the members of the subgovernment without involving a large number of other participants. Subgovernment members have a high degree of motivation to reach some form of compromise among their various initial positions on issues in order to help prevent "outsiders" such as the secretary of defense or the president or a congressional party leader from intervening. The compromises they reach are likely to contain more subcommittee preferences than bureaucratic preferences, although the interests of neither—nor of their clients—will be badly treated.

In strategic policy, we expect the the importance of the subgovernment relationship to be only modest. Only a few narrow aspects of an issue will be dealt with definitively through bureau–subcommittee interactions. Rarely are final decisions made at this relatively invisible institutional level. Most decisions will instead be made in the higher reaches of the executive branch, where strategic policy usually originates. Conflict based on ideological differences between congressional and executive branch actors may occur. Such conflict is not usually resolved at the level of a subgovernment but is passed along to a higher level for final decisions. At that higher level, conflict is resolved by a broad compromise or it may remain unresolved. Executive branch views typically dominate final decisions. Congress may, in some instances, push for redefinition of issues as structural rather than strategic because the former is an area in which members of Congress feel most comfortable and also in which they have a better chance of prevailing if there is disagreement with the executive branch.

In the case of crisis policy, we expect that the subcommittee–bureau level of interaction will not be a factor in the decision-making process. Decisions about responses to crises are made within the confines of the presidency, with the participation of those few individuals the president chooses to include. There is little chance for either cooperation or conflict, except in the confines of the small group summoned by the president. Conflict between the president and Congress may develop after an event and the reaction to it, of course. Formal statements after the event and decision usually take the form of either congressional resolutions disagreeing with or supporting presidential action, or executive orders that either formalize a course already being followed or impose a solution despite congressional dissent. Genuine compromise on controversial actions is generally not reached, largely because it is irrelevant to decisions that have already been made and actions that have already been taken. Sometimes sham compromise is effected in the name of "national unity." Some differences of opinion are, in effect, eliminated through an imposed solution—either a congressional action with teeth or an executive order. Generally, the presidential view of issues left in controversy prevails.

Structural Policy

The Defense Budget

Many aspects of the defense budget, especially those related to ongoing procurement decisions, provide good examples of structural policy. The defense budget also has a strategic component as it helps determine the total structure of U.S. forces and specific decisions about whether to acquire new weapons systems and at what pace. To some extent, procurement decisions are driven by strategic decisions—and, in theory, that should be the dominant relationship. In practice, however, many strategic decisions are in effect foreordained by a series of structural decisions. As we would expect with structural decisions, Congress is heavily involved in virtually all aspects of defense budget decisions (Lindsay 1987, 1988).

Since the onset of massive federal deficits in the early 1980s and the continuing political salience of those deficits, broad treaties have been hammered out between the executive branch and Congress each year putting some general caps on defense spending (and also domestic spending). Both strategic decisions and structural decisions have had to come within the general caps, and thus the large growth in defense budgets that characterized the early 1980s gave way to stability and even shrinkage when budgets are measured in constant dollars (Adams and Cain 1989; Korb and Daggett 1988). Figure 7–1 summarizes annual changes (adjusted for inflation) in

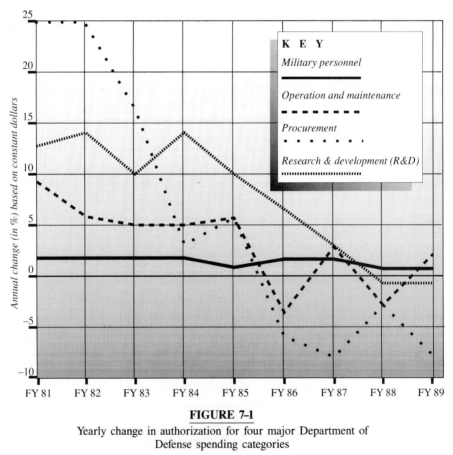

FIGURE 7–1

Yearly change in authorization for four major Department of
Defense spending categories

SOURCE: Adapted from Congressional Budget Office data in *New York Times,* April 3, 1988.

spending authorization in the four major categories into which the defense budget is broken: military personnel, operation and maintenance, procurement, and research and development. The growth in military personnel (essentially salaries) has always been slow but declined near the end of the decade. Growth in operation and maintenance declined steadily and even shrank during some years. The most dramatic change took place in procurement, beginning the decade with two massive annual increases of 25 percent and ending the decade with four straight years of decline. Research and development began with sizable increases that were the last to suffer, but by the last two years of the decade this budget also declined a small amount each year.

Defense budgets are still huge. Department of Defense authorizations for the ten years from Fiscal Year 1981 through Fiscal Year 1990, for example, averaged $292 billion annually in constant 1989 dollars (*Congressional Quarterly Weekly Report,* November 11, 1989, 3089, for 1990; Korb and Daggett 1988, 45, for 1981–1989). They reached their peak in Fiscal Year 1985 ($326 billion) and declined gradually thereafter to about the average for the decade. But patterns of relative growth and shrinkage put different pressures on the interaction between strategic considerations and structural considerations in the defense budget. In years of great growth, the strain is relatively light. The strategists can get new weapons systems, and those who look on defense spending in a more structural (that is, pork barrel) light can also engineer many public works and defense contracts for favored congressional districts and companies. But when budget growth is slight or even negative, the competing claims of strategic considerations and structural considerations meet head-on. More often than not, structural interests prevail.

Procurement subgovernments Very close links exist between Pentagon procurement officials, private sector contractors, and members of the House and Senate whose states and districts benefit from defense contracting. The links were so close that many of them between contractors and the Pentagon became illegal. Major government prosecutions in the late 1980s resulted in a number of convictions of contractors. President Bush's new secretary of defense, Richard Cheney, continued to seek changes in the procurement system that would prevent abuses in the future.

The close ties among those interested in defense procurement and the benefits they share for making decisions involving massive amounts of money create a great deal of momentum for an expanded arsenal. Contractors are approached by defense procurement officials, and they jointly work out the specifications to be met when specific weapons systems are planned. Members of Congress who are interested in a weapons system—usually because pieces of it are manufactured in their states or districts—are kept abreast of such discussions and negotiations. They are given the privilege of announcing awards of contracts in their states and districts. A recent study of "the Government relations practices of military contractors" reached the following general conclusion (Adams 1982, 207):

> Decisions on defense policy and weapons procurement rest almost entirely in the hands of insiders and policy experts, walled off from outsiders and alternative perspectives. The policy-makers, whose expertise is real and necessary, are also people and

organizations with interests to protect and promote: (1) defense contractors whose success is measured by weapon sales, (2) the defense department, with positions and a future to protect and, (3) members of Congress who share in making military policy and are prime targets of industry–Government relations."

In early 1985, Georgetown University's Center for Strategic and International Studies released a major report that severely criticized the Defense Department's procurement system. It pointed out that the individual services are allowed to develop weapons systems "independently, each according to its own sense of national priorities." The report also pointed out that individual contractors can "buy into" a weapons program by keeping the initial cost estimates low. Once they are in the program, the Pentagon and the affected senators and representatives happily fund cost overruns more accurately reflecting what the contractors should have bid in the first place, plus a healthy profit (*Washington Post*, February 26, 1985).

Presumably they were chastened by some of the convictions of contractors and some of the temporary bans on specific companies doing business with the Pentagon. Other evidence, however, suggests that "business as usual" was the dominant response of procurement subgovernments to the challenges to their autonomy. All of the participants in these subgovernments could be expected to profit in one or more senses: current earnings for companies, bureaucratic credit for Pentagon bureaucrats in the short run and plush postretirement jobs in private industry in the somewhat longer run, and political and electoral credit for members of the House and Senate for directing lucrative job-sustaining contracts to companies important to the economies of specific localities. Thus the subgovernments had large stakes in taming Secretary of Defense Richard Cheney's procurement reform proposals in 1989. By mid-November 1989, about eight months after Cheney had taken office, the score seemed to be procurement subgovernments (captained by the Pentagon bureaucracy) 1, Cheney 0. As the *Wall Street Journal* (November 17, 1989) reported:

> . . . Mr. Cheney is expected to announce a package of "reforms" in the next few weeks that effectively leaves intact the structure and authority of the entrenched Pentagon procurement bureaucracy.
>
> Instead of spearheading the "cultural changes" he promised, top civilian and military leaders at each of the armed services have managed to block Mr. Cheney from fundamentally revamping the $100 billion-a-year acquisition system. . . .

Also in 1989 the power of the subgovernments to continue procuring weapons deemed essentially useless (except for keeping the subgovernments purring) was again demonstrated. Even in a year in which the Gramm–Rudman–Hollings automatic budget-cutting mechanism took effect and in which there was continuing heartrending rhetoric about the need for budgetary responsibility, Congress insisted on continuing procurement of the V-22 Osprey aircraft for the Marine Corps and the F-14D fighter plane for the Navy. New concern with the budget produced little change in the politics of procurement. These expensive obsolete weapons were simply the current counterparts of earlier weapons throughout the 1970s and into the 1980s such as the Orion patrol plane for the U.S. Navy and the F-111 and A-7D aircraft. In reporting on the latest reprieve for the A-7D in 1981, the *Washington Post* (March 13) identified the core of the pro-A-7 coalition: the National Guard, which used the plane as a trainer; Vought, the company that produced it; and the congressional delegation from Texas, the site of the plant producing the plane. A similar coalition could be found behind any of the other flying anachronisms.

When two weapons systems are put into competition, rival subgovernments will sometimes spring up, at least temporarily. Typically, each of the competing weapons systems will have a Pentagon sponsor (usually with one service favoring one system and a different service favoring a competing system), favored contractors as allies, and members of the House and Senate linked with given contractors in or near their districts or states as additional allies. The Pentagon rivals will deliberately seek to mobilize the largest group of allies, even though such mobilization includes non-experts in decisions that have strategic impact (Armacost 1969).

When a weapons system has been decided on, there may still be competing contractors with their respective congressional supporters giving them at least ritualistic support. Once the basic decision is made about what kind of system is going to be developed, however, the Pentagon has a relatively free hand in making the final choice of contractors. Over time, these procurement decisions are made to build as large a constituency as possible, which means that lots of companies will get contracts (Smith 1973).

The decentralized nature of governmental procurement, especially within the Department of Defense (DOD), enhances the latitude of groups of interacting DOD officials, contractors, and senators and representatives. In the absence of a central clearinghouse, defense procurement subgovernments operate with a high degree of autonomy. The federal procurement structure in general (two-thirds of the expenditures of which are for defense) was described by a former head of the General Services Administration as a "garage sale" with no one in charge.

The procurement subgovernments aim to keep companies profitable and stable. If that goal is achieved, all of the members of the subgovernment benefit—companies, the military services, and members of Congress with large defense contractor payrolls. Only the general taxpayer foots the bill. A study released in 1985 showed that the ten largest defense contractors were about twice as profitable as American corporations in general (*New York Times*, April 9, 1985). The least profitable of these ten companies—Grumman—was given an extra infusion of support from the DOD in 1985 to help keep it healthy economically (*New York Times*, August 5, 1989). Two planes manufactured by Grumman for the Navy were no longer providing much work. The production of the A-6 had almost ceased, and the F-14 had experienced shrinking sales. New Navy contracts were then given to Grumman that provided more than $1 billion to upgrade both planes, even though defense experts questioned the wisdom of that decision from the standpoint of national defense. But, in fact, defense procurement addresses national defense concerns only in part. Procurement decisions also reflect concerns with jobs, local economic welfare, and campaign contributions to members of Congress.

Congressional priorities within the defense budget Congressional activity on the defense budget tends to concentrate on procurement and research and development items and to place much less emphasis on personnel and operations and maintenance categories. In the areas on which they concentrate, the input of congressional defense appropriations subcommittees is significant; it has also been more in accord with the views of the individual services than with any differing views of the secretary of defense. The congressional focus on these budget categories is enhanced by the deliberate appeals of Pentagon officials for allies, even though they have to grant those allies some impact on strategic decisions. Kanter (1972) suggested that Congress is deliberately used by the military services to provide critical support so that military preferences will dominate. Because of interservice rivalries, any one service is likely to suffer some temporary setbacks.

Members of Congress seek, with considerable success, to influence DOD decisions in geographically specific ways—both the location of weapons contractors and the location of bases and other DOD facilities. The payrolls of contractors and the DOD itself are important political assets to members of the House and Senate.

DOD congressional liaison structure   The congressional liaison structure of the DOD promotes the development and maintenance of independent subgovernments (Holtzman 1970, 137–141, 167–168; Pipe 1966). Each service has its own large liaison staff that works directly with relevant committees, subcommittees, and senators and representatives. Each of the individual service liaison staffs is much larger than the liaison staff of the Office of the Secretary of Defense. Holtzman (1970, 138) described the implications of this situation well:

> Each military department cooperated with the SOD [Secretary of Defense] in relation to the Congress when its interests coincided with his, but each attempted to play its own game when their interests conflicted. Control and coordination from the secretarial level were very difficult to impose, in large measure because key individuals in the Congress had long opposed such domination by the senior political executive within Defense. . . . [W]hen a military department was in rebellion against the policies of the SOD, that service's legislative liaison staff withdrew from the usual cooperative arrangements with the DOD liaison officer. Under such circumstances, the latter could not rely upon the service's liaison staff as a resource for intelligence or as an aid in working with the Congress.

DOD–OMB relations   The relations between the DOD and the Office of Management and Budget (OMB) facilitate the existence of strong subgovernments. The OMB has deliberately structured its relations with the DOD so the latter has a freer hand in its budgeting decisions than do the domestic agencies. The OMB budget examiners work directly with Pentagon and service budget officers (usually physically located in the Pentagon) to arrive at a recommendation for the president. The secretary of defense and the White House still exercise some control, but the vastness of the military establishment lends itself to the official recognition of fragmentation.

In the Reagan years, the already weak national security division in the OMB became even weaker as it lost more staff and permanent positions than any other part of the OMB. The pro-DOD stance of the Reagan administration reduced still further the already small efforts to control defense spending by the OMB. Said one inside source, "The administration is kind of ignoring this small division, reducing a source of advice for reform. If we were stronger, not all the problems would be solved. But now that there's no one around to say to the emperor that he has no clothes, I don't think things are going to get any better" (*Washington Post*, March 9, 1983).

Conference committee procedures   The practices of the House and Senate conferees on defense authorization and appropriations bills maximize congressional support for specific military policies that are highly valued by either the House or the Senate. Kanter (1972) analyzed 161 differences between House and Senate positions on DOD appropriations bills that were resolved by conference committees between Fiscal Year 1966 and Fiscal Year 1970. In examining the relative influence of the two houses, he found that only about 20 percent of the time did the conferees adopt a "split-the-difference" approach to resolve a disagreement. Rather, the usual approach was to give each house all of what it wanted on some issues, but none of what it wanted on other issues. In this way, each house got its way on what was most important to it. Each would "sacrifice" its position on less important matters. These norms of how to reach conference committee decisions allowed the highest priorities of the military services and their contractor allies the greatest chance of success. Mutual deference characterized this final decision making, a pattern also found in foreign aid decision making (Ripley 1965).

Reprogramming funds   The DOD has considerable leeway to reprogram appropriated funds within appropriation accounts during a fiscal year. It can transfer money and use it for purposes other than those for which it was originally appropriated (Fisher 1974). Reprogramming maximizes the ability of the military parts of defense subgovernments to make decisions that allow them to pursue their highest priorities despite competing priorities that might be articulated by the president, the secretary of defense, or Congress. The relevant committees have to be informed about most reprogrammings, but this keeps the flow of information to "insiders" and does not inform "outsiders." Typically, reprogrammings for procurement have to obtain prior approval from the Armed Services and Appropriations Committees in both houses. Reprogramming is not trivial: it involves at least several billion dollars annually.

Weapons Systems

Initial decisions about whether to proceed with new weapons sytems are usually made within the DOD at the service level. Congress must act on executive branch requests for new weapons. The broad decision about whether to proceed in the first place is in the realm of strategic policy, but once a weapons system has been approved for prototype research or pilot testing, subsequent decisions regarding its continuation, expansion, or alterations become a matter of structural policy.

The B-1 bomber   An article in the *New York Times* (October 17, 1988) nicely summarized the long-running political show occasioned by the bomber designated as the B-1:

Over the last 20 years, few weapons in the United States arsenal have been blown about by political crosswinds as often as the B-1 bomber. Even though it has been built and paid for, the aircraft continues to be the subject of partisan contention.

Inside the Beltway, that highway that sometimes seems to separate Washington from the rest of the world, the B-1 is essentially perceived as a "Republican bomber." It was originated by President Nixon, a Republican, killed by President Carter, a Democrat, and revived by President Reagan, a Republican who made it a campaign issue in 1980.

Controversy and politics engulfed the building and procurement of the plane. Controversy continued over whether the plane worked very well after it was built (see Kotz 1988; *Washington Post*, August 10, 1987).

The Air Force began lobbying in the 1960s for the development and production of the B-1 to succeed the B-52 as the mainstay of the manned bomber fleet of the United States. The path to arriving at a fleet of one-hundred finished bombers— although operational problems seemed severe even then—was long and arduous. The coalition that supported the Air Force throughout more than two decades always included the contractors and subcontractors who would make the plane, all of the Republican presidents during the period (Nixon, Ford, and Reagan), and—with a temporary exception in the late 1970s—a majority of the House of Representatives. Only in 1978—when President Carter became the focus of an anti–B-1 coalition—did the Air Force appear to lose. But the fortunes of the B-1 were quickly revived when Ronald Reagan made the B-1 the first main symbol of his drive to expand the military arsenal of the nation.

Three glimpses of this long-running political show follow. The first is from 1973 to 1974, when the supporters of the aircraft were in control and had the president on their side. The second glimpse is from 1977 to 1978, when President Carter intervened in this basically structural matter by stressing its strategic aspects and claiming that the president should have a major role in making any decision about the aircraft. The third glimpse summarizes the final push to production in the Reagan years.

1973–1974 In 1973 the Air Force requested an authorization of $473.5 million for the B-1 in order to continue funding the development of prototypes. The House Armed Services Committee recommended the entire amount, and an attempt on the floor to delete it was defeated easily by a vote of 96 to 313. The Senate Armed Services Committee recommended a reduction of $100 million, which was sustained on the Senate floor. However, an amendment adding $5 million to finance a study of alternatives to the B-1 was rejected. The Senate was willing to practice some economy, but not at the expense of jeopardizing the whole project. The conference committee was even less inclined to economize, and the B-1 program emerged with only $25 million less than the administration had requested. The final bill also carried the stipulation that no money could be saved by firing employees of the contractor (Rockwell International).

In 1974 the Air Force asked for $499 million for continued prototype development in Fiscal Year 1975. The House Armed Services Committee again recommended the full authorization. An amendment on the House floor to delete all of the money for the B-1 failed 309 to 94. The Senate Armed Services Committee recommended a cut of $44 million from the request, but the language of the committee report indicated that the cut was simply related to producing only three prototypes instead of four, not to lack of enthusiasm for the project itself. The Senate defeated a floor amendment to cut another $225 million by a vote of 59 to 31. The conference committee adopted the Senate figure of $455 million. The Air Force, however, lost nothing because the statute provided that the $44 million that had been "cut" could be reinserted by the reprogramming procedure as soon as the first prototype had been successfully tested in flight. The defense appropriations bill contained virtually full funding ($445 million of the $455 million authorized). In its lobbying efforts, Rockwell stressed explicitly and convincingly the public works nature and the geographical distribution of contracts and jobs.

1977–1978 After his defeat in November 1976, one of President Ford's last acts as president was to order initial production of the B-1, even though the incoming president, Jimmy Carter, had already expressed opposition to the plane. Congress had stipulated that full-scale production would have to await review by the new president.

In his first few months in office, Carter was subjected to the arguments of both supporters and opponents of the B-1. By mid-1977 he had become firmly convinced that the money would be better spent on a cruise missile, and he made that position public. He moved to rescind the $462 million appropriated for Fiscal Year 1977 to build the first two planes. The Senate, which had displayed some skepticism about the B-1 for several years, went along with President Carter. The House, however, refused to accept the rescission by a vote of 191 to 166 in December 1977.

For the next several months after the House vote, the administration orchestrated a concentrated campaign against the B-1. Gradually the administration won over the Air Force and the key defense establishment figures in Congress, especially senior members of the House Defense Appropriations Subcommittee and the House Armed Services Committee. The administration's major argument was to stress that national defense, especially the Air Force, would not lose resources because of negative action on the B-1. Instead, the resources would be shifted to other Air Force projects, such as the cruise missile. Procedurally, the rescission was attached to an omnibus $7.8 billion supplemental appropriations bill that contained funding for an assortment of activities important to a large number of House members. When the House voted on the B-1 rescission in this format in late February 1978, it upheld the administration by a vote of 234 to 182. Supporters of the Air Force lost nothing; only the group specifically supporting the B-1 itself appears to have lost. Even that loss turned out to be temporary.

The Reagan years After Ronald Reagan became president in 1981, Congress quickly succumbed to his blandishments to put the B-1 into production. Reagan, of course, had strong support from the Air Force and Rockwell International and its subcontractors. The death of the B-1 in 1978 had been an illusion. Congress agreed to build one hundred planes, the last of which was delivered in 1988. The final price tag was close to $30 billion. Subgovernments do not give up easily. The Air

Force–B-1 coalition—especially when nourished by presidential support—prevailed. Rockwell even began making serious noises about asking for planes beyond the one hundred authorized, but by 1990 that idea was probably dead, both because the stealth bomber had become the new darling of the manned bomber subgovernment and because events in Eastern Europe and U.S. budget problems put some constraints on what even a defense subgovernment could achieve.

The stealth bomber In scientific terms, stealth technology is the quest for an aircraft that is as close to invisible as human engineering can devise, using low-detectable aerodynamics, sophisticated electronics, and radar-absorbent coatings. In political terms, stealth technology, which began life as a well-funded, underscrutinized "black program" in the Pentagon, is becoming a vulnerable strategic bargaining chip whose future is far from secure (Atkinson 1989a, 1989b, 1989c).

Stealth development began in secrecy in 1977 amidst a small, closed circle limited to "need to know" participants in the Air Force, Lockheed, the White House, and Congress (the chairmen of the House and Senate Armed Services and Appropriations Committees). Prevailing SAR (special access required) restrictions meant that debate was limited to a tiny band of insiders. There was no public scrutiny of the project. The belief that radar-elusive offensive weapons could be developed to strengthen America's defensive position guided project participants' decisions to develop a stealth bomber (the B-2), a fighter (the F-117), and a cruise missile. Northrup was brought in as an additional contractor in 1981. The B-2 is a bomber capable of delivering a payload of twenty atomic bombs while cruising at 500 miles per hour with a range of over 6,000 miles.

Until the mid-1980s, the stealth program enjoyed "no strings" secret funding and a free hand in development decisions. Operations were secret. Not until 1986 did the first ripple of congressional misgiving emerge in the form of a slight trimming of the budget for the B-2 and a stretching out of the scheduled completion of the full production run of bombers. But these budget negotiations between the SAR-approved congressional participants and the Air Force were amicable. The Pentagon estimate was for completion of 132 bombers at a cost of just over $37 billion. But this was the first crack in the quiet coalition that had functioned unhampered thus far.

Less than a year later, congressional disillusionment with the reliability of several expensive strategic weapons programs began to set in when problems with MX missile guidance systems and B-1B bomber (a special model of the B-1) electronics were revealed to the House Armed Services Committee. Consternation directed at the B-2 grew when the select congressional circle informed of B-2 developments learned that Air Force accounting practices were commingling monies for development and procurement. Northrup's credibility suffered because it managed both the MX and B-2 projects.

Northrup's and the Air Force's main priority was to get the first plane built. Despite massive technological challenges—Northrup and its team developed nine hundred new processes and materials in the course of bringing the plane to reality— Air Vehicle One (AV-1) was rolled out by the Air Force from a closely guarded hangar to be photographed and viewed from discreet distances in November 1988. In the same month, Northrup and the Air Force agreed on terms of a contract for production of at least thirteen of the bombers.

Seeing AV-1, even from a distance, opened up the question of future expenditures on the plane to a level of public debate that had never before existed. The B-2's creators and supporters had never questioned its value as a nuclear deterrent, nor did they doubt that it would be built. In their minds, its maiden flight in July 1989 proved its technological soundness.

The public debate following the revelation of the previously highly secret program brought its future very much into question. The heightened visibility and publicity destroyed quiet decision making. Massive federal deficits and a shrinking defense budget became major constraints in the late 1980s, in sharp contrast to the relative ease of funding very expensive defense programs in the late 1970s and early 1980s. Relations with America's major potential military adversary were also in a state of flux. Under Gorbachev, the military threat from the Soviet Union no longer seemed so ominous.

Perhaps most damaging was the simple transition from a secret program to a public program. Former Secretary of Defense Harold Brown noted that the magnitude of the secrecy helped generate the magnitude of the negative reaction. Senator John Glenn (D–Ohio) noted that members of Congress may have been "derelict in our duty...in not being on top of those things more" (quoted in the *Washington Post*, October 10, 1989). Pentagon estimates for completing the 132 planes had risen to $70 billion—over $500 million per plane. The schedule had been stretched out to 1999. Increased costs in a time of fiscal belt tightening were a big liability.

The admission by the Air Force in mid-1989 that the B-2 would not be capable of striking and destroying mobile enemy targets increased congressional frustration and skepticism about the utility of the project. Many critics felt that this capability had been an integral selling point of the original project. These constraints are reflected in Fiscal Year 1990 funding for the B-2, which reduced the executive branch request from production of three planes to production of two and reduced the funding of the program from $4.3 billion to $3.5 billion (*Congressional Quarterly Weekly Report*, November 18, 1989, 3187). Further congressional restrictions were imposed for start-up of production and for required flight test data. Congress also asked the Pentagon to prepare an impact report on implications of cutting production by one-half or one-third.

Like many strategic weapons decisions, the B-2 story will play out over many years. Production of the aircraft was unquestionably seriously damaged in moving from a secret, black status to the light of public scrutiny. B-2 proponents argue it is essential to guarantee a reliable nuclear deterrent into the twenty-first century. Its critics doubt its efficacy and fear its budget-breaking potential. In the absence of both strong presidential leadership and a national consensus about how to arm the nation, Congress vacillates, trimming but not eliminating the program.

Reserve Forces

Since World War II, the subgovernment deciding on the size, status, and perquisites of the reserve military forces has operated in classic distributive fashion (Levantrosser

1967). A close liaison has been forged between the chief interest group (the Reserve Officers Association), the Armed Services Committees in the House and Senate, other members of Congress who are either members of or have an interest in the reserves, and selected members of the executive branch, especially regular officers in the military services. The concerns of this subgovernment have been to retain a large reserve force and give its members generous pay, retirement income, and other benefits. The subgovernment has been successful in pursuing these preferences.

The Reserve Officers Association (ROA) is an interest group that functions directly as a policy maker. It initiates legislation in addition to monitoring legislative proposals emerging from the executive branch or Congress. Its representatives participate directly in the "mark-up" sessions held by committees on bills pertaining to the reserve. It has a Legislative Advisory Committee composed of members of Congress who are reserve officers. This committee aids in the passage of favorable legislation and passes out awards to particularly important and supportive members of the House and Senate.

In the executive branch, the ROA seeks allies in the military services by inducing regular officers to become associate members. The ROA also confers regularly with service officials who follow reserve legislation.

In the late 1980s the reserve forces remained in fine shape. The proportion of all U.S. military strength in the reserves stood at about one-third. In 1984 Congress created a new post in the DOD, an assistant secretary for reserve affairs. This position was a good symbol of the strength of the reserve subgovernment.

Food for Peace

Since its passage in 1954, the Food for Peace program (also known as P.L. 480) has expanded in times of domestic crop surpluses and contracted when those surpluses have disappeared. P.L. 480 was designed as a means of disposing of agricultural surpluses abroad. The program has been used for both humanitarian and diplomatic and political purposes by the State Department and the administration. From the viewpoint of the subsidized producers of farm commodities in the United States, P.L. 480 represents a major subsidy in years in which a crop surplus is generated.

The supportive subgovernment has been consistently successful in continuing and expanding the program. The major members of the subgovernment have been bureaucrats in the Foreign Agricultural Service of the Department of Agriculture, most members of the relevant subcommittees of the House and Senate committees dealing with agricultural authorization and appropriations bills, virtually all of the agricultural interest groups, and U.S. shipping interests, which obtain a guaranteed portion of the shipping of the commodities to other nations. Earl Butz, secretary of agriculture for Presidents Nixon and Ford, stated the viewpoint of the Department of Agriculture and the subsidized farmers succinctly when he referred to P.L. 480 primarily as a way of "getting rid of the stuff" (*National Journal*, November 23, 1974, 1761; "stuff" is a technical term used by Butz to identify surplus commodities).

The world of P.L. 480 is, however, more complex than Butz's comment implies. P.L. 480 has both structural and strategic aspects. A major debate erupted in late

1974 and 1975 over the purposes of the program that revealed the tension between them. Commodity exports under the program were being increasingly used to reward political allies abroad (at that time, for example, South Korea, South Vietnam, Pakistan) and to encourage desired behavior from other nations. Critics of the strategic uses of the program (who included Democratic Senator Hubert Humphrey of Minnesota, one of the original sponsors of the program) opposed what they viewed as the excessive use of food aid for political and diplomatic purposes. These critics combined a focus on humanitarianism with an implicit focus on stabilizing the subsidy aspects of the program at home—an unusual but not uncomfortable stance. Opponents of the critics (who included then Secretary of State Henry Kissinger) were interested in more than just the U.S. image as a humanitarian nation and the provision of increased and stabilized farm subsidies at home. They wanted to preserve the flexibility in P.L. 480 to use it for diplomatic and international political purposes.

A healthy P.L. 480 program moved past its thirty-fifth birthday in 1989. It continued to serve the twin purposes of buying agricultural surpluses at home and serving the foreign policy interests of the United States as defined by the administration of the day. It seemed ill-suited to achieving these purposes simultaneously because of fluctuations in the domestic and international food markets. Problems with the program also became apparent when critics asked whether the people most in need in the recipient countries actually got the food (Bird 1978; Rothschild 1977). But the supportive subgovernment could shrug off these criticisms, as did the Reagan administration. Spending for the program continued to grow.

Strategic Policy

In general, the congressional posture in dealing with strategic foreign and defense policy issues has been either (1) to support the administration's requests directly or indirectly (as in the case of the strategic implications of new weapons systems that are approved primarily as structural policy), or (2) to register a competing point of view in a way that does not remove all administration flexibility. Congress usually gives support, either willing or at least grudging, to the administration's view of strategic matters. This pattern does not mean that congressional impact on these issues is missing, however.

Troop Cuts

In recent years, even before the major political changes in Eastern Europe that broke out with startling rapidity in 1989, Congress has expressed considerable concern about the numbers of U.S. troops stationed overseas.

For many years, one of the leading critics of a large American military contingent in Europe was Mike Mansfield of Montana, the Democratic floor leader in the Senate from 1961 until his retirement after the 1976 session. Arguments for reductions in U.S. troops overseas have focused on balance-of-payments problems, the responsibility of U.S. allies for their own defense, and the dangers of incidents involving U.S. troops that might lead to war. Despite efforts to reduce troop levels and to specify the location of those reductions, Congress has ultimately contented itself with specifying overall troop levels that usually represent, at most, only modest cuts from existing levels. Congress has not specified where even these small overseas troop cuts should take place, but has continued to leave the principal strategic decisions in the hands of the executive branch. Specific examples from the last several decades support this general point.

In 1974 the defense appropriations bill contained a provision requiring a total troop withdrawal of 12,500 from overseas locations by May 31, 1975, about eight months after the passage of the bill. This reduced the total authorized U.S. troop strength abroad to 452,000, which included 300,000 in Europe, 125,000 in East Asia, and the remainder in scattered locations. The decision on where the 12,500 should be removed was left to the executive branch.

The conference committee had produced the number 12,500 when reconciling the Senate bill, which called for a cut of 25,000, and the House bill, which had no provision for a cut. The Senate Appropriations Committee indicated it would prefer to mandate the cuts in Europe, but the secretary of defense and his staff worked very hard, and successfully, to convince the conference committee not to specify location.

The troop reduction issue had also been debated during the consideration of the 1974 authorization bill for procurement and research and development funds for the DOD. In the House, the majority leader, Thomas P. O'Neill, a Massachusetts Democrat, proposed an amendment reducing overseas troops by 100,000 by the end of 1975. The House defeated the O'Neill amendment 240 to 163. The House Armed Services Committee had recommended against unilateral troop withdrawal from Europe.

During the Senate consideration of the defense procurement bill, that body defeated a proposal for a troop reduction of 125,000 by a vote of 54 to 35. This vote came on an amendment offered by Senator Mansfield. Strenuous activities of high-ranking administration officials, including both Secretary of State Kissinger and Secretary of Defense James Schlesinger, helped ensure the defeat. The Senate barely defeated, 46 to 44, a second proposal—also made by Mansfield—to mandate a cut of 76,000.

The one provision dealing with overseas troop strength in the defense procurement bill adopted in 1974 required a reduction of 18,000 support troops specifically from Europe. But the bill also allowed the secretary of defense to replace these support troops with combat troops and gave him until June 30, 1976, to accomplish the reduction. The Senate bill had set the reduction at 23,000 troops, but the conference committee cut that figure. Again the twin urges of Congress on this issue were apparent: the desire to have an impact on a strategic issue—U.S. troop levels abroad—and the desire not to bind the executive branch too tightly.

In 1977 and 1978 some members of Congress exhibited a different concern in this policy area when President Carter announced a phased withdrawal of United States ground troops from South Korea. The opponents of this move did not generate any concrete activity, however, in part because the Joint Chiefs of Staff had been successful in getting Carter to accept some conditions surrounding the withdrawal they thought were essential. These conditions included provisions that the withdrawal would be carried out in a manner that would not "destabilize" the military situation between North Korea and South Korea, that the United States would publicly renew its obligations to South Korea under a mutual security treaty, and that the United States would make a public statement that it intended to remain a military power in East Asia. Congressional reaction to the presidential announcement was essentially symbolic.

In 1977 Congress added language to the bill that authorized funds for the State Department that declared that U.S. policy toward South Korea should "continue to be arrived at by joint decision of the President and Congress" and that implementation of the phased troop withdrawal plan should be "carried out in regular consultation with Congress." In 1978 the military aid appropriations bill continued a provision that it was the sense of Congress that additional withdrawal of U.S. troops from South Korea might upset the military balance in the region and that such moves require full consultation with Congress. But these provisions put no effective limits on the administration's power in this strategic area. Rather, they simply served notice on Carter that Congress was watching this area carefully and might become troublesome if members did not receive appropriate stroking.

More important, in votes on concrete matters, Congress supported the president. By a vote of almost two to one, the House rejected an amendment to the defense authorization bill that would have barred a reduction in U.S. troops in South Korea to a level lower than 26,000. The military aid bill contained a provision allowing the president to give about $800 million worth of weapons of U.S. units in Korea to the Koreans when the U.S. troops departed.

In 1982, even under a president very different from Carter—Reagan—and even with a Congress dominated by ideological conservatives, the congressional interest in limiting the number of troops stationed abroad (and/or forcing foreign nations to increase their own defense efforts or perhaps their money contributions to maintaining U.S. overseas garrisons) was once again made evident. But, as in the past, Congress also made it clear that it wished to leave lots of flexibility in the hands of the president. Two specific issues were debated and finally resolved in this typically schizophrenic fashion by Congress in 1982. In both cases, congressional anxieties and preferences were evident. In neither case did Congress take action that, ultimately, would force the president or the DOD to do anything that conflicted with their best judgment.

The first issue again involved U.S. troop levels in Europe. The conferees on the appropriations bill (a continuing resolution in form, but like a new bill in content) agreed to limit the number of U.S. military personnel in Europe to 315,600 (a cut from existing levels), *but* they also provided that the president could waive this limit if he found and stated that "overriding national security requirements" necessitated expansion or retention beyond the limit.

The second issue involved a tiny amount of money ($35 million) and the attempt to disband one specific brigade (which had about 4,000 troops in it) of a cavalry division stationed in West Germany. The provision in the bill produced by the conference committee and signed by the president deleted the money, which represented the operating funds for the brigade. But once again Congress deferred to executive branch flexibility. The bill gave the DOD several months to decide whether to save the $35 million by disbanding the brigade *or* by making the cuts elsewhere if it judged the brigade to be "essential." Finding $35 million in a budget the size of the U.S. Army's was not much of a challenge.

Turkish Aid

Two hostile ethnic communities (Greeks and Turks) live on the island of Cyprus. Turkey and Greece have long disputed which country has rightful claim to the island. In July 1974 Turkey invaded the island, using weapons supplied through the U.S. military assistance program. Such use of these weapons violated provisions of U.S. statutes restricting use of the weapons to defensive purposes only.

During the autumn of 1974 Congress engaged in a running battle with the Ford administration over what response the United States should make to this action. The final decisions were made on the floor of the House and Senate rather than in a quiet subcommittee setting. Congress got involved in part because of the presence of a group of American voters of Greek extraction who were vocal in demanding anti-Turkish action. There was no competing set of American voters of Turkish ancestry. Despite the fervent protests of President Ford, the secretary of state, and other high-ranking executive branch officials, Congress made the strategic policy decision that a cutoff of aid to Turkey, presumably coupled with U.S. mediation of the Greek–Turkish dispute over Cyprus, would be a better means of forcing a solution to the military situation on Cyprus than quiet diplomatic moves alone. But there was enough self-doubt in Congress about the strategic decision that it still allowed the administration some flexibility by giving it the option of postponing the aid cutoff date.

The parliamentary manuevering over Turkish aid from mid-September through mid-December 1974 was elaborate and intricate. Each chamber took numerous roll calls on the issue and always took an anti-Turkey, anti-administration position. The entire story need not be told here, but even a partial account reveals the reluctance of Congress to be overly rigid in binding the executive branch on strategic issues when caught between the cross pressures brought by an active subset of Greek-American voters and forceful arguments about the national interest and national security made by the president and secretary of state with reference to a valued and important ally, Turkey.

The first restriction Congress voted, which was accepted unhappily by the administration, was contained in a temporary law—a resolution continuing appropriations signed in mid-October. The key congressional concession was to delay the cutoff in aid to Turkey until December 10, which gave Ford and Kissinger time to put diplomatic pressure on Turkey that might force Turkish action and render the cutoff unnecessary. The final Ford agreement to the compromise came in a telephone call to the House minority leader. The language of the bill allowed the president to delay imposing the ban as long as Turkey observed the cease-fire and did not add either troops or U.S. weapons to its forces already on Cyprus.

The debate resumed when Congress reconvened after the 1974 election for a lame-duck session. Proponents of an aid cutoff sought to add mandatory language to the foreign aid and military assistance authorization bill that made the cutoff part of permanent law rather than part of a continuing resolution. Both houses voted in favor of the cutoff. The House insisted on making the cutoff take effect December 10. However, the Senate passed a provision allowing the president to suspend the cutoff until February 14, 1975, to give the president and Secretary of State Kissinger more time to continue quiet work with both Turkey and Greece. The conferees chose February 5 as the cutoff date, and both houses approved. The new law provided that, if the cutoff took place on February 5, it could be lifted if the administration could certify that "substantial progress" was being made toward a solution to the Cyprus problem.

As February 5 approached, Kissinger met with four Democratic leaders of the cutoff forces in Congress, one senator and three House members. He asked them to arrange another extension of the deadline in the interests of national security and to avoid jeopardizing American bases in Turkey and the Turkish–American alliance. But he indicated he could not certify substantial progress in the Cyprus negotiations. The four members of Congress refused his request and indicated that the cutoff would have to take place on schedule. They also indicated, however, their support for speedy resumption of aid once the certification of substantial progress could be made.

After the aid cutoff went into effect on February 5, 1975, the administration continued to press for lifting the ban. In the next three months an impressive coalition backing the administration was built in the Senate. It included the majority leader, the minority leader, the minority whip, and the chairmen and ranking minority members of the Foreign Relations Committee and the Armed Services Committee. These individuals co-sponsored a bill allowing resumption of aid but retaining an active oversight role for Congress. The Senate passed this bill 41 to 40. The House, however, by a vote of 223 to 206 upheld the ban in late July 1975. The Turkish government retaliated by ordering that American bases in Turkey be closed.

In October 1975 Congress agreed to lift the arms embargo partially, in order to give the president latitude in negotiations designed to prevent Turkey from making the base closings permanent. Reporting requirements preserved an important congressional role in monitoring U.S. relations with both Greece and Turkey. The sales that were permitted had to be related to North Atlantic Treaty Organization (NATO) defenses.

In his 1976 campaign for the presidency, Jimmy Carter supported the partial arms embargo. But as president in 1978 he took the position that the partial embargo should be lifted because it was threatening Turkey's continued membership in NATO and because Turkey was considering making the closing of U.S. bases permanent (Maxfield 1978a, 1978b, 1978c, 1978d, 1978e). Turkey had not, however, changed its position on Cyprus and remained in control of about 40 percent of the island. In early June 1978, the president personally lobbied members of the House and Senate on this issue and was aided by other high-ranking officials such as NATO commander Alexander Haig, Secretary of State Cyrus Vance, and Secretary of Defense Harold Brown.

The resolution of the 1978 debate took place along lines familiar when strategic issues are at stake. Decisions in congressional committees were not final but were subject to change on the floor of the House and Senate after heated debate. The floor decisions required compromises that left Congress with the illusion of being important in continued decision making. The president got the essence of what he wanted.

The Senate Foreign Relations Committee voted 8 to 4 against ending the embargo. When the issue came to the floor of the Senate, it was clear that some compromise language to accompany the repeal would be needed. The majority leader and others offered such language, which provided that when the president requested any funds for Turkey, Greece, or Cyprus, he must simultaneously certify that U.S. goals for resolving the conflict over Cyprus were being achieved. The language also noted disapproval of continuing Turkish military presence on Cyprus. The president was required to report to Congress every sixty days on progress on the Cyprus question.

The House had always taken a tougher pro-embargo stance than the Senate. The House International Relations Committee (a name it used for a short time before reverting to the long-standing appellation of Foreign Affairs Committee) voted 18 to 17 to end the embargo only because two pro-embargo members did not vote. On the House floor the pro-embargo forces would have won had not an even more "pro-Congress" compromise been found than the one the Senate had forged. Even then, the House passed it only 208 to 205. This compromise, drafted by the majority leader, who worked closely with the White House, did not formally repeal the embargo but allowed it to be put aside by the president if he certified to Congress that resumption of aid was in the "national interest of the United States and in the interest of NATO." He also had to certify to Congress that Turkey was "acting in good faith" in settling a number of Cyprus-related issues on a permanent basis. Like the Senate, the House required the president to report every sixty days.

The conference committee took the harder House line in framing the final bill—calling it a "de facto repeal" rather than an outright, clear-cut repeal. This was done to avoid another bruising battle on the House floor.

By 1981 the issue had receded so far that the conferees on a foreign aid bill simply dropped a House amendment that required the president to take into account whether Greece, Turkey, and Cyprus were working toward a peaceful settlement in Cyprus before supplying aid to any of them. Even this mild reminder of the stresses of the past—which now put Greece and Cyprus in the same category with Turkey—proved to be more meddling in a strategic issue than Congress ultimately wanted to undertake. In 1982 the president requested $465 million in military aid for Turkey. He got $400 million; more important, Congress offered no language that continued to insert itself into the attempt to pressure Turkey on Cyprus. The tempest was over.

The importance of the Greek-American community in generating congressional interest in a cutoff and in sustaining that cutoff despite strong appeals from the president and the secretary of state from 1974 to 1976 should be underscored. This community had never been particularly politically active before, but on this issue an impressive organization was put together on short notice to lobby members of the House and Senate. Several members of the House and Senate, including some of

Greek ancestry, were willing to take the lead in pressing the issue. The issue was, of course, more complex than a matter of simple ethnicity, but ethnicity made this a hot issue involving Congress and top executive branch officials, including the president, in a running and heated debate for about five years. The strength of the Greek-American lobby contined to be apparent in Congress in the mid-1980s as Congress successfully insisted on maintaining a 7-to-10 ratio in the military aid dollars given by the United States to Greece and Turkey, even though that ratio substantially understated the military importance of Turkey to the United States and NATO when compared to Greece.

Foreign Economic Policy

A careful study of the making of foreign economic policy from 1929 through 1976 (Pastor 1980) reaches a number of important conclusions that are consonant with our expectations about strategic policy. It finds, for example, that interest groups have a limited role. The study also finds that both the executive branch and the Congress have reasonably well-established corporate views of issues such as trade, foreign aid, and international investment. Sometimes these views clash, sometimes they are quite similar. In all cases, bargaining and compromise produced final policy results.

Another finding is that the internal divisions in executive branch views of these issues seem to be relatively few and of low intensity. This suggests that disaggregated pieces of the bureaucracy have only a modest influence on these issues. More centralized parts of the executive branch, including the president, have more influence. The author suggests that there is a "natural" tendency on the part of the various pieces of the executive branch to see the world of foreign economic policy in a common way:

> The foreign economic policies analyzed in this study were the product of a continuous interactive process involving both the legislative and executive branches. While coalitions were sometimes organized between bureaus and committees, the rule in many of the policies analyzed was that Congress and the Executive approached issues as coherent, unitary organizations with decided preferences and predispositions in each issue. Whether these preferences were molded into a single policy depended to a great extent on the degree of trust and responsiveness which flowed in both directions between the branches (p. 345).

Pastor also identifies a number of specific instances in which interest groups and classic bureau–subcommittee alliances sprang up and isolated some aspect of foreign economic policy they could then treat as structural. Those in both branches pushing for broad policy outcomes sought to keep issues defined as strategic as a way of keeping decision making relatively centralized and at a high level. Those trying to pursue narrower domestic policy interests continually tried to redefine pieces of the total turf as structural, where subgovernments would have more influence. Congress and the executive branch could both withstand these parochial pressures better when the president and executive branch were providing constant pressure to keep the issues in the strategic realm rather than letting them slip into the structural realm.

Pastor's study demonstrates that the executive branch tended to prevail when there was conflict between the two branches but, at the same time, that congressional impact on policy in this realm was also sizable, although not controlling, because it could force compromises when disagreement appeared. Congress made a difference in the substance of many specific policies. When interest groups appeared in force, got access to the decision process, and were taken seriously, then some issue was usually redefined as structural.

Aid to Nicaraguan Contras

In dealing with administration policy toward Nicaragua in the 1980s, Congress was a major and strong-willed partner. It questioned, restricted, and at times denied administration requests. However, the administration was able to continue to offer at least some military aid to the contras during much of the decade, until President Bush tacitly acknowledged that the chances of contra success in ousting the Sandinista government of Nicaragua were slim, to say the least.

Throughout the Reagan presidency, congressional–presidential disagreement in this strategic area arose repetitively over the same issues: the use of the Central Intelligence Agency (CIA) in dispensing aid; the role of the U.S. government in efforts to destabilize and overthrow another government; the reliance on military rather than diplomatic solutions to achieve policy aims; and the possibility that the United States would become involved in another Vietnam-like civil war.

Reagan came to office in 1981 enunciating a hard-line, anti-Communist policy for Central America. He consistently espoused that position with regard to Nicaragua throughout his presidency. His initial goal was articulated as stopping the flow of arms from Nicaragua to El Salvador's leftist guerrillas, but his rhetoric quickly expanded to a denunciation of the Sandinista government as the source of political instability for the entire region. His goal clearly became to replace the government of Nicaragua with one more to his liking. He authorized covert CIA actions to overthrow the Sandinista government of Daniel Ortega.

In 1982 Congress added the Boland amendment (named for Democratic congressman Edward Boland of Massachusetts, a consistent critic of administration policy in Nicaragua) to a 1983 appropriations bill. That amendment prohibited the CIA and the DOD from participating in activities designed to overthrow the Nicaraguan government. Congress did not, however, eliminate or even reduce aid for the contras. In the following year, Congress granted only half the amount of aid for the contras sought by Reagan but did not include any restrictions on the CIA.

In 1984 the administration's policy suffered a major setback because of publicity about the role of the CIA in mining Nicaraguan harbors. The action had been taken without consultation with the intelligence committees in Congress. Congress retaliated by cutting off all contra aid, although it expressly included a provision in the cutoff that allowed the president to seek funding again in 1985.

The battle continued in 1985 when the president again asked for aid. Facing stiff opposition in both houses, Reagan compromised, asking for "humanitarian" aid rather than military aid. The House continued to resist, voting against the president twice in April. In June, however, the House voted for humanitarian aid. The House shift was based on a negative reaction to Daniel Ortega's visit to Moscow in the spring to seek funds from the Soviet Union. The shift also reflected the fears of some members that they would be perceived as lacking the will to fight communism in Central America. The Reagan administration also compromised on two important political issues in order to gain the victory—agreeing to ask for humanitarian aid only and agreeing to prohibit the CIA from dispensing the aid. In several different bills the administration got $27 million in humanitarian aid, acquiesced in a prohibition of CIA and DOD involvement in distributing the aid, got permission to use the CIA to provide advice and information to the contras, and got the definition of "humanitarian" broadened to include such quasi-military items as trucks and radios. Congress exhibited the schizoid behavior that is usual when its majority disagrees with the administration on a strategic issue: it seeks victory on some core issues but retains or even gives back flexibility to the administration rather than pressing its advantage.

The tug of war on this issue between Congress and Reagan continued in the last years of the Reagan administration, from 1986 through 1989. Reagan remained adamant in trying to push for as much aid to the contras as possible. Congress remained skeptical but was unwilling to cut off contra aid altogether. In these years Congress seemed to be engaged in endless debate and endless voting on the issue. Nonmilitary aid was approved in limited amounts, and in 1987 some military aid was also approved.

The Bush administration and Congress reached accommodation on the matter in April 1989, when both branches and both parties agreed on authorization of almost $50 million in nonmilitary aid to be administered by the Agency for International Development, the foreign aid agency of the United States government. This authorization lasted through the end of February 1990. The administration and Congress also agreed that no money would be spent after November 30, 1989, without the express consent of the leaders of both parties and relevant authorizing committees and appropriations subcommittees in both houses. Such consent was forthcoming in late November. Congress agreed with the administration that aid should be available until after the elections scheduled by the government of Nicaragua for February 25. Central American presidents continued to push for the cessation of all American aid to the contras, but, on this strategic matter, Congress was willing to let the administration choose the timing it found most congenial.

Star Wars

Speaking in a nationally televised broadcast on March 23, 1983, President Reagan announced his administration's commitment to a new concept he called the Strategic Defense Initiative (SDI) as a major part of future U.S. defense policy with regard to the Soviet Union. The press immediately gave it the sobriquet "Star Wars." The proposal represented a stunning departure from decades of defense policy grounded in nuclear deterrence, the threat of retaliation, and mutual assured destruction. It generated immediate controversy.

Reagan personally and ardently embraced the concept of a space shield to render the United States invulnerable to Soviet missile attacks. Conceptually, the idea of space-based defensive weaponry was not new. It can be traced back to the Eisenhower administration's BAMBI (Ballistic Missile Boost Intercepts) proposal (Boffey and others 1988, 255). What was new was Reagan's willingness to invest in the concept and deploy it. No other president had been willing to do so. The program's proponents believed that SDI offered a technological fix that would permanently free the United States from the specter of a USSR nuclear attack. President Reagan was a tireless and fervent lobbyist for this project in Congress. Allied with him were civilian and military bureaucrats in the Department of Defense, whose power and influence would increase if SDI became real, and a number of defense contractors, some members of the scientific community, and political conservatives enraptured by Reagan's hard-line stance toward the communist "evil empire."

Skeptics existed in Congress, in other parts of the executive branch, and in the scientific community. They argued that the complexity of the project would require decades of research, that the cost would be too high, and that the deployment would alienate the Soviets and forestall the possibility of progress in arms reduction talks with them.

Despite misgivings, Congress deferred to the president. Within a year of his speech, a bureaucracy dedicated to overseeing the Star Wars project had been estab-lished and was on its way to becoming entrenched in the basement of the Pentagon—the Strategic Defense Initiative Organization. Congressional appropriations began to flow in Fiscal Year 1985 ($1.4 billion) and rose steadily for five years to about $4 billion annually. These funds were all for research. Ultimately deployment would cost hundreds of billions of dollars. Congress expressed skepticism, however, by tinker-ing with SDI's research priorities. In the Fiscal Year 1989 authorization bill, for example, Congress directed that emphasis be shifted from space-based to ground-based antimissile weapons during the 1990s by setting spending ceilings and ear-marking funds for specific technologies such as ERIS (exoatmospheric reentry vehicle interceptor system) and HEDI (high endoatmospheric defense interceptor) (*Aviation Week & Space Technology,* July 25, 1988, 21).

Star Wars was conceived and nurtured in an atmosphere of hostile official percep-tions of the Soviets in the early 1980s under the direct leadership of a president who was a true believer. By the end of the 1980s, the situation was altered, and Star Wars was no longer a preeminent feature of American defense policy (*New York Times,* September 28, 1989). In a significant symbolic and political gesture, Congress reduced appropriations for SDI below the appropriations for the previous fiscal year for the first time in Fiscal Year 1990, following five years of growth.

A number of factors help explain this congressional action. Relations between the United States and the Soviet Union were significantly improved in an era of glasnost, perestroika, and the turmoil in Warsaw Pact nations that seemed to promise political pluralism in those countries. The difficulties of developing and testing SDI components proved to be more complex than even skeptics had predicted. SDI proponents were forced to admit the "space shield" would be at best only a partial defense against some missile attacks. The most significant change was the role played by the president. Bush was restrained in his support for SDI and did not lobby for its funding as Reagan had done. His secretary of defense acknowledged that the program was politically vulnerable to congressional budget cutters.

The effect of the cutback remains to be seen. The program is still popular with conservatives, the views of whom are taken quite seriously, at least for political reasons, by President Bush. The reduction will force delays in undertaking research on new technologies and will lengthen the implementation plan for the entire project. In an era of shrinking resources for defense, Star Wars will be weighed against competing programs such as the B-2 Stealth bomber, Midgetman missiles, mobile MX missiles, and Trident submarines. SDI is far from abandoned, but it is no longer the jewel in the defense crown.

SDI conforms to the general pattern of how strategic policies get made. Congress, when confronted with a determined president (Reagan), deferred to him, despite grumblings and some cuts in his requests. However, when a new president (Bush) became less committed and insistent, Congress felt free to act more in accord with its own doubts, though it was still not willing to tell the president he could not make any forward movement on this program at all.

Crisis Policy

The typical pattern of decision making in crisis situations involves congressional legitimation of presidential action after that action has occurred. When President Johnson decided in 1965 to send U.S. marines to the Dominican Republic, allegedly to prevent a Communist takeover (Evans and Novak 1966, Chapter 23), he had not engaged in even symbolic consultation with any members of Congress. Instead he simply told some of the leaders an hour after the landing was ordered that he had made a decision. No formal congressional legitimating action was either requested or received. The event marked the public defection of the chairman of the Senate Foreign Relations Committee, William Fulbright, an Arkansas Democrat, from the president's foreign policy in general, first with regard to the Dominican Republican and soon thereafter with regard to Vietnam.

It is also possible that congressional leaders will be consulted before action is taken in a crisis. Prior consultation is completely at the discretion of the president. When such consultation occurs, the congressional leaders included in the consultation may take a variety of positions, although those positions may or may not have any impact. Again, the decision on what weight those views will have is up to the president. In the first case that follows, which concerns a decision about Vietnam in 1954, when France still nominally controlled the country, the response of a few congressional leaders to an administration proposal was critical. The administration proposed action to support the French; the congressional leaders opposed any action. The administration bowed to the congressional view, in part because other international factors also pushed in that direction and in part because President Eisenhower was not firmly committed to a course of action before he initiated the consultation. In the second case that follows, which concerns the U.S. response to the presence of Soviet missiles in Cuba in 1962, congressional response was also critical. In this instance, congressional leaders wanted more action than that proposed by the administration. But President Kennedy remained firm in supporting his initial decision about the best course of action.

In an effort to prevent a repetition of U.S. involvement in a foreign war because of executive action without formal congressional consent, as happened in Vietnam in the 1960s and 1970s, Congress in 1973 passed the War Powers Act, which required the president to consult with Congress when making decisions to commit U.S. forces abroad. The act was envisioned by its supporters as a tool for ensuring congressional participation in crisis decisions involving armed forces before policy commitments could be made. The final two examples both involve or could have involved the War Powers Act.

Vietnam, 1954

In 1954 the Eisenhower administration pondered becoming involved militarily in Southeast Asia in support of what proved to be the losing French effort to keep Indochina French and non-Communist (Roberts 1973). In April of that year, Secretary of State John Foster Dulles called a meeting attended by five senators and three representatives (leaders from both parties in both houses) and a few DOD officials, including the chairman of the Joint Chiefs of Staff, Admiral Arthur Radford. Dulles proposed at this meeting that Congress pass a resolution giving the president the authority to use American sea and air power to support the French in Indochina. The members of Congress who had been summoned questioned Dulles and Radford searchingly. Two key points were established. First, the other members of the joint chiefs did not agree with Radford that military action was needed. Second, the United States had not consulted any allies about their views on the matter. As events spun out, it became evident that the United States could not generate support—especially in the important case of Great Britain. Dien Bien Phu, the French stronghold in Southeast Asia, fell to those fighting the French before further action could be taken.

The general point of this episode should not be overstated. This war was primarily a crisis for France. It would become a crisis for the United States only if we willfully treated it as such. Radford and Dulles tried unsuccessfully to give the war a crisis label in relation to U.S. interests. But the resistance and skepticism of the congressional leaders helped persuade President Eisenhower not to take action. After the collapse of Dien Bien Phu, action became irrelevant; the game was over. This vignette shows that when top administration officials consult congressional leaders ahead of time, the questions or advice they receive may have considerable impact, although such impact is certainly not guaranteed.

Cuban Missiles

On October 16, 1962, President John Kennedy received undeniable proof that the Soviet Union had established offensive missile bases in Cuba. He and his closest advisors viewed these bases as a grave threat to American security. They pondered their response for six days before deciding on a naval quarantine and a demand that the existing bases be closed and the missiles be dismantled and returned to the Soviet Union. If the Soviets did not bow to these demands, the president was prepared to take direct military action against the bases. In his own private calculations, he figured the chances of a general nuclear war with the Soviet Union at something between one in two and one in three. But he thought that what was at stake demanded such a gamble. His advisors agreed.

Until he had decided to make a public announcement concerning the U.S. reaction to the discovery of the missiles, President Kennedy's consultations had been limited to a group of fewer than twenty individuals from the highest levels of the executive branch (Kennedy 1971, 8). Some congressional critics of the administration had been claiming knowledge of the existence of Soviet missiles in Cuba for more than a month before the president was convinced of their presence. They had also been demanding strong American action. The president, however, did not choose to consult anyone from Congress until he had made his decision and was ready to announce it to the American people. Shortly before making the announcement, the president met with congressional leaders to inform them of the course of action he was going to take. Robert Kennedy, the president's brother and a participant in the deliberations of the administration in response to this crisis, described that meeting (Kennedy 1971, 31–32):

> Many congressional leaders were sharp in their criticism. They felt that the President should take more forceful action, a military attack or invasion, and that the blockade was far too weak a response. Senator Richard B. Russell of Georgia said he could not live with himself if he did not say in the strongest possible terms how important it was that we act with greater strength than the President was contemplating.
>
> Senator J. William Fulbright of Arkansas also strongly advised military action rather than such a weak step as the blockade. Others said they were skeptical but would remain publicly silent, only because it was such a dangerous hour for the country.
>
> The President, after listening to the frequently emotional criticism, explained that he would take whatever steps were necessary to protect the security of the United States, but that he did not feel greater military action was warranted initially. Because it was possible that the matter could be resolved without a devastating war, he had decided on the course he had outlined. Perhaps in the end, he said, direct military action would be necessary, but that course should not be followed lightly. In the meantime, he assured them, he had taken measures to prepare our military forces and place them in a position to move.

The Mayaguez Incident

After disillusionment with policy in Vietnam had set in, many individuals in Congress were discontented with the minimal role of Congress in crisis situations that involved the use of armed force. Even if the use of such force began on a limited basis, there was always the threat that it would expand. Therefore, in November 1973 Congress passed, over a veto by President Nixon, the War Powers Act. This law provides that the president must report overseas commitments of American troops to combat within forty-eight hours. He must order the end of such combat after sixty days unless Congress has given specific approval for continuation, although he is given the power of extending the period for thirty days if he determines that American troops are in danger. The act also provides that the president should "in every instance possible consult with Congress" before ordering actions that might risk military hostilities.

An early test of the act, fortunately quite limited, occurred in 1975. Forces of the new Communist government of Cambodia seized an American merchant ship, the *Mayaguez*, in waters claimed by Cambodia but viewed by the United States to be international. The president, as is typical in crisis situations, consulted with officials from the White House, State Department, and Defense Department. The president opted for a limited use of force, although more force than recommended by the Department of Defense. He then informed a few leading members of Congress of his decision. He used marines to seize the ship and rescue the crew from an island where they were being held. He also ordered the bombing of selected Cambodian mainland targets as a preemptive measure to prevent retaliation.

President Ford's decision, however, was made without the consultation urged by the War Powers Act. Senator Mansfield put the situation succinctly: "I was not consulted. I was notified after the fact about what the administration had already decided to do. . . . I did not give my approval or disapproval because the decision had already been made" (*Congressional Quarterly Weekly Report*, May 17, 1975, 1008).

The Republican floor leader in the Senate, Hugh Scott of Pennsylvania, agreed that he had not been consulted either. He said he had merely been advised of the administration's intentions after the course of action was already set. It was not until after the administration had decided on a course of action that any members of Congress were informed.

President Ford, although he did not consult with Congress prior to his action, complied with the reporting requirements of the act by sending a letter to the full Congress explaining the Cambodian provocation and the response of the United States to it. By the time the letter was received, the incident was over. Marines had rescued the ship and its crew, although twenty American servicemen had died in the process. Congressional reaction to the letter was irrelevant to what happened, since hostilities had already ceased.

The reaction from Congress to the president's handling of the crisis was generally congratulatory. The praise for the president was extensive and came from both parties and members with differing ideological commitments. The only exceptions were some not too seriously voiced skeptical remarks about having been "informed" rather than consulted and some questions about whether negotiation had been explored sufficiently before force was used. The Senate Foreign Relations Committee passed a resolution of support as a symbolic gesture.

There is no agreement within Congress on what the War Powers Act is supposed to do. On the one hand, critics of the act argue that if consultation with Congress were taken literally, executive flexibility to maneuver in a crisis would be seriously reduced. Supporters of the act argue that at a minimum the act guarantees Congress the right to review executive decisions involving the armed forces and to decide whether or not to continue them. Potentially, the War Powers Act gives to Congress a greater role in crisis decision making, but the *Mayaguez* incident does not reflect any change from the usual very limited congressional role. The euphoria of having escaped a serious international incident was so great that serious reflection on the efficacy of the War Powers Act did not take place.

After he left the presidency, Gerald Ford did reflect on the use of the War Powers Act during his administration (Ford 1977). He made it clear that the provisions had very little impact on how he conducted himself in six specific incidents, including the *Mayaguez* case. The most accurate comment on the War Powers Act, given Ford's testimony and what else we know of the six incidents he discussed, is that it remains an unclear and probably ineffective congressional attempt to control war-making powers. It is a symbol of congressional frustration in facing a world in which a genuine large-scale crisis could destroy much of the world's population in a short period of time.

The Aborted Rescue of the Iran Hostages

The seizure of more than fifty American hostages in the U.S. embassy in Teheran, Iran, in late 1979 set off a continuing crisis. The longer it lasted, the greater the number of U.S. actors who became involved in trying to figure out a way to free the hostages. Only the first few days or weeks were truly a crisis. But presidential dominance of the problem was again demonstrated forcefully in April 1980 when President Carter and those few people he chose to involve decided to rescue the hostages in a commando raid using helicopters. The raid failed even to reach Teheran. Eight would-be rescuers died. It was successful, however, in being carried out without any prior public knowledge. It was also successful in driving another nail into the coffin of the War Powers Act. These events demonstrated again that the act contained rhetoric that would be ignored by a president facing real situations.

After the raid, a brief public debate over whether the War Powers Act applied and, therefore, had been illegally ignored, produced no definitive results. Both constitutional and legal opinion on the meaning of the act and its applicability in this case were divided and inconclusive (Kaiser 1980). The strongest analytic message from the incident, however, is clear: the president dominates in crisis situations; the War Powers Act is not likely to have much operational importance in the real world.

Conclusions

In general, the expected patterns of congressional–executive interaction can be observed in the examples used in this chapter. Subgovernments are very important in structural decisions, although when those decisions also have major strategic implications—as in the case of most major weapons systems—the scope of conflict is widened. Congress as a whole typically gets involved in strategic decisions, although the tendency to defer to the executive branch or at least to preserve considerable flexibility for the executive branch is very strong. Where Congress wants more clout it pushes, in effect, to redefine matters as structural. In crisis situations congressional participation tends to be only symbolic, if it is present at all. The War Powers Act makes broad claims for a congressional role in crises, but there is a good deal of évidence that those claims will not become operational. Congress is likely to become important in a crisis only if the president chooses to make selected congressional leaders important and chooses to listen to them.

The largest deviation from our initial expectations about congressional–executive relations in foreign and defense policy is the degree to which Congress gets involved in strategic decisions. This deviation can be explained largely on two grounds. First, strategic and structural issues are often blurred. The defense budget, for example, presents a number of structural decisions to Congress each year. But some of those decisions, particularly those on new weapons systems, are also strategic in impact. At the nadir of congressional willingness to challenge the executive branch on strategic matters, a period from roughly 1955 to 1965 (Ripley 1988, 409–413), Congress tended to back off from any involvement in strategic matters. Since then, Congress has been much less timid, although still generally intent on leaving considerable executive branch flexibility, especially on the part of the president.

Second, if domestic political considerations are involved, then Congress is usually willing to render judgments on strategic issues that may vary from those coming from the executive branch, including the military services. Ethnic considerations, as in the case of aid to Turkey, or domestic economic considerations, as in the case of balance-of-payments deficits related to the stationing of U.S. troops overseas, can help make Congress relatively more aggressive in strategic matters. But congressional concern for flexibility remains even under these conditions.

Presidents who wish to have an impact on structural decisions can enhance their chances of success by stressing the strategic aspects of those decisions. When Congress wishes to intervene in strategic matters, it is most likely to oppose the president when it focuses on structural aspects, especially when domestic political considerations intrude.

Figures 7-2, 7-3, and 7-4 summarize the most important relationships between executive, legislative, and private sector actors in formulating and legitimating the three different types of foreign and defense policy: structural, strategic, and crisis.

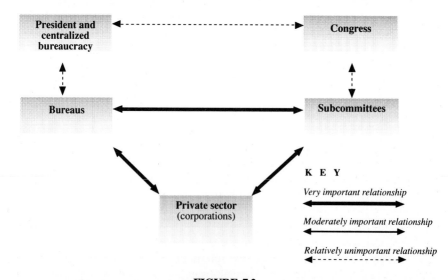

FIGURE 7-2

Relative importance of relationships for determining structural policy

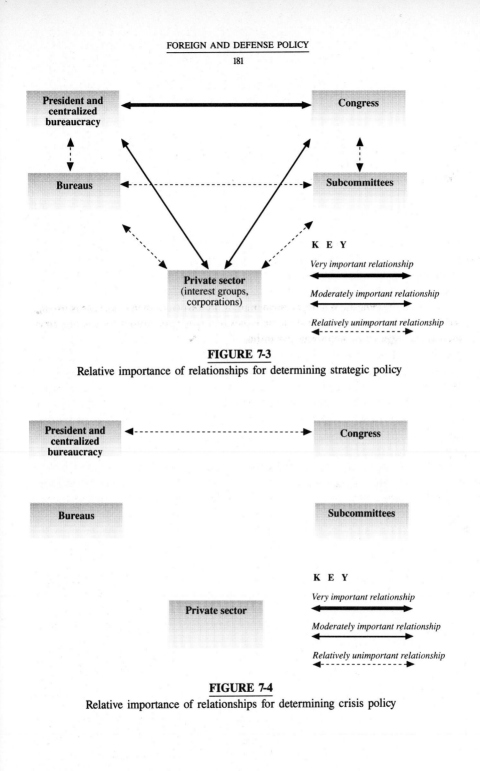

FIGURE 7-3

Relative importance of relationships for determining strategic policy

FIGURE 7-4

Relative importance of relationships for determining crisis policy

CHAPTER EIGHT

Congress, the Bureaucracy, and the Nature of American Public Policy

In general, American public policy can be accurately characterized as (1) slow to change, (2) more responsive to special interests than to general interests, (3) more responsive to the privileged in society than to the underprivileged, and (4) likely to be defined and treated as distributive in the domestic realm or structural in the foreign and defense realm, when possible. These features of American policy can be explained by a number of factors, chief among which include the importance of subgovernments in much of American policy making, the strong incentives for Congress and the bureaucracy to cooperate whenever possible, the lack of meaningful continuous congressional oversight for many policies, and the fact that political forces pushing for no change or minimal change in policy are stronger than forces pushing for greater change.

When the United States is compared to other economically developed, politically open nations (the nations of Western Europe, Canada, Japan), the U.S. bureaucracy looks quite different from those in the other countries. Central departmental management is weaker in the United States. The strength of disaggregated bureaucratic units (we use the generic term *bureaus*) is simultaneously much greater. This difference also helps foster the general characteristics of American public policy we have discussed throughout this book and that we have summarized in the first sentence of this chapter.

In addition, when the United States is compared to the nations of Western Europe, Canada, and Japan, it becomes evident that the lack of a strong, coherent left-wing (*social democratic* would be the best descriptor) political party, coupled with the presence of a consistently strong, generally right-wing party (the Republicans), helps keep the already privileged protected and also helps explain the stress in the United States on distributive policy. The American "left-wing" party (the Democrats) is, in fact, moderate and is constantly pulled to the right by the need to compete with the Republicans for the middle of the American political spectrum. But the American "middle" is ideologically considerably more to the right than the "middle" in the other economically developed, politically open nations. That basic partisan situation in the United States also helps explain why the politically meaningful definition of "redistribution" runs only in one direction—toward the disadvantaged—and why, collectively, Americans usually suspect that redistributive proposals are illegitimate much of the time.

We do not, however, see the world as black and white. It is, in fact, gray, no matter how unsettling that fact may be to individuals who do not tolerate ambiguity well. Features of man-made institutions, processes, and policies are at least partially manipulatable even in the short run. Thus, although we think the generalizations about the nature of American policy summarized in the first sentence are usually true, they are not true in every instance. Nor are they immutable.

Our aim in this final chapter is to summarize briefly the prinicipal analytic themes we have developed in the preceding chapters in order to explain the predominance of slowly changing, largely distributive and structural policy that caters mainly to special interests and the more well-off members of society. We also want to summarize our explanation of the exceptional conditions that can produce policies that do not fit the predominant mold. In addition, we want to underscore some normative concerns in the course of this summary discussion, although we do not pretend to have "final" answers to the questions we raise.

In the sections that follow we will first address in summary fashion the relative influence of various participants in different policy areas. Second, we will discuss the rewards of congressional–bureaucratic cooperation in policy making compared to the rewards of conflict. Third, we will offer some final thoughts on congressional oversight of bureaucratic policy performance. Fourth, we will summarize the relative strength of the forces pushing for stable policy and the forces pushing for changes in policy.

Participants, Influence, and Issues

We have made the argument in Chapters 4 through 7 that different relationships have varying degrees of importance in determining final policy statements, depending on the kind of issue at stake. At the end of each of those chapters we summarized the relative importance of relationships in diagrammatic form. Those six diagrams— one for each of the six basic policy types we have analyzed—are reproduced in Figure 8–1. These diagrams portray the relationships between five clusters of actors in those policy areas. The five clusters are (1) the president and centralized bureaucracy (the president personally, his top advisors, and cabinet members); (2) the bureaus (that is, the bureaucracy in its decentralized components); (3) Congress (as a whole); (4) subcommittees (Congress in its decentralized components); and (5) the private sector (the exact nature of which varies from policy area to policy area and is specified on the diagrams).

The diagrams reproduced in Figure 8–1, when coupled with the material in Tables 1–3 and 4–1, present an overview of the relative influence of all participants in the six different policy areas and also specify the changing role of the bureau-subcommittee–private sector subgovernments from area to area. The expectations we summarized in Table 4–1 were, in general, supported by the policy examples we examined. Ordinarily, subgovernments dominate distributive and structural policy making. They play lesser roles in three other policy areas and disappear only in the

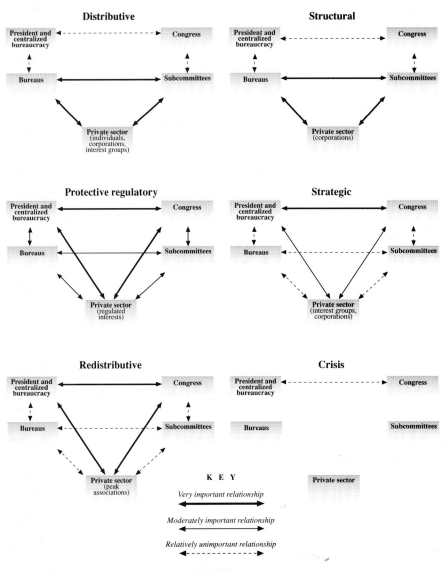

FIGURE 8–1
Relative importance of relationships for determining different kinds of policy

case of crisis policy. They play a moderately important role in protective regulatory policy and are sporadically important in the redistributive and strategic arenas.

Some would argue that the dominance of subgovernments in much policy making is beneficial and works in the public interest because genuine experts are placed in charge of issues. In addition, it is sometimes argued that the mechanisms for redressing excesses of subgovernment self-indulgence exist because broader access to various pressure points is open to "outsiders."

We do not agree with this totally apologetic and sanguine view. The incentives for using any mechanisms that may be available for redress are low most of the time. Simultaneously, the self-defense mechanisms in the hands of subgovernments are very strong. We would not argue that subgovernments can or should be eliminated from the policy-making process in the United States. However, we think that better and more responsive public policy can result from broader oversight of subgovernment functioning and the involvement of "outsiders" in at least some subgovernment deliberations. At minimum, the policies generated by the subgovernments that dominate distributive and structural policy making have implications for many sectors of society and the economy well beyond the direct beneficiaries of the policies. Expanding the participants in subgovernment deliberations would help spell out those impacts. Examples of such impacts would be that of subsidies for growing and processing various food products on the price of those items at the grocery or subsidies for the development of water resources on the environment. Such expansion of who is included in decision making might also help to relate the disaggregated policies of numerous dispersed subgovernments into a more coherent pattern. Bargaining, negotiation, and compromise are the hallmarks of the American decision-making system about policy matters. Our preference is to open the bargaining and negotiation that occur within subgovernments more broadly than is often the case, particularly in the distributive and structural arenas.

One general pattern we found that did not quite conform to our initial expectations is summarized in Table 4–1. After analyzing a number of policy areas (only some of which find their way into any specific edition of this book), we found that Congress in general—not just disaggregated into subcommittees—was a more important actor in all policy areas than the literature had led us to expect. In the protective regulatory domain, for example, members of Congress get involved not only in seeking weaker regulation for favored interests but also, in some cases, in seeking stiffer regulation than that being sought by the relevant regulatory agencies or the administration. In the redistributive arena we found, as expected, that presidential support was virtually always essential to producing concrete outcomes. However, in several of the redistributive cases, we observed an important role for Congress in quiet negotiations. These quiet negotiations often took place directly within what might be called a redistributive subgovernment—individuals from relevant congressional committees and subcommittees, bureaus, and interest groups (often peak associations). An important role for subgovernments in redistributive policy is not nearly as frequent as in the case of distributive policy. But such a role was, in some cases, essential at a critical juncture in a debate that might have gone on much longer and without resolution had quiet discussions involving parts of Congress not taken place.

Congress also played an unexpectedly large role in strategic decisions, both because there was a blurring of strategic and structural issues and because domestic political considerations often motivated congressional involvement. Even in crisis situations we noted that individuals from Congress—senior leaders from the committees primarily responsible for foreign policy and defense matters and also the party leaders—might give relevant advice that could be important *if* the president chose to ask for the advice and chose to listen to it. Presidents often have neither the time nor inclination to ask for congressional participation, but occasionally they do. The War Powers Act is at least a paper reminder from Congress that it would like to be consulted and a stronger reminder that it does not again want the United States to drift into war without full congressional involvement.

Some analyses of the role of Congress in policy making proceed as if the source of the initiation of legislative ideas is all that matters and that somehow Congress and the executive branch are involved in a zero-sum game over initiation. The conclusion in such analyses is usually that because the executive branch initiates more than Congress, it has "won" the game, and the importance of Congress in policy making has declined. At least three serious problems suggest that this view is wrong.

First, Congress can and does get involved in policy initiation on a broad range of issues (Chamberlain 1946; Moe and Teel 1970; and Orfield 1975). For example, Congress was responsible for initiation in the following policy areas in recent years: medicare, social security disability insurance, pension reform, voting rights for eighteen-year olds, political campaign reform, reduction and cessation of the U.S. military role in Indochina, chemical additives in foods, the creation of a consumer-protection agency, mandatory automobile safety standards, food programs for the poor, increases in the minimum wage, sanctions against the South African government, and highway development. Congress also initiated major investigations of the drug industry, multinational corporations, organized crime, and labor racketeering.

Second, Congress does much more than initiate. Even granting that the executive branch initiates a great deal on a piecemeal basis and that the president is probably the only possible source for a genuinely comprehensive and integrated legislative program, the power that Congress has and uses to legitimate, amend, or reject executive and presidential initiatives is both extensive and extremely important.

Third, congressional–executive relations cannot reasonably be interpreted as a zero-sum game. Congress and the executive branch (both the president and the bureaucracy) can be creative together or can fall on their faces together. In most instances, policy making involves at least some efforts from both of them. Much of the time it is a cooperative venture. To analyze a cooperative venture in terms of a zero-sum game produces gross distortions.

A more systematic way of thinking about the interaction of the executive branch and Congress in making policy is to posit four basic "models" of the relationship (Ripley 1988, 399–417).

The first model is one of *executive dominance.* In this relationship, the executive branch is the principal source of the initiation of legislative ideas and also shapes most of the details. Congressional participation in the shaping of details is low. Legislation results.

The second model is one of *joint program development.* In this relationship, either the executive branch or Congress can be the principal source of initiation. Both branches are heavily involved in shaping the details of the final decision. Legislation results.

The third model is one of *congressional dominance*. In this relationship, Congress provides the chief source of initiation and also shapes most of the details of the final legislation, which is passed.

The fourth model is one of *stalemate*. In this relationship, principal initiative can come from either branch. Often it comes from both branches simultaneously, but they disagree about what they want. Both branches also try to shape the details of legislative proposals. Again they do not agree. The short-term result at least is that no legislation results because the disagreements are too great.

Table 8–1 summarizes the four models of policy formulation and legitimation. Table 8–2 lists domestic policy decisions from recent years that illustrate the different patterns.

Cooperation and Conflict between Congress and the Bureaucracy

In Chapter 1 we specified six conditions that promote either cooperation or conflict between Congress and the bureaucracy, depending on the state of the conditions at any given time. These were level of personal compatibility, level of ideological or programmatic agreement, level of genuine congressional participation in decision making, level of salience of an issue to constituents and organized groups, relative aggressiveness of agencies in requesting expansion, and nature of party control of the executive branch and Congress. The relative importance of these conditions varies by type of policy. Smooth subgovernment relations are dominant in the distributive

TABLE 8–1
Models of Policy Formulation and Legitimation

Model	Principal source of initiation	Degree of congressional participation in shaping details	Degree of executive participation in shaping details	Final legislative product
Executive dominance	Executive	Low	High	Yes
Joint program development	Executive or Congress or both	High	High	Yes
Congressional dominance	Congress	High	Low	Yes
Stalemate	Executive or Congress or both	HIgh	High	No

SOURCE: R. B. Ripley, *Congress: Process and Policy,* 4th ed. (New York: W. W. Norton, 1988), 402.

and structural policy areas because personal compatibility is high, programmatic agreement is high (with ideology almost totally irrelevant to all parties), the level of congressional participation is high, the issues are salient to constituents and organized groups that congressional and bureaucratic figures in key positions are eager to serve, there is a mutually agreed on level of agency expansion, and differing party control of the two branches is often only a minor irritant.

In the protective regulatory, strategic, and redistributive arenas, there is more likely to be ideological or programmatic disagreement; the executive branch may

TABLE 8–2

Examples of Recent Domestic Policy Making Generally Fitting Different Models

---

Executive dominance
 Economic Opportunity Act, 1964
 Model Cities, 1966
 Juvenile delinquency, 1963
 Tax Act, 1981
 Budget reconciliation, 1981

Joint program development
 Area Redevelopment Act, 1961
 Humphrey–Hawkins bill, 1978
 Appalachia program, 1964
 Food stamps, 1963
 Aid to airports, 1950s and 1960s
 Mass transit, 1960s and 1970s
 Numerous education programs, 1940s–1960s
 Job Training Partnership Act, 1982
 Farm supports and farm credit, 1985
 Tax Act, 1986
 Minimum wages, 1989

Congressional dominance
 Air-pollution control, 1950s–1970s
 Water-pollution control, 1950s–1970s
 Strip mining regulation, 1977
 Health research, 1950s, 1960s
 Tax Act, 1982
 Highway bill, 1987

Stalemate
 Housing, early 1970s
 Air to elementary and secondary education, 1940s–early 1960s
 Medicare, 1940s–early 1960s
 Creation of an Urban Affairs Department, 1961–1962
 Welfare reform, 1970s
 Enterprise-zone bill, 1980s
 Tax bill, 1985
 Deficit reduction, 1983–1985

---

try to exclude Congress or at least diminish its role; the salience of issues is likely to encompass larger groups and sets of individuals rather than small, tightly knit groups with common interests; desires for expansion will be articulated without prior agreement; and differing party control of the two branches makes increased conflict much more likely.

Cooperation is certainly needed, or else effective government cannot exist in the United States. We do not denigrate the value of cooperation. But we also do not denigrate the values that are sometimes promoted by conflict. Conflict can produce incisive questions about public policy, more oversight and evaluation of program performance, and more awareness of what is at stake in public policy decisions. The desire of most participants, however, is for cooperation whenever possible, sometimes at all costs. The price paid for this desire is often an uncritical attitude about specific public policies on the part of public officials, both elected and nonelected. The incentives are heavily loaded in favor of cooperation. As suggested in Chapter 2, the background of our officials, both in Congress and in the executive branch, is such that a fairly homogeneous group of mostly middle-aged, middle-class, white males makes most decisions. This may mean there is a built-in bias to see things from a relatively common perspective. This point should not be overstated. Obviously, individuals and clusters in this set of decision makers differ markedly on some policy matters. We, unlike some critics, do not suggest that a "conspiracy" exists. We do raise the possibility, however, that relative homogeneity in background in a set of officials may help produce relative homogeneity in outlook on *some* crucial policy questions.

Even more important, as suggested in Chapter 3, a number of institutional incentives contribute to the desire to see policy in a nonconflictive light. Both members of Congress and members of the bureaucracy usually have more to gain from cooperation than from conflict (Ripley 1988, Chapter 10).

Legislative Oversight

Why Oversight Is Less than Systematic: Resources and Motivations

Oversight of bureaucratic behavior and performance as a congressional activity can be thought of in two senses. First, in a random and nonsystematic—although not trivial—sense, oversight can be described as a constant activity. This is the case because individual members, staff members, subcommittees, and committees all have many opportunities to engage in oversight, and they take advantage of a number of those opportunities. Congress is in a position to be relatively well informed about agency behavior if it wants to be so informed (Aberbach 1987, 1989; Foreman 1988).

Second, however, more systematic, planned, continuous oversight by Congress is relatively rare. We have already suggested some of the reasons. In general, members of the House and Senate have a variety of interests. The motivation for them to engage in systematic, planned, continuous oversight is often missing or weak at best. (For a good review of the literature on oversight see Rockman 1984, 414–439.)

Ogul (1973, 2–3; see also Ogul 1976, 1981) discussed specific legislative oversight activities in terms of these motivations:

> When any action is perceived to contribute directly and substantially to political survival as well as to other legitimate functions, it is likely to move toward the top of any member's priority list. Extra incentives to oversee come from problems of direct concern to one's constituents or from issues that promise political visibility or organizational support. Conversely, problems not seen as closely related to political survival are more difficult to crowd onto the member's schedule. . . .
>
> Not all congressional activity is linked directly to political survival. A congressman seems to gain interest in pushing oversight efforts onto his active calendar under the following conditions: New executive requests are forthcoming calling for massive new expenditures or substantial new authorizations in controversial policy areas; a crisis has occurred that has not been met effectively by executive departments; the opposition political party is in control of the executive branch; he has not been treated well either in the realm of personal attention or in the servicing of his requests; he has modest confidence in the administrative capacity of departmental or agency leaders.

Ogul also pointed out that when a member has high confidence in a set of leaders or agrees with the policies they are pursuing, the motivation for oversight lessens. If favored policies are being ignored or contradicted, however, the member has relatively high incentive to get involved with the bureaucracy to try to alter its policy behavior in a desired direction.

Davis (1970, 133–134) added some reasons that oversight is weak and sporadic:

> For all the formal power of Congress, Congress does operate under important restraints in playing its role of administrative overseer. Congress is relatively small compared to the executive branch; it does not meet continuously, it is made up (at best) of intelligent laymen, and it has limited staff. These characteristics mean that Congress is unable to review the performance of executive branch organizations in any regular and systematic way. Because of its limited staff Congress cannot collect all the information it would need to review agency performance systematically and, if it could collect the needed information, it could not analyze and interpret it. It can react to complaints, respond to fires. But it may be able to spot fires only when they have reached considerable proportions. . . .
>
> An additional limit on Congress's ability to oversee administration is the potential ability of a government executive to avoid the close examination of his organization and its budget by maintaining friendly personal relations with relevant committee chairmen. If a bureau chief can build an atmosphere of confidence and trust, then Congressmen may not ask him many questions and may accept on faith his answers to any questions asked.

Ralph K. Huitt (1966, 20), a careful student of Congress and a former assistant secretary in the Department of Health, Education, and Welfare, reached much the same conclusion as Davis about the extent of congressional oversight and also indicated the conditions under which it is most likely:

> Not much "oversight" of administration, in a systematic and continuous enough manner to make it mean very much, is practiced. The appropriations committees probably do more than the legislative committees. . . . Most legislative oversight occurs when hearings on new bills or authorizations occur. Closer scrutiny is likely to result from the personal interest of a chairman or ranking member, the sudden interest of the public in a program or a member's hunch that interest can be aroused, or the relationship (amounting virtually to institutional incest in a separation-of-powers system) which arises when a chairman fills the agency's top jobs with his own former staff members. The individual member's interest in administration is likely to be spurred by a constituent's protest, which subsides when the matter is taken care of.

Only a few studies of congressional oversight have been undertaken that have been systematic in the sense of collecting and rigorously using data on both congressional behavior (including both members and staff members) and bureaucratic behavior. Other studies have focused on only the congressional side or only on a subset of congressional actors, such as staff members.

One systematic study was of the relations between three congressional committees and seven independent regulatory commissions from 1938 to 1961 (Scher 1963). Another was a study of the relations between the Senate Banking and Currency Committee and three agencies (the Small Business Administration, the Federal Reserve Board, and the Housing and Home Finance Agency) from 1954 through 1962 (Bibby 1966). The Scher study supported the Davis and Huitt positions by observing that long periods of time passed between serious reviews of the various agencies by the committees. The Bibby study examined specific conditions promoting greater oversight. These include the presence of a committee chairperson devoted to "serving" the other members of the committee rather than imposing personal views on the committee; a relatively high degree of subcommittee autonomy within the committee; a sufficient and aggressive staff for the committee; members highly interested in the work of the committee and experienced in Congress and in interacting with the executive branch; and a committee with a basic orientation toward oversight of the administration of existing statutes rather than with the development of new basic legislation. Because few committees meet all of these conditions often or for long periods of time, the relative paucity of systematic oversight is easy to understand and explain.

A study by Ogul (1976) of three House committees (the Post Office and Civil Service Committee, a subcommittee of the Judiciary Committee, and a special subcommittee of the Government Operations Committee) in the mid- and late 1960s produced similar findings. The one committee engaged in oversight that had much impact was a short-term special subcomittee. Ogul also summarized the conditions most likely to foster oversight, although the presence of any one or all of these conditions in no way guarantees a strong oversight performance. His general conclusion is that nothing can guarantee effective oversight, and idiosyncratic features probably explain a great deal about its occurrence.

A thorough study of the intergovernmental grant system—one of the largest and most important sets of domestic programs—concluded that congressional oversight performance in this area, despite congressional rhetoric alleging great interest in oversight, had been "disappointing" (Advisory Commission on Intergovernmental Relations 1978, 86). Specifically, Congress had simply ignored a provision for periodic review of grants contained in the Intergovernmental Cooperation Act of 1968.

General and special revenue-sharing programs and block grants also present new challenges to already weak oversight. Because these programs are not directly controlled or implemented by federal bureaucracies, but are instead controlled largely by seemingly innumerable state and local governments, Congress has great trouble in getting a handle on how to oversee them and also has little incentive to do so. When Ronald Reagan became president, he pushed for even more devolution of federal power to states and localities. Oversight of various forms of special revenue sharing and block grants has been minimal, because, for one reason, the federal agencies did not collect data that would allow systematic evaluation of programs, *even if* Congress asked the right questions. The block grant programs created under the Reagan presidency were even less likely to require data appropriate for systematic evaluation and oversight.

Even in the area of covert intelligence, in which extremely disturbing revelations about the practices of the Central Intelligence Agency, the Federal Bureau of Investigation, and other agencies have been made in recent years, protestations of changed congressional attitudes toward the intelligence function—which took considerable time to develop (Elliff 1977; Ransom 1975)—were followed up with little concrete, sustained oversight (Horrock 1978; Marro 1977). Both houses have demonstrated interest by creating select committees on intelligence, but these committees have been sporadically rather than continuously influential and active in the design and use of oversight. Structural protections for covert agencies and shifting public attention, as well as shifting personal interest, views, experience, and stamina on the part of individual members of Congress, all work to minimize continuous oversight in this realm (Johnson 1980).

One concrete problem Congress faces in trying to oversee many programs is that the delegations of power by Congress to the executive branch are so broad that they contain no standards against which performance can be measured, even at a very general level (Lowi 1979; Woll 1977). Broad delegations of power also blur the intended focus of oversight. As a result, oversight can ask widely varying questions, focusing on issues such as management efficiency, bureaucratic procedures, programmatic impact on clients and beneficiaries, degree of programmatic goal achievement, or justification for a program. Yet another obstacle to oversight is an attitude among legislators who agree that, in the abstract, oversight is necessary and important but who do not want their pet programs to be overseen. This attitude can lead to a form of backscratching that diminishes the incentives for and the frequency of oversight. "Don't investigate my program and I won't investigate yours," is the implied form of mutual agreements.

In the 1970s, after Watergate, there was a clear increase in interest in oversight on the part of Congress. There was also a conclusion reached rapidly by some journalists (and even a few political scientists, who should have known better) that a new, permanently high level of congressional oversight had become part of the American political landscape. However, the post-Watergate burst of interest proved to be largely temporary. It did not lead to a permanent increase in oversight or the removal of any of the fundamental constraints on mounting continuous oversight (Dodd and Schott 1979). Oversight does not come naturally or easily to Congress, and there is no reason to expect that it ever will.

Altering Patterns of Resources and Motivations to Promote Oversight

The reasons for sporadic or absent congressional oversight relate both to the resources of Congress on the one hand and to the motivations of legislators on the other. Problems of resources are easier to affect than problems of motivation, but are still not easy.

Resources At both the verbal level and the formal statutory level, Congress has demonstrated considerable interest in oversight since World War II, and that interest has intensified in the 1970s and 1980s (Aberbach 1989, 1979; Freed 1975; Havemann 1976).

The first explicit congressional legislative attempt to create both an oversight mandate and capacity came in the Legislative Reorganization Act of 1946. In that act (which also reduced the number of standing committees, rationalized their jurisdiction in relation to the governmental agenda in 1946, and provided professional staffs for committees and members) all committees were charged with "continuous watchfulness" of executive branch performance in administering public laws and with studying agency reports submitted to Congress. The Government Operations Committees in both houses were given a special mandate to make sure that all government programs were meeting the traditional criteria of economy and efficiency.

In the Intergovernmental Cooperation Act of 1968, committees were specifically required to oversee the operations of federal grant-in-aid programs to states and localities, including those that had no firm expiration dates in the initial statutes. Congress has ignored this provision. The Legislative Reorganization Act of 1970 gave oversight capacity, at least in principle, to the General Accounting Office (GAO) and the Congressional Research Service. It also required virtually all committees to report every two years on their oversight activities.

In 1974 Congress passed two statutes that showed substantial concern with oversight. The Congressional Budget and Impoundment Control Act created staff capacity in the two budget committees and the Congressional Budget Office. In addition, the GAO was mandated to establish an Office of Program Review and Evaluation and to recommend to Congress methods to be used in such review and evaluation. The Treasury and the OMB in the executive branch were also required to provide special information to committees, the GAO, and the Congressional Budget Office.

Perhaps most important, the 1974 Budget Act got at least some members of the House and Senate—the members of the Budget Committees—intimately involved in the details of the federal budgets. This involvement could lead to a greater concern with systematic oversight. Given the procedures of the Budget Act requiring that budget resolutions be passed each year by the entire House and Senate, there was at least some potential in the act for creating a similar concern in all members of the House and Senate.

One critical resource Congress has done well in providing for itself in recent years is adequate and high-quality professional staff (Fox and Hammond 1977; Ripley 1988, 239-251). Staff limits are no longer a major constraint on oversight potential in most substantive areas. Individual senators and representatives and all committees and subcommittees have sizable staffs.

In addition, Congress has created some new central support offices in recent years and has strengthened some preexisting ones in an effort, in part, to create a more professional staff structure that could help sustain more effective and continuous oversight. The Congressional Budget Office has already been mentioned as one relatively new office that has some potential for enhancing congressional oversight. Another relatively new office with at least limited potential of that kind is the Office of Technology Assessment.

An older organization that was renamed, the Congressional Research Service, was required by the 1970 Legislative Reorganization Act to provide committees of Congress (in effect, chairpersons) with lists of expiring legislation and also with "a list of subjects and policy areas which the committees might profitably analyze in depth." Another established organization, the GAO, was authorized by the same law "to review and analyze 'the results of government programs and activities, including the making of cost and benefit studies,' on its initiative or when ordered by either house or a committee." The use of the GAO is not governed by a rational plan, however. A Wisconsin Republican member of the House, William Steiger, complained that the GAO "is not used properly because there is no comprehensive, rational approach to how it should be used. By and large, a congressman will tell GAO, 'Here's a problem, look at it and report back.' There's no understanding of the types of questions that should be asked or how programs should be evaluated." (All quotations in this paragraph are from Freed 1975, 597-598.)

Both houses reorganized their committee systems in the 1970s—the House in 1974 and the Senate in 1977. The Senate reorganization had no particular relationship to oversight potential. In the House, one provision required standing committees with more than twenty members to set up special oversight subcommittees or to require their standing subcommittees to engage in oversight. It also gave special oversight responsibilities and powers to seven standing committees (Budget, Armed Services, Education and Labor, International Affairs, Interior and Insular Affairs, Science and Technology, and Small Business). These committees were specifically authorized to cross normal jurisdictional boundaries in pursuing their oversight duties. This formal requirement has not improved either the quality or quantity of oversight, however.

Motivations A more subtle and difficult problem in improving oversight lies in altering the motivations of members to conduct or avoid it. The motivations of members are set in institutional contexts that are slow, although not impervious, to change. One way to increase the amount of oversight that gets done would be to stress the linkages between oversight and other, higher-priority tasks of legislators. This would help improve members' motivations to perform oversight. The performance of oversight should have payoffs for members' other priorities or goals, such as getting reelected. For example, constituents' problems raise issues that spark oversight. By seeking patterns among constituents' problems with agencies' programs (such as social security eligibility and payments), more systematic oversight of client-oriented programs would result. Staff and others can argue that such patterns are present, but ultimately members have to see the patterns themselves to change their behavior.

Congressional perception of the public mood may help stimulate oversight, as the burst of post-Watergate activity demonstrates. But the normal lack of public interest in oversight also helps promote congressional apathy because there is no apparent political reward for pursuing activities diligently if few in the voting public value those activities. There may be political incentives for pursuing what amounts to phony or toothless oversight conducted primarily to impress the home folks. Some congressional questions about and inquiries into the performance of some bureaucracies and programs are almost purely to build an image of no-nonsense effectiveness back in the district. Such "oversight" is, by definition, much too sporadic to have any genuine impact on the agencies or programs presumably involved.

Another way of creating motivation for legislative oversight would be to tie oversight to the desire of members to initiate and develop legislation. Because most members derive a feeling of accomplishment from authorizing legislation, that pride of parenthood might be tapped to motivate committee members involved in creating legislation to follow through on oversight of the implementation and impact of that legislation. This would be facilitated if the legislation mandated stiff reporting and evaluation requirements for the administering agency.

In those areas in which Congress has been most important in initiating, it has often been most aggressive in oversight. Air and water pollution legislation offer good examples. We disagree at least partially with Huitt (1966) and Bibby (1966) when they suggest there is a necessary trade-off between performing oversight and developing new legislation and that a committee interested in the latter will not have much time for the former. This may be true if the committee is not subsequently forced, in effect, to consider performance of the receipt of agency reports and evaluations. But with the automatic, scheduled receipt of such reports and evaluations, the opportunity for oversight would be created, and we would place our bets on the most aggressive initiating committees also performing most aggressively as overseers.

An additional provision of new statutes that might also enhance oversight would be an automatic termination date coupled with reporting and evaluation requirements that would force the committee to consider the statute periodically and at the same time provide data and agency views that would be considered in the deliberations about whether to terminate, extend, or amend a program (Lowi 1973b). This notion of "sunset" legislation was relatively popular in Congress in the late 1970s, although it faded from view in the 1980s and into the early 1990s. Through a combination of attention to developing congressional resource capacity and increasing members' motivations for performing legislative oversight, the quality and continuity of oversight could improve. No magic formula will cure all problems, however, and congressional oversight is never likely to become everything critics want.

Forces for and against Change

A number of powerful forces work against policy change of any sizable magnitude, yet some sizable shifts do occur.

The forces supporting the status quo in any policy area are likely to be higher-level civil servants—especially those in older, larger, well-established agencies—and members of Congress and staff members in Congress working on the subcommittees dealing with individual agencies and their programs. The disposition of these bureaucrats and legislators and legislative staff to make only moderate or small changes in policies is seconded by the impact of the representatives of interest groups that receive particular benefits and advantages from existing policy. All of these individuals, both from public units and from the private sector, tend to be character-ized by long service and a long history of interacting with each other. They are highly specialized in the substantive business of their particular subgovernment, and their loyalties tend to be primarily institutional (that is, to the subcommittee or agency or interest group itself) or to a limited constituency (the "most important" voters in the case of a member of Congress or the "most important" clients or support groups in the case of bureaucrats).

The forces that are more likely to be mobilized in support of substantial policy change consist of a few bureaucrats, congressional staff members, members of Congress (usually outside of the subgovernment dominating policy in the area) and—selectively—the president and some of his appointees in relevant positions in the executive establishment. These individuals tend to have less tenure in their positions than those more likely to favor the status quo. This is most evident in the case of presidents and their appointees. They probably do not have long-established patterns of personal relations with one another. The forces that coalesce to work in favor of major policy change are likely to do so *ad hoc*, whereas the forces supporting the status quo with only minor changes tend to be more institutionalized and permanent. The degree of specialization is much lower in the forces pushing for change than in the forces pushing for the status quo. The principal loyalties of those working for fairly major change are more likely to be ideological or programmatic (tied to a vision of "good policy") than narrowly institutional. The president and at least some members of Congress who seek to relate to a national constituency (this applies especially to senators and representatives who think they might want to be president) take some policy initiatives to gain support from some portion of the national electorate.

The sheer complexity of getting new policies adopted in the United States when compared to a number of other developed countries with open political systems also helps explain why "new departures" in policy seem to be relatively rare in the United States. After studying policies on regional development and population distribution in the United States, Great Britain, France, Italy, the Netherlands, and Sweden, one careful student of policy making (Sundquist 1978, 79) reached these conclusions:

> Because the institutional structure of policymaking in the United States is more complex and pluralized than those of the other industrial democracies of the Atlantic

community, because the policymaking circle is broader and more amateur and less disciplined, public participation more intense, and the points of potential veto of policy innovation more numerous, and because political parties are weaker as integrating mechanisms, a higher degree of national consensus and a more intense commitment of political leadership are necessary before new departures can be developed and approved, and a narrower range of innovation can be successfully attempted at any one time.

What effect did the Reagan presidency have on the basic patterns of policy making analyzed in this book? How much change did Reagan bring to the underlying patterns of policy formulation and legitimation in the United States?

At one level, the answer is that Reagan was just another president and that the underlying patterns and activities we have analyzed continued throughout his presidency and remain in place today. Change and marginal adjustments occur constantly. They did so during the Reagan years too. But there were no major changes in the basic patterns of policy formulation and legitimation that process the nation's business. At the same time, however, although the processes of decision making changed by relatively small increments, the substance of the agenda being addressed changed more. Reagan insisted on a different policy agenda from the one that had become familiar for the preceding half century. But President Bush has already made it clear that he has some different policy priorities from Reagan. His agenda looks more like a pre-Reagan Republican agenda than it looks like a Reaganite agenda. Even in the realm of substance, therefore, the "Reagan revolution" appears to have been a temporary interlude.

As the Reagan years fade from memory, it is worth noting the essence of the temporary changes in the policy agenda wrought by his administration. Three major points stand out. First, Reagan's antipathy to social programs brought a halt to redistributive policy making aimed at greater social equality. Without presidential backing, such initiatives either are not taken or go only a short distance before running out of gas. Reagan's efforts were aimed at redistributing in favor of the already well-off. But, in American political parlance, such policy preferences do not generate political patterns associated with redistributive policy.

Second, he was generally opposed to protective regulatory legislation. That position effectively blocked the consideration of any new legislation of this type. He was not successful in getting Congress to "de-regulate" in this arena by eliminating or weakening existing statutes. Various coalitions, with sufficient congressional support, protected the laws already on the books. However, the president and some of his appointees did all they could to weaken enforcement of some of those laws by using their control over implementation processes.

Third, Reagan engaged in rhetoric condemning subgovernments. When examined, however, his statements were primarily attacks on coalitions supporting various redistributive policies and programs. He rarely attacked the classic subgovernments clustered around subsidy programs. The Reagan passion for increased defense spending strengthened the hand of most of the subgovernments active in the structural policy arena.

Two major impacts of the Reagan era on the organs of government can be discerned. First, Reagan appointments to federal judgeships have produced a dramatic conservative tilt in the entire federal judiciary. The Supreme Court's new conservative majority is most visible, but it also needs to be remembered that over half of all federal district judges and appellate judges are also Reagan appointees. The Reagan administration was assiduous in appointing only dedicated conservatives to all of these openings.

Second, and most relevant to the analysis in this book, is the impact of the Reagan era on the federal bureaucracy: its personnel, structure, morale, and capacity for governing fairly and efficiently. Analytically, there is little certain knowledge about the impact of elections—especially elections that reveal changing political beliefs—on bureaucracy in the United States (Meier and Kramer 1980). Nor is anyone sure how quickly pieces of the domestic bureaucracy can reestablish pre-Reagan equilibrium upset by reductions in force (both voluntary and involuntary), major shifts of senior- and middle-level personnel in terms of assignment and geographical location, budget cuts, high turnover, and executive branch attitudes unsupportive of agency missions and purposes. There are signs that the legacy of the Reagan years in the bureaucracy will be with us for some time.

In effect, the Reagan presidency produced a widespread and often successful attack on the capacity, self-esteem, and status of the federal civil service. The revelations of massive corruption in the Department of Housing and Urban Development during the Reagan years that began to come to light throughout 1989 suggest how far a bureaucracy can collapse when it is run by appointees who have little competence and are dealing with policies the political masters in the White House did not want or care about. The facts being revealed about Pentagon procurement during the Reagan years present yet another gruesome spectacle of treating government like a private and very fat piggy bank for the enrichment of favored parts of the private sector.

Not all federal agencies came out of the Reagan years in such sorry shape as HUD or the procurement units in the Department of Defense. But the Reagan administration's practices of using the Senior Executive Service (created in 1978 as a "reform" measure; used by the Reagan administration for political ends) to promote the conservative agenda by moving senior civil servants thought to be unsympathetic, ignoring pay equity for civil servants, and suggesting that government is the problem rather than any part of the solution have had deleterious effects that will not go away quickly. Departure of many competent people from federal service, diminished morale of the survivors, and supervision by incompetents or those hostile to the programs and missions of agencies (or both) have all taken place on a grand scale.

It will take many years to repair the damage. Does the government want to do it? Does the executive branch after Reagan perceive that damage has occurred? Does it want to repair it? There are some favorable hints from President Bush. But until major repairs are well under way, the bureaucracy can, in general, expect to play its roles in policy formulation and policy implementation with less than usual vigor and competence.

A Closing Word

We end both this chapter and the book on an analytical note that is moderately hopeful about the future. Conservatism in the sense of support for the status quo is dominant in the national policies of the United States for reasons we hope are clear in this volume: the pervasive need for compromise built into the system, the widespread desire to minimize conflict, and the desire to protect personal careers on the part of individuals throughout the executive and legislative branches. At the same time, however, these facts are not intended to be taken as an indictment of the system. Not all of the status quo is bad or undesirable policy. More important, status quo policy is not completely impervious to change, nor are the forces supporting the status quo dominant to the exclusion of all chances for change. Bursts of policy creativity can and do occur and may be initiated in either the legislative or executive branches.

Too much is often claimed for the "genius of American government." Likewise, indictments of American government and policy are often too sweeping. Conservative distributive or structural policies are likely to prevail unless deliberate action to pursue other ends is carefully and energetically pursued. Even though the political system of the nation does not *encourage* such action, it *permits* it when men and women with requisite political skills and policy commitments work hard and together to achieve desirable change.

REFERENCES

ABERBACH, J. D. (1979) "Changes in Congressional Oversight." *American Behavioral Scientist* 22 (May/June): 493–515.

ABERBACH, J. D. (1987) "The Congressional Committee Intelligence System: Information, Oversight, and Change." *Congress & the Presidency* 14 (Spring): 51–76.

ABERBACH, J. D. (1989) *Keeping a Watchful Eye: The Politics of Congressional Oversight.* Washington, D.C.: Brookings Institution.

ABERBACH, J. D., R. D. PUTNAM, and B. A. ROCKMAN. (1981) *Bureaucrats and Politicians in Western Democracies.* Cambridge, Mass.: Harvard University Press.

ABERBACH, J. D. and B. A. ROCKMAN. (1976) "Clashing Beliefs within the Executive Branch: The Nixon Administration Bureaucracy." *American Political Science Review* 70 (June): 456–468.

ABERBACH, J. D. and B. A. ROCKMAN. (1977) "The Overlapping Worlds of American Federal Executives and Congressmen." *British Journal of Political Science* 7 (January): 23–47.

ABERBACH, J. D. and B. A. ROCKMAN. (1978) "Bureaucrats and Clientele Groups: A View from Capitol Hill." *American Journal of Political Science* 22 (November): 818–832.

ADAMS, G. (1982) *The Politics of Defense Contracting: The Iron Triangle.* New Brunswick, N.J.: Transaction Books.

ADAMS, G. and S. A. CAIN. (1989) "The Defense Budget in the 1990s." In J. Kruzel (ed.), *1989–1990 American Defense Annual.* Lexington, Mass.: Lexington Books.

ADVISORY COMMISSION ON INTERGOVERNMENTAL RELATIONS. (1978) *Categorical Grants: Their Role and Design* (publication A-52). Washington, D.C.: U.S. Government Printing Office.

ANDERSON, J. E. (ed.). (1970) *Politics and Economic Policy-Making.* Reading, Mass.: Addison-Wesley.

ARMACOST, M. H. (1969) *The Politics of Weapons Innovation.* New York: Columbia University Press.

ARNOW, K. S. (1954) *The Department of Commerce Field Service.* Indianapolis: Bobbs-Merrill. ICP Case #21.

ATKINSON, R. (1989a) "Stealth: From 18-inch Model to $70 Billion Muddle." *Washington Post* (October 8).

ATKINSON, R. (1989b) "Unraveling Stealth's 'Black World.'" *Washington Post* (October 9).

ATKINSON, R. (1989c) "How Stealth's Consensus Crumbled." *Washington Post* (October 10).

BAUMER, D. C. and C. E. VAN HORN. (1984) *The Politics of Unemployment.* Washington, D.C.: Congressional Quarterly Press.

BEAM, D. R. (1984) "New Federalism, Old Realities: The Reagan Administration and Intergovernmental Reform." In L. M. Salamon and M. S. Lund (eds.), *The Reagan Presidency and the Governing of America.* Washington, D.C.: The Urban Institute.

BENDINER, R. (1964) *Obstacle Course on Capitol Hill.* New York: McGraw-Hill.

BERNSTEIN, M. H. (1958) *The Job of the Federal Executive.* Washington, D.C.: Brookings Institution.

BIBBY, J. F. (1966) "Committee Characteristics and Legislative Oversight of Administration." *Midwest Journal of Political Science* 10 (February): 78–98.

BIRD, K. (1978) "Food for Peace—or Politics?" *Washington Post* (January 4).

BOFFEY, P. M. et al. (1988) *Claiming the Heavens: The New York Times Complete Guide to the Star Wars Debate.* New York: Times Books.

BONAFEDE, D. (1979) "The Tough Job of Normalizing Relations with Capitol Hill." *National Journal* (January 13): 54–57.

BOSSO, C. J. (1987) *Pesticides and Politics: The Life Cycle of a Public Issue.* Pittsburgh: University of Pittsburgh Press.

BRADY, D. W. (1981) "Personnel Management in the House." In J. Cooper and G. C. Mackenzie (eds.), *The House at Work.* Austin: University of Texas Press.

BROWNE, W. P. (1988) *Private Interests, Public Policy, and American Agriculture.* Lawrence: University of Kansas Press.

CARPER, E. (1965) *The Reorganization of the Public Health Service.* Indianapolis: Bobbs-Merrill.

CARROLL, H. N. (1966) *The House of Representatives and Foreign Affairs,* rev. ed. Boston: Little, Brown.

CATER, D. (1964) *Power in Washington.* New York: Random House.

CHAMBERLAIN, L. H. (1946) *The President, Congress and Legislation.* New York: Columbia University Press.

CHUBB, J. E. (1985) "Federalism and the Bias for Centralization." In J. E. Chubb and P. E. Peterson (eds.), *The New Direction in American Politics.* Washington, D.C.: Brookings Institution.

CLARKE, J. N. and D. McCOOL. (1985) *Staking Out the Terrain: Power Differentials among Natural Resource Management Agencies.* Albany: State University of New York Press.

COOPER, A. (1978) "Congress Approves Civil Service Reform." *Congressional Quarterly Weekly Report* (October 14): 2945–2950.

CORSON, J. J. and R. S. PAUL. (1966) *Men Near the Top.* Baltimore: Johns Hopkins University Press.

CRAIG, B. H. (1983) *The Legislative Veto: Congressional Control of Regulation.* Boulder, Colorado: Westview Press.

CRAIG, B. H. (1988) *Chadha: The Story of an Epic Constitutional Struggle.* New York: Oxford University Press.

CULHANE, P. J. (1981) *Public Lands Politics: Interest Group Influence on the Forest Service and the Bureau of Land Management.* Baltimore: Johns Hopkins University Press.

DAVIDSON, R. H. (1967) "Congress and the Executive: The Race for Representation." In A. DeGrazia (ed.), *Congress: The First Branch of Government.* Garden City, N.Y.: Doubleday.

DAVIDSON, R. H. (1969) *The Role of the Congressman.* New York: Pegasus.

DAVIDSON, R. H. (1972) *The Politics of Comprehensive Manpower Legislation.* Baltimore: Johns Hopkins University Press.

DAVIDSON, R. H. (1975) "Policy Making in the Manpower Subgovernment." In M. P. Smith et al. (eds.), *Politics in America.* New York: Random House.

DAVIDSON, R. H. (1977) "Breaking Up Those 'Cozy Triangles': An Impossible Dream?" In S. Welch and J. G. Peters (eds.), *Legislative Reform and Public Policy.* New York: Praeger.

DAVIDSON, R. H. and W. J. OLESZEK. (1977) *Congress against Itself.* Bloomington: Indiana University Press.

DAVIS, J. W. (1970) *The National Executive Branch.* New York: Free Press.

DAVIS, J. W. and R. B. RIPLEY. (1967) "The Bureau of the Budget and Executive Branch Agencies: Notes on Their Interaction." *Journal of Politics* 29 (November): 749–769.

DESTLER, I. M. (1980). *Making Foreign Economic Policy.* Washington, D.C.: Brookings Institution.

DESTLER, I. M. (1985) "Executive–Congressional Conflict in Foreign Policy: Explaining It, Coping with It." In L. C. Dodd and B. I. Oppenheimer (eds.), *Congress Reconsidered,* 3rd ed. Washington, D.C.: Congressional Quarterly Press.

DODD, L. C. and B. I. OPPENHEIMER (eds.). (1977) *Congress Reconsidered.* New York: Praeger.

DODD, L. C. and R. L. SCHOTT. (1979) *Congress and the Administrative State.* New York: Praeger.

DONOVAN, J. C. (1973) *The Politics of Poverty,* 2nd ed. Indianapolis: Pegasus.

DREW, E. B. (1970) "Dam Outrage: The Story of the Army Engineers." *Atlantic* (April): 51–62.

DREW, E. B. (1982) "Legal Services." *New Yorker* (March 1): 97–113.

EIDENBERG, E. and R. D. MOREY. (1969) *An Act of Congress.* New York: W. W. Norton.

ELDER, S. (1978) "The Cabinet's Ambassadors to Capitol Hill." *Congressional Quarterly Weekly Report* (July 29): 1196–1200.

ELLIFF, J. T. (1977) "Congress and the Intelligence Community." In L. C. Dodd and B. I. Oppenheimer (eds.), *Congress Reconsidered.* New York: Praeger.

EVANS, R. and R. NOVAK. (1966) *Lyndon B. Johnson: The Exercise of Power.* New York: New American Library.

FENNO, R. F., Jr. (1959) *The President's Cabinet.* New York: Vintage.

FENNO, R. F., Jr. (1966) *Power of the Purse.* Boston: Little, Brown.

FENNO, R. F., Jr. (1973) *Congressmen in Committees.* Boston: Little, Brown.

FENNO, R. F., Jr. (1978) *Home Style: House Members in Their Districts.* Boston: Little, Brown.

FIORINA, M. P. (1977) *Congress: Keystone of the Washington Establishment.* New Haven, Conn.: Yale University Press.

FISHER, L. (1974) "Reprogramming of Funds by the Defense Department." *Journal of Politics* 36 (February): 77–102.

FISHER, L. (1985) "Judicial Misjudgments about the Lawmaking Process: The Legislative Veto Case." *Public Administration Review* 45 (November): 705–711.

FISHER, L. L. (1987) "Fifty Years of Presidential Appointments." In C. G. Mackenzie (ed.), *The In-and-Outers.* Baltimore: Johns Hopkins University Press.

FORD, G. R. (1977) "The War Powers Resolution: Striking a Balance between the Executive and Legislative Branches." *Reprint #69.* Washington, D.C.: American Enterprise Institute.

FOREMAN, C. H., Jr. (1988) *Signals from the Hill: Congressional Oversight and the Challenge of Social Regulation.* New Haven, Conn.: Yale University Press.

FOSS, P. O. (1960) *Politics and Grass.* Seattle: University of Washington Press.

FOX, H. W., Jr. and S. W. HAMMOND. (1977) *Congressional Staffs: The Invisible Force in American Lawmaking.* New York: Free Press.

FRANCK, T. M. and E. WEISBAND. (1979) *Foreign Policy by Congress.* New York: Oxford University Press.

FRANKLIN, G. A. and R. B. RIPLEY. (1984) *CETA: Politics and Policy, 1973–1982.* Knoxville: University of Tennessee Press.

FREED, B. F. (1975) "Congress May Step Up Oversight of Programs." *Congressional Quarterly Weekly Report* (March 22): 595–600.

FREEMAN, J. L. (1965) *The Political Process,* rev. ed. New York: Random House.

FRIEDMAN, K. M. (1975) *Public Policy and the Smoking-Health Controversy.* Lexington, Mass.: Lexington Books.

FRITSCHLER, A. L. (1989) *Smoking and Politics,* 4th ed. Englewood Cliffs, N.J.: Prentice-Hall.

FROMAN, L. A., Jr. (1968) "The Categorization of Policy Contents." In A. Ranney (ed.), *Political Science and Public Policy.* Chicago: Markham.

FRYE, A. (1975) *A Responsible Congress: The Politics of National Security.* New York: McGraw-Hill.

GIST, J. R. (1978) "Appropriations Politics and Expenditure Control." *Journal of Politics* 40 (February): 163–178.

GOLDENBERG, E. N. (1984) "The Permanent Government in an Era of Retrenchment and Redirection." In L.M. Salamon and M.S. Lund (eds.), *The Reagan Presidency and the Governing of America.* Washington, D.C.: The Urban Institute.

GREEN, H. P. and A. ROSENTHAL. (1963) *Government of the Atom: The Integration of Powers.* New York: Atherton.

GREENBERG, D. S. (1967) *The Politics of Pure Science.* New York: New American Library.

HAAS, L. J. (1988a) "Unauthorized Action." *National Journal* (January 2): 17–21.

HAAS, L. J. (1988b) "New Rules of the Game." *National Journal* (March 19): 732–734.

HAAS, L. J. (1988c) "The Deficit Culture." *National Journal* (June 4): 1460–1467.

HAAS, L. J. (1988d) "What OMB Hath Wrought." *National Journal* (September 3): 2187–2191.

HAAS, L. J. (1989) "Fiscal Catastrophe." *National Journal* (October 7): 2453–2456.

HARRIS, J. P. (1964) *Congressional Control of Administration.* Washington, D.C.: Brookings Institution.

HARRIS, R. A. and S. M. MILKIS. (1989) *The Politics of Regulatory Change: A Tale of Two Agencies.* New York: Oxford University Press.

HAVEMANN, J. (1976) "Congress Tries to Break Ground Zero in Evaluating Federal Programs." *National Journal* (May 22): 706–713.

HAVEMANN, J. (1977) "Congress Opens Floodgates in the SBA's Disaster Loan Program." *National Journal* (December 31): 2001–2003.

HAVEMANN, J. (1978) *Congress and the Budget.* Bloomington: Indiana University Press.

HAYES, M. T. (1981) *Lobbyists and Legislators: A Theory of Political Markets.* New Brunswick, N.J.: Rutgers University Press.

HECLO, H. (1977) *A Government of Strangers: Executive Politics in Washington.* Washington, D.C.: Brookings Institution.

HECLO, H. (1984) "In Search of a Role: America's Higher Civil Service." In E. N. Suleiman (ed.), *Bureaucrats & Policy Making.* New York: Holmes & Meier.

HECLO, H. (1987) "The In-and-Outer System: A Critical Assessment." In C. G. Mackenzie (ed.) *The In-and-Outers.* Baltimore: Johns Hopkins University Press.

HOLTZMAN, A. (1970) *Legislative Liaison: Executive Leadership in Congress.* Skokie, Ill.: Rand McNally.

HORN, S. (1970) *Unused Power: The Work of the Senate Committee on Appropriations.* Washington, D.C.: Brookings Institution.

HORROCK, N. M. (1978) "Intelligence Oversight: Congress Tries Again." *New York Times* (February 12).

HUITT, R. K. (1966) "Congress, the Durable Partner." In E. Frank (ed.), *Lawmakers in a Changing World*. Englewood Cliffs, N.J.: Prentice-Hall.

HUNTINGTON, S. P. (1961) *The Common Defense*. New York: Columbia University Press.

HUNTINGTON, S. P. (1973) "Congressional Responses to the Twentieth Century." In D. B. Truman (ed.), *Congress and America's Future*, 2nd ed. Englewood Cliffs, N.J.: Prentice-Hall.

JOHANNES, J. R. (1976) "Executive Reports to Congress." *Journal of Communication* 26 (Summer): 53–61.

JOHNSON, L. (1980) "The U.S. Congress and the CIA: Monitoring the Dark Side of Government." *Legislative Studies Quarterly* 5 (November): 477–499.

JONES, C. O. (1984) *An Introduction to the Study of Public Policy*, 3rd ed. Pacific Grove, Calif.: Brooks/Cole.

JONES, C. O. (1988) *The Trusteeship Presidency: Jimmy Carter and the United States Congress*. Baton Rouge: Louisiana State University Press.

KAISER, R. G. (1980) "In Stunned Congress Wariness and Concern over War Powers Act." *Washington Post* (April 26).

KANTER, A. (1972) "Congress and the Defense Budget, 1960–1970." *American Political Science Review* 66 (March): 129–143.

KATZMANN, R. A. (1980) *Regulatory Bureaucracy: The Federal Trade Commission and Antitrust Policy*. Cambridge, Mass.: Harvard University Press.

KAUFMAN, H. (1981) *The Administrative Behavior of Federal Bureau Chiefs*. Washington, D.C.: Brookings Institution.

KEEFE, W. J. and M. S. Ogul. (1985) *The American Legislative Process*, 6th ed. Englewood Cliffs, N.J.: Prentice-Hall.

KEISLING, P. (1982) "Old Soldiers Never Die." *Washington Monthly* (March): 20–29.

KELLER, B. (1980) "How a Unique Lobby Force Protects over $21 Billion in Vast Veterans' Programs." *Congressional Quarterly Weekly Report* (June 14): 1627–1634.

KELLER, B. (1981a) "Fast-Food Industry Expands Its Lobby Franchise to Cover Jobs and Commodities Issues." *Congressional Quarterly Weekly Report* (June 20): 1095–1098.

KELLER, B. (1981b) "Executive Agency Lobbyists Mastering the Difficult Art of 'Congressional Liaison.'" *Congressional Quarterly Weekly Report* (December 5): 2387–2392.

KELLER, B. (1981c) "Many Invincible Programs Again Spared the Budget Ax in Spite of Reagan Campaign." *Congressional Quarterly Weekly Report* (July 18): 1271–1282.

KELLER, B. (1982) "Some Sacred Cows of the Past Turn Out Not to Be Immortal as a Year of Budget Cuts Ends," *Congressional Quarterly Weekly Report* (January 2): 6–8.

KENNEDY, R. F. (1971) *Thirteen Days*. New York: W. W. Norton.

KESSEL, J. H. (1984) *Presidential Parties*. Pacific Grove, Calif.: Brooks/Cole.

KETTL, D. F. (1988) *Government by Proxy: (Mis?)Managing Federal Programs*. Washington, D.C.: CQ Press.

KIRST, M. W. (1969) *Government without Passing Laws*. Chapel Hill: University of North Carolina Press.

KLUGER, R. (1976) *Simple Justice*. New York: Knopf.

KOFMEHL, K. (1977) *Professional Staffs of Congress*, 3rd ed. West Lafayette, Ind.: Purdue University Studies.

KOLODZIEJ, E. A. (1966) *The Uncommon Defense and Congress, 1945–1963*. Columbus: The Ohio State University Press.

KOLODZIEJ, E. A. (1975). "Congress and Foreign Policy: The Nixon Years." In H. C. Mansfield, Sr. (ed.), *Congress against the President.* New York: Academy of Political Science.

KORB, L. J. and S. DAGGETT. (1988) "The Defense Budget and Strategic Planning." In J. Kruzel (ed.), *1988–1989 American Defense Annual.* Lexington, Mass.: Lexington Books.

KOTZ, N. (1988) *Wild Blue Yonder: Money, Politics, and the B-1 Bomber.* New York: Pantheon.

KRISTOF, N. D. (1982) "Scorned Legal Services Corporation on the Rebound." *Washington Post* (July 21).

KRIZ, M. E. (1988) "Pesticidal Pressures." *National Journal* (December 10): 3125–3127.

LANDIS, J. M. (1938) *The Administrative Process.* New Haven, Conn.: Yale University Press.

LANOUTTE, W. J. (1978) "Who's Setting Foreign Policy—Carter or Congress?" *National Journal* (July 15): 1116–1123.

LAWRENCE, S. A. (1965) "The Battery Acid Controversy." In E. A. Bock (ed.), *Government Regulation of Business.* Englewood Cliffs, N.J.: Prentice-Hall.

LeLOUP, L. T. (1980) *The Fiscal Congress: Legislative Control of the Budget.* Westport, Conn.: Greenwood Press.

LeLOUP, L. T. (1988) *Budgetary Politics,* 4th ed. Brunswick, Ohio: King's Court.

LEVANTROSSER, W. F. (1967) *Congress and the Citizen-Soldier.* Columbus: Ohio State University Press.

LEVITAN, S. A. (1969) *The Great Society's Poor Law.* Baltimore: Johns Hopkins University Press.

LEWIS, E. (1977) *American Politics in a Bureaucratic Age: Citizens, Constituents, CLients, and Victims.* Cambridge, Mass.: Winthrop.

LIGHT, L. (1979) "White House Lobby Gets Its Act Together." *Congressional Quarterly Weekly Report* (February 3): 195–200.

LINDSAY, J. L. (1987) "Congress and Defense Policy: 1961 to 1986." *Armed Forces & Society* 13 (Spring): 371–401.

LINDSAY, J. L. (1988) "Congress and the Defense Budget." *The Washington Quarterly* (Winter): 57–74.

LOFTUS, J. A. (1970) "How the Poverty Bill Was Saved in the House." In J. E. Anderson (ed.), *Politics and Economic Policy-Making.* Reading, Mass.: Addison-Wesley.

LOWI, T. J. (1964) "American Business, Public Policy, Case-Studies, and Political Theory." *World Politics* 16 (July): 677–715.

LOWI, T. J. (1967) "Making Democracy Safe for the World: National Politics and Foreign Policy." In J. N. Rosenau (ed.), *Domestic Sources of Foreign Policy.* New York: Free Press.

LOWI, T. J. (1972) "Four Systems of Policy, Politics, and Choice." *Public Administration Review* 32 (July/August): 298–310.

LOWI, T. J. (1973a) "How the Farmers Get What They Want." In T. J. Lowi and R. B. Ripley (eds.), *Legislative Politics U.S.A.,* 3rd ed. Boston: Little, Brown.

LOWI, T. J. (1973b) "Congressional Reform: A New Time, Place, and Manner." In T. J. Lowi and R. B. Ripley (eds.), *Legislative Politics U.S.A.,* 3rd ed. Boston: Little, Brown.

LOWI, T. J. (1979) *The End of Liberalism,* 2nd ed. New York: W. W. Norton.

LOWI, T. J. (1988) "Foreword: New Dimensions in Policy and Politics." In R. Tatalovich and B. W. Daynes (eds.), *Social Regulatory Policy: Moral Controversies in American Politics.* Boulder, Colo.: Westview Press.

LYNN, L. E. (1984) "The Reagan Administration and Renitent Bureaucracy." In L. M. Salamon and M. S. Lund (eds.), *The Reagan Presidency and the Governing of America.* Washington, D.C.: The Urban Institute.

LYTLE, C. M. (1966) "The History of the Civil Rights Bill of 1964." *The Journal of Negro History* 51 (October): 275-296.

MAASS, A. A. (1950) "Congress and Water Resources." *American Political Science Review* 44 (September): 576-593.

McCOOL, D. (1987) *Command of the Waters: Iron Triangles, Federal Water Development, and Indian Water.* Berkeley, Calif.: University of California Press.

MANLEY, J. F. (1970) *The Politics of Finance.* Boston: Little, Brown.

MANLEY, J. F. (1971) "The Rise of Congress in Foreign Policy-Making." *Annals of the American Academy of Political and Social Science,* no. 337: 60-70.

MARMOR, T. R. (1973) *The Politics of Medicare,* rev. ed. Chicago: Aldine.

MARRO, A. (1977) "Watching over Intelligence Involves New Fears and Doubts." *New York Times* (March 22).

MAXFIELD, D. M. (1978a) "Carter Plan to End Turkey Arms Sale Embargo Faces Tough Opposition in House." *Congressional Quarterly Weekly Report* (April 15): 872-873.

MAXFIELD, D. M. (1978b) "Carter Steps Up Lobbying for Turkey Arms Sales." *Congressional Quarterly Weekly Report* (June 10): 1464.

MAXFIELD, D. M. (1978c) "Senate Backs End to Turkey Arms Embargo." *Congressional Quarterly Weekly Report* (July 29): 1919-1920.

MAXFIELD, D. M. (1978d) "House Votes End to Turkey Arms Embargo." *Congressional Quarterly Weekly Report* (August 5): 2041.

MAXFIELD, D. M. (1978e) "Military Aid Bill Cleared Authorizing $2.8 Billion; Turkey Arms Ban Lifted." *Congressional Quarterly Weekly Report* (September 23): 2561.

MAYHEW, D. R. (1974) *Congress: The Electoral Connection.* New Haven, Conn.: Yale University Press.

MEIER, K. J. (1987) *Politics and the Bureaucracy: Policymaking in the Fourth Branch of Government,* 2nd ed. Pacific Grove, Calif.: Brooks/Cole.

MEIER, K. J. and K. W. KRAMER. (1980) "The Impact of Realigning Elections on Public Bureaucracies." In B. A. Campbell and R. J. Trilling (eds.), *Realignment in American Politics: Toward a Theory.* Austin: University of Texas Press.

MEIER, K. J. and L. G. NIGRO. (1976) "Representative Bureaucracy and Policy Preferences: A Study in the Attitudes of Federal Executives." *Public Administration Review* 36 (July/August): 458-469.

MEISOL, P. (1978) "Has Disaster Loan Program Hit Its High-Water Mark?" *National Journal* (September 16): 1462-1463.

MOE, R. C. and S. C. TEEL. (1970) "Congress as Policy-Maker: A Necessary Reappraisal." *Political Science Quarterly* 85 (September): 443-470.

MOE, T. M. (1985) "The Politicized Presidency." In J. E. Chubb and P. E. Peterson (eds.), *The New Direction in American Politics.* Washington, D.C.: Brookings Institution.

MOE, T. M. (1987) "An Assessment of the Positive Theory of 'Congressional Dominance'." *Legislative Studies Quarterly* 12 (November): 475-520.

MORELAND, W. B. (1975) "A Non-Incremental Perspective on Budgetary Policy Actions." In R. B. Ripley and G. A. Franklin (eds.), *Policy-Making in the Federal Executive Branch.* New York: Free Press.

MORGAN, R. J. (1965) *Governing Soil Conservation.* Baltimore: Johns Hopkins University Press.

MORROW, W. L. (1969) *Congressional Committees.* New York: Scribner's.

MUNGER, F. J. and R. F. FENNO. (1962) *National Politics and Federal Aid to Education.* Syracuse, N.Y.: Syracuse University Press.

NADEL, M. V. (1971) *The Politics of Consumer Protection.* Indianapolis: Bobbs-Merrill.

NELSON, G. (1975) "Change and Continuity in the Recruitment of U.S. House Leaders, 1789-1975." In N. J. Ornstein (ed.), *Congress in Change.* New York: Praeger.

NEUSTADT, R. E. (1954) "Presidency and Legislation: The Growth of Central Clearance." *American Political Science Review* 48 (September): 641-671.

NEUSTADT, R. E. (1955) "Presidency and Legislation: Planning the President's Program." *American Political Science Review* 49 (December): 980-1021.

NEUSTADT, R. E. (1973) "Politicians and Bureaucrats." In D. B. Truman (ed.), *Congress and America's Future,* 2nd ed. Englewood Cliffs, N.J.: Prentice-Hall.

NICE, D. C. (1987) "State Regulation of Railroads." *Transportation Research* 21A (No. 6): 411-420.

OGUL, M. S. (1973) "Legislative Oversight of the Bureaucracy." Paper prepared for the Select Committee on Committees, U.S. House of Representatives, 93rd Congress, 1st session. Washington, D.C.: U.S. Government Printing Office.

OGUL, M. S. (1976) *Congress Oversees the Bureaucracy.* Pittsburgh: University of Pittsburgh Press.

OGUL, M. S. (1981) "Congressional Oversight: Structures and Incentives." In L. C. Dodd and B. I. Oppenheimer (eds.), *Congress Reconsidered,* 2nd ed. Washington, D.C.: Congressional Quarterly Press.

OLESZEK, W. J. (1978) *Congressional Procedures and the Policy Process.* Washington, D.C.: Congressional Quarterly Press.

ORFIELD, G. (1975) *Congressional Power: Congress and Social Change.* New York: Harcourt, Brace, Jovanovich.

ORNSTEIN, N. J., T. E. MANN, and M. J. MALBIN. (1987) *Vital Statistics on Congress 1987-1988.* Washington, D.C.: Congressional Quarterly.

PAGE, B. I. (1983) *Who Gets What from Government.* Berkeley: University of California Press.

PALMER, J. L. and I. V. SAWHILL (eds.). (1982) *The Reagan Experiment.* Washington, D.C.: The Urban Institute.

PALMER, J. L. and I. V. SAWHILL (eds.). (1984) *The Reagan Record.* Cambridge, Mass.: Ballinger.

PASTOR, R. A. (1980) *Congress and the Politics of U.S. Foreign Economic Policy.* Berkeley: University of California Press.

PECHMAN, J. A. (ed.) (1983) *Setting National Priorities: The 1984 Budget.* Washington, D.C.: Brookings Institution.

PECHMAN, J. A. (1987) *Federal Tax Policy,* 5th ed. Washington, D.C.: Brookings Institution.

PENNER, R. G. and A. J. ABRAMSON (1988) *Broken Purse Strings: Congressional Budgeting, 1974-88.* Ann Arbor and Grand Rapids, Mich.: The Gerald R. Ford Foundation; and Washington, D.C.: The Urban Institute Press.

PETERSON, G. E. (1984) "Federalism and the States: An Experiment in Decentralization." In J. L. Palmer and I. V. Sawhill (eds.), *The Reagan Record.* Cambridge, Mass.: Ballinger.

PETRACCA, M. P. (1986) "Federal Advisory Committees, Interest Groups, and the Administrative State." *Congress & the Presidency* 13 (Spring): 83-114.

PINCUS, W. (1974) "Reforming Oversight Functions." *Washington Post* (December 23).

PIPE, G. R. (1966) "Congressional Liaison: The Executive Branch Consolidates Its Relations with Congress." *Public Administration Review* 26 (March): 14-24.

POLSBY, N. W. (1968) "Institutionalization in the House of Representatives." *American Political Science Review* 62 (March): 144–168.

PRICE, H. D. (1971) "The Congressional Career—Then and Now." In N. W. Polsby (ed.), *Congressional Behavior.* New York: Random House.

RABINOVITZ, F., J. PRESSMAN, and M. REIN (1976) "Guidelines: A Plethora of Forms, Authors, and Functions." *Policy Sciences* 7: 399–416.

RANSOM, H. H. (1975) "Congress and the Intelligence Agencies." In H. C. Mansfield, Sr. (ed.), *Congress against the President.* Proceedings of the Academy of Political Science 32: 153–166.

RAPP, D. (1988) "Is Anyone Really Trying to Balance the Budget?" *Congressional Quarterly Weekly Report* (November 26): 3379–3387.

RAUCH, J. (1985) "Farmers' Discord over Government Role Produces a Farm Bill That Pleases Few." *National Journal* (November 9): 2535–2539.

RAUCH, J. (1987) "Is It Really Working?" *National Journal* (January 31): 244–248.

RAUCH, J. (1988) "Sugary Shakedown." *National Journal* (April 30): 1131–1134.

RICH, S. (1980) "America as a 'Depressed Area.'" *Washington Post* (May 4).

RIESELBACH, L. N. (1977) *Congressional Reform in the Seventies.* Morristown, N.J.: General Learning Press.

RIESELBACH, L. N. (1986) *Congressional Reform.* Washington, D.C.: Congressional Quarterly Press.

RIPLEY, R. B. (1965) "Congressional Government and Committee Management." *Public Policy* 14: 28–48.

RIPLEY, R. B. (1969a) *Power in the Senate.* New York: St. Martin's.

RIPLEY, R. B. (1969b) "Congress and Clean Air: The Issue of Enforcement, 1963." In F. N. Cleaveland and Associates, *Congress and Urban Problems.* Washington, D.C.: Brookings Institution.

RIPLEY, R. B. (1972) *The Politics of Economic and Human Resource Development.* Indianapolis: Bobbs-Merrill.

RIPLEY, R. B. (1988) *Congress: Process and Policy,* 4th ed. New York: W. W. Norton.

RIPLEY, R. B. and G. A. FRANKLIN. (1986) *Policy Implementation and Bureaucracy,* 2nd ed. Homewood, Ill.: Dorsey Press.

ROBERTS, C. M. (1973) "The Day We Didn't Go to War." In T. J. Lowi and R. B. Ripley (eds.), *Legislative Politics, U.S.A.,* 3rd ed. Boston: Little, Brown.

ROCKMAN, B. A. (1984) "Legislative–Executive Relations and Legislative Oversight." *Legislative Studies Quarterly* 9 (August): 387–440.

ROTHMAN, S. and S. R. LICHTER. (1983) "How Liberal Are Bureaucrats?" Regualtion (December): 16–22.

ROTHSCHILD, E. (1977) "Is It Time to End Food for Peace?" *New York Times Magazine* (March 13): 43–48.

ROVNER, J. (1989a) "Both Chambers in Retreat on 1988 Medicare Law." *Congressional Quarterly Weekly Report* (October 7): 2635–2638.

ROVNER, J. (1989b) "The Catastrophic-Costs Law: A Massive Miscalculation." *Congressional Quarterly Weekly Report* (October 14): 2712–2715.

ROVNER, J. (1989c) "Catastrophic-Coverage Law Is Dismantled by Congress." *Congressional Quarterly Weekly Report* (November 25): 3238–3239.

RUDDER, C. E. (1977) "Committee Reform and the Revenue Process." In L. C. Dodd and B. I. Oppenheimer (eds.), *Congress Reconsidered.* New York: Praeger.

RUTTENBERG, S. H. and J. GUTCHESS. (1970) *Manpower Challenge of the 1970's: Institutions and Social Change.* Baltimore: Johns Hopkins University Press.

REFERENCES

SALISBURY, R. H. (1968) "The Analysis of Public Policy: A Search for Theories and Roles." In A. Ranney (ed.), *Political Science and Public Policy*. Chicago: Markham.

SAWYER, K. (1982) "A 'Tough Cop' on Private Sector, but Few Arrests in Own Precinct." *Washington Post* (April 13).

SCHATTSCHNEIDER, E. E. (1960) *The Semi-Sovereign People*. New York: Holt, Rinehart & Winston.

SCHER, S. (1963) "Conditions for Legislative Control." *Journal of Politics* 25 (Augest): 526–551.

SCHICK, A. (1980) *Congress and Money: Budgeting, Spending and Taxing*. Washington, D.C.: The Urban Institute.

SCHICK, A. (1981) *Reconciliation and the Congressional Budget Process*. Washington, D.C.: American Enterprise Institute.

SCHLOZMAN, K. L. and J. T. TIERNEY. (1986) *Organized Interests and American Democracy*. New York: Harper & Row.

SCOTT, A. (1977) "Veterans' Clout Extracts Extraordinary Benefits." *Washington Post* (November 1).

SEIDMAN, H. (1980) *Politics, Position, and Power: The Dynamics of Federal Organization*, 3rd ed. New York: Oxford University Press.

SHARKANSKY, I. (1965a) "Four Agencies and an Appropriations Subcommittee: A Comparative Study of Budget Strategies." *Midwest Journal of Political Science* 9 (August): 254–281.

SHARKANSKY, I. (1965b) "An Appropriations Subcommittee and Its Client Agencies: A Comparative Study of Supervision and Control." *American Political Science Review* 59 (September): 622–628.

SMITH, R. A. (1973) "TFX: $7 Billion Contract That Changes the Rules." In M. H. Halperin and A. Kanter (eds.), *Readings in American Foreign Policy*. Boston: Little, Brown.

STANLEY, D. T. (1964) *The Higher Civil Service*. Washington, D.C.: Brookings Institution.

STANLEY, D. T., D. E. MANN, and J. W. DOIG. (1967) *Men Who Govern*. Washington, D.C.: Brookings Institution.

STRICKLAND, S. P. (1972) *Politics, Science, and Dread Disease*. Cambridge, Mass.: Harvard University Press.

STOKES, B. (1985) "A Divided Farm Lobby." *National Journal* (March 23): 632–638.

SUNDQUIST, J. L. (1968) *Politics and Policy*. Washington, D.C.: Brookings Institution.

SUNDQUIST, J. L. (1978) "A Comparison of Policy-Making Capacity in the United States and Five European Countries: The Case of Population Distribution." In M. E. Kraft and M. Schneider (eds.), *Population Policy Analysis*. Lexington, Mass.: Lexington Books.

TALBOT, R. B. and D. F. HADWIGER. (1968) *The Policy Process in American Agriculture*. San Francisco: Chandler.

TATALOVICH, R. and B. W. DAYNES (eds.). (1988) *Social Regulatory Policy: Moral Controversies in American Politics*. Boulder, Colo.: Westview Press.

TATE, D. (1982) "Use of Omnibus Bills Burgeons Despite Members' Misgivings; Long-Term Impact Is Disputed." *Congressional Quarterly Weekly Report* (September 25): 2379–2383.

TOLCHIN, M. (1989) "How the New Medicare Law Fell on Hard Times in a Hurry." *New York Times* (October 9).

U.S. CIVIL SERVICE COMMISSION. (1976) *Executive Personnel in the Federal Service*. Washington, D.C.: U.S. Government Printing Office.

WARREN, M. and K. CHILTON. (1989) "The Regulatory Legacy of the Reagan Revolution: An Analysis of 1990 Federal Regulatory Budgets and Staffing." St. Louis: Center for the Study of American Business, Washington University (May, OP 72).

WELCH, S. and J. G. PETERS (eds.). (1977) *Legislative Reform and Public Policy.* New York: Praeger.

WILDAVSKY, A. (1984) *The Politics of the Budgetary Process,* 4th ed. Boston: Little, Brown.

WILDAVSKY, A. (1988) *The New Politics of the Budgetary Process.* Glenview, Ill.: Scott, Foresman.

WILENSKY, H. L. (1967) *Organizational Intelligence.* New York: Basic Books.

WILSON, J. Q. (1975) "The Rise of the Bureaucratic State." *The Public Interest* (Fall): 77–103.

WILSON, J. Q. (ed.). (1980) *The Politics of Regulation.* New York: Basic Books.

WITMER, T. R. (1964) "The Aging of the House." *Political Science Quarterly* 79 (December): 526–541.

WOLL, P. (1977) *American Bureaucracy,* 2nd ed. New York: W. W. Norton.

YATES, D. (1982) *Bureaucratic Democracy.* Cambridge, Mass.: Harvard University Press.

INDEX